New Indian Cinema in Post-Independence India

Shyam Benegal is an Indian director and screenwriter whose work is considered central to New Indian Cinema. By closely analysing several of Benegal's films, this book provides an understanding of India's post-independence history.

The book examines the filmmaker's focus on women by highlighting his subtle and critical engagement with a truism of Indian nationalism: women's centrality to the (nation-)state's negotiation with modernity. It looks at the importance Benegal accords to history – its little known, contested, or iconic events and figures – in crafting national culture and identities, and goes on to discuss the filmmaker's nuanced representation of the developmental agendas of the nation-state. The book presents an account of the relationship of historical film and fiction to official history, and provides a fuller understanding of Indian cinema, and how it is shaped by, as well as itself shapes, national imperatives.

Filling a gap in the literature, the book offers an analysis of the cinematic treatment of post-independence narratives and gives important insights into the imagination of the time. It is a useful contribution for students and scholars of Film Studies, South Asian History, and South Asian Culture.

Anuradha Dingwaney Needham is Donald R. Longman Professor of English at Oberlin College, USA. She is the author of *Using the Master's Tools: Resistance and the Literature of the African and South Asian Diasporas* (2000), and has co-edited *Between Languages and Cultures: Translation and Cross-Cultural Texts* (1996) and *The Crisis of Secularism in India* (2007).

Intersections: colonial and postcolonial histories
Edited by Gyanendra Pandey
Emory University, USA

This series is concerned with three kinds of intersections (or conversations): first, across cultures and regions, an interaction that postcolonial studies have emphasized in their foregrounding of the multiple sites and multi-directional traffic involved in the making of the modern; second, across time, the conversation between a mutually constitutive *past* and *present* that occurs in different times and places; and third, between *colonial* and *postcolonial* histories, which as theoretical positions have very different perspectives on the first two "intersections" and the questions of intellectual enquiry and expression implied in them. These three kinds of conversations are critical to the making of any present and any history. Thus the new series provides a forum for extending our understanding of core issues of human society and its self-representation over the centuries.

While focusing on Asia, the series is open to studies of other parts of the world that are sensitive to cross-cultural, cross-chronological, and cross-colonial perspectives. The series invites submissions for single-authored and edited books by young as well as established scholars that challenge the limitations of inherited disciplinary, chronological, and geographical boundaries, even when they focus on a single, well-bounded territory or period.

1 **Subaltern Citizens and their Histories**
Investigations from India and the USA
Edited by Gyanendra Pandey

2 **Subalternity and Religion**
The prehistory of Dalit Empowerment in South Asia
Milind Wakankar

3 **Communalism and Globalization in South Asia and its Diaspora**
Edited by Deana Heath and Chandana Mathur

4 **Subalternity and Difference**
Investigations from the north and the south
Edited by Gyanendra Pandey

5 **Mixed-Race and Modernity in Colonial India**
Changing concepts of hybridity across Empires
Adrian Carton

6 **Medical Marginality in South Asia**
Situating subaltern therapeutics
Edited by David Hardiman and Projit Bihari Mukharji

7 **Hindi Cinema**
Repeating the subject
Nandini Bhattacharya

8 **New Indian Cinema in Post-Independence India**
The cultural work of Shyam Benegal's films
Anuradha Dingwaney Needham

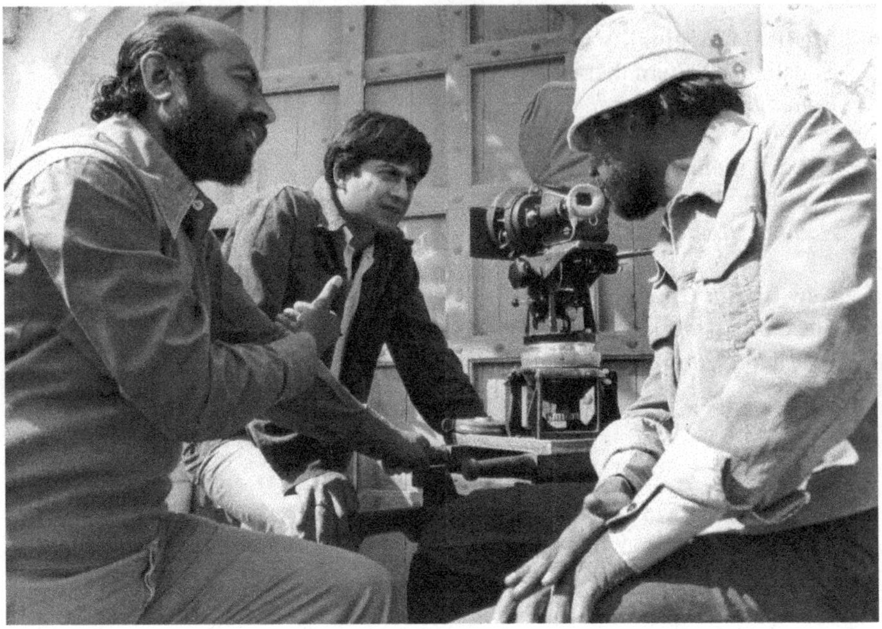

Frontispiece Benegal on a film shoot with cameraman Govind Nihalani and actor Anant Nag.

New Indian Cinema in Post-Independence India

The cultural work of Shyam Benegal's films

Anuradha Dingwaney Needham

Routledge
Taylor & Francis Group
LONDON AND NEW YORK

First published 2013
by Routledge

2 Park Square, Milton Park, Abingdon, Oxfordshire OX14 4RN
711 Third Avenue, New York, NY 10017

Routledge is an imprint of the Taylor & Francis Group, an informa business

First issued in paperback 2017

British Library Cataloguing in Publication Data
A catalogue record for this book is available from the British Library

Library of Congress Cataloging in Publication Data
A catalog record has been requested for this book

ISBN: 978-0-415-69397-4 (hbk)
ISBN: 978-1-138-57545-5 (pbk)

Typeset in Times New Roman
by Wearset Ltd, Boldon, Tyne and Wear

This book is dedicated to the memory of my late mother Krishna Dingwaney, without whose urging it would not have been undertaken and my two sisters, Devana Naik and Manjari Dingwaney, without whose enthusiastic welcome of my many India visits, it would not have been written.

Contents

Figures

Preface

One of the starting points of this study of Shyam Benegal's feature and documentary films derives from a curious paradox: For a prolific filmmaker, who provides important insights into the post-independence imagination of India; who has achieved significant commercial success with films considered pioneering efforts of art or parallel cinema; who has introduced a repertory of exceptional actors, technicians, and cinematographers to both art and mainstream Indian cinema; and who is nationally and internationally renowned, Benegal's *oeuvre* remains remarkably under-examined and under-theorized.[1]

Another point of departure for this study is the context in which it was begun, which has subsequently had an impact on the contexts it activates for an understanding of Benegal's films. It was conceived while I was in the midst of co-organizing a conference on secularism in India with Rajeswari Sunder Rajan. The varied, rich and extensive scholarship on the subject of Indian and other secularism(s) we studied in preparation for this conference (in order to determine the shape it would take, the topics and perspectives it would address and the collection of essays, which resulted from the conference) became an important lens through which I began to see Benegal's films.

Finally, some of the subjects this book engages and the emphases it privileges owe much to the critical analyses that see Benegal's films as (supportive of) statist enterprises. On the one hand, because I did not recognize my own responses to Benegal's films in these analyses, they compelled me to articulate for myself (and for others) the sources of my disagreement. On the other hand, as the most serious interlocutors of Benegal's films' (presumed) political alignments, these analyses provided a valuable counterpoint against which to test my own responses. More importantly, however, by embedding their discussion of Benegal's (early) films in a theoretically sophisticated "master narrative" that highlighted the "political and ideological contexts" (Vasudevan 2001: 119), these analyses both provided intellectual heft to a discussion of Benegal's *oeuvre* and opened up the possibility of a substantive engagement with arguments for and against the state, developmental ideologies, and realism that I believe Benegal's films complicate in significantly meaningful ways.

Vasudevan notes that while "Indian art film and author cinema" both of which Benegal is associated with, "continues to be showcased at home and abroad," it "has become somewhat marginal both to public discussion and scholarly engagement"; "popular cinema," on the other hand, "seems to have emerged as a powerful vehicle for Indian identity requirements in the newly defined global space of Indian national interests" (2011: 1, 3). This study can then be seen as constituting a recuperative gesture, focusing on a cinema (and the historical moment it invokes and itself seeks to recuperate) whose time may be considered to be over. My expectation and hope, however, is that both are worth recovering in order to grasp precisely those moments of struggle and contestation that went into the history of the nation and its cinemas.

Acknowledgments

While working on this book, I have accumulated many debts, among the more significant of these being to its subject, Shyam Benegal, whose generosity in opening up his time and home, and making hard-to-find materials available, made the task of research and developing ways of thinking about his films remarkably productive. I also wish to thank Nira Benegal for her hospitality.

Because this work departs so markedly from my prior research and teaching, it necessitated that I begin virtually from scratch in educating myself about visual media in general and film in particular, and within these, Indian cinema, especially Parallel and New Indian Cinema and their contexts. In this task, I was helped enormously by Arvind Rajagopal, who proved to be a great sounding board for my initial speculations regarding this work's framework and whose own suggestions about scholarship I should consult and ideas I should reflect on have also left their indelible imprint on the entire undertaking. Ravi Vasudevan, through a course he taught at Oberlin College, and through his own scholarship and generous response to my many queries, enabled in major ways an informed and fine-grained encounter with film analysis. I really could not have asked for better teachers than Rajagopal and Vasudevan.

Rajeswari Sunder Rajan, Bishnupriya Ghosh, Priya Kumar, Rashmi Bhatnagar, and Rashmi Sawhney provided encouragement and support in tangible and intangible ways by reading and commenting on discrete segments of this work, and through the example of their own work. To Raji, I owe a significant debt of another kind as well: She provided three different venues in which I presented different versions of the first two chapters – conferences at New York University ("Postcolonialism and the Hit of the Real") and Delhi University ("Postfeminist Postmortems? Gender, Sexualities and Multiple Modernities") and a public talk at the New York University Abu Dhabi campus, in conjunction with a retrospective on Benegal's films organized by NYU/AD, the Indian Film Society and the cultural wing of the Indian Embassy in Abu Dhabi. With regard to to the last venue, I also must acknowledge the wonderfully generative conversations and help of Sheetal Majthia and Dale Hudson, who helped organize the NYU/AD event. I am grateful to the audiences at all these venues for their comments and suggestions. For related reasons, I wish to thank K. Sivaramakrishnan, who by inviting me to present my analysis of Benegal's *Nishant* in conjunction with

Girish Karnad's residency at the South Asia Studies Council at Yale University provided both a rare opportunity to meet with Karnad and a lively, engaged audience.

I owe a big debt to my colleague Michael Fisher, who was an indispensable resource for all matters regarding South Asia's colonial and postcolonial history. I also owe a debt to Albert Borroni for his help with the illustrations.

I have been very lucky in research assistants who, apart from doing all sorts of drudge-work, contributed substantively by conducting the much-needed literature searches and watching Benegal films with me, on which they commented extensively. They were often valued interlocutors, and I have incorporated many of their ideas into my own analysis. So, my infinite gratitude to: Pooja Rangan, Margarida Malarkey, Max Wolcott, Josh Davidson, Meagan Day, and Srijit Ghosh.

I was the fortunate recipient of many internal grants that enabled me to travel to and from India several times while conducting my research. A year long Research Status award from Oberlin in 2010–2011, enabled me to write the bulk of this book. My thanks for these grants go to the Dean of the College of Arts and Sciences, Sean Decatur, and to the various Research and Development Committees that oversaw them. Thanks also to the director of Sponsored Programs at Oberlin College, Pamela Snyder, for her ongoing and very welcome support.

Larry Needham has lived with this book for longer than anyone else, but without his willingness to read different drafts, be a sounding board for its many arguments and, most importantly, editing skills, I would still most likely be struggling with it.

To Gyan Pandey, I owe a debt of a different sort: In encouraging me to submit a proposal for the series he edits for Routledge, he, in effect, made sure that I not only wrote the book I had promised but also completed it in a timely manner. To my commissioning editor, Dorothea Schaefter and her assistant Jillian Morrison, I owe a big thank you for their prompt responses to my many queries and also for their encouraging emails. Thanks also to the production team at Wearset, especially the senior project manager, Allie Hargreaves, and the copyeditor for this project, Denise Bannerman.

The dedication page responds to a somewhat idiosyncratic debt: my mother did not live to see this project come to fruition, but she was, in some sense, its instigator, urging me to write a book on Hindi film because she was based in Bombay; all my research trips, she said, would involve coming home. My sisters provided a home away from home on all my trips to India once my mother had passed away.

I am indebted to Saksham Khosla, my student assistant, for his assiduous work on the index, and to my colleague, Michael Fisher, once again, for his help with it.

An earlier version of the first half of chapter one appeared in 2011 as "Statist Realism and its Discontents: Another Optics for Shyam Benegal's *Ankur* (The Seedling, 1973)" in a special issue of *South Asian Review* devoted to "Transnational Realism in South Asian Literature and Culture," (32: 1). I owe a debt of gratitude to its editors, Rashmi Bhatnagar and Rajendar Kaur for all the effort they put in to make it work for the special issue. I thank its general editor, K.D. Verma, for permission to reprint it here.

For permission to reprint extracts as epigraphs framing individual chapters and sections within each, I wish to acknowledge the following:

University of Texas Press for extract from *National Identity in Indian Popular Cinema, 1947–1987* by Sumita Chakravarty, Copyright ©, 1993.

Geeta Kapur and Tulika Books, New Delhi, for extract from *When Was Modernism: Essays on Contemporary Cultural Practice in India* by Geeta Kapur, Copyright ©, 2000.

Columbia University Press for extract from *Primitive Passions: Visuality, Sexuality, Ethnography, and Contemporary Chinese Cinema* by Rey Chow, Copyright ©, 1995.

Women Unlimited, New Delhi, for extract from Karen Gabriel, "The Importance of Being Gandhi," from *South Asian Masculinities: Contexts for Change, Sites of Continuity*, edited by Radhika Chopra, Caroline Osella, and Fillipo Osella, Copyright ©, 2004.

University of California Press, for extract from Velcheru Narayana Rao, "A Ramayana of Their Own: Women's Oral Tradition in Telegu," from *Many Ramayanas: The Diversity of a Narrative Tradition,* edited by Paula Richman, Copyright © by the Regents of the University of California, 1991.

Oxford University Press India for extracts from Ranajit Guha, "Chandra's Death," from *Subaltern Studies V*, edited by Ranajit Guha, Copyright ©, 1987; and K. Sivaramakrishnan and Arun Agarwal, "Regional Modernities in Stories and Practices of Development," from *Regional Modernities: The Cultural Politics of Development in India*, edited by K. Sivaramakrishnan and Arun Agarwal, Copyright ©, 2003.

Berg Publishers, an Imprint of Bloomsbury Publishing PLC for extracts from *Bollywood Babylon: Interviews with Shyam Benegal*, edited by William van der Heide, Copyright ©, 2006.

Sage Publications India Pvt., Ltd, New Delhi, for extract from Lata Singh, "Retrieving Voices from the Margins: The Courtesan and the Nation's Narrative," from *Indian Journal of Gender Studies*, Vol. 14: 1, Copyright © by Centre for Women's Development Studies, New Delhi, 2007.

Orient Blackswan, New Delhi, for extract from Venna Das, "Femininity and the Orientation of the Body," from *Socialization, Education and Women*, edited by Karuna Chanana, Copyright © by Nehru Memorial Museum and Library, 1988.

Marcia Landy for extract from her "Introduction" to *The Historical Film: History and Memory in Media*, edited by Marcia Landy, published by Rutgers University Press, Copyright © Marcia Landy, 2001.

Doris M. Srinivsan for extract from "Royalty's Courtesans and God's Mortal Wives: Keepers of Culture in Pre-colonial India," from *The Courtesan's Arts: Cross-Cultural Perspectives*, edited by Martha Feldman and Bonnie Gordon, published by Oxford University Press, New York, Copyright © Doris M. Srinivasan, 2006.

Routledge (Taylor & Francis) for extract from *Hindi Music in a Musical Genre: Thumri Lyrics* by Lalita du Perron, Copyright ©, 2002.

Primus Books, Delhi, for extract from *Class, Power and Consciousness in Indian Cinema and Television* by Anirudh Deshpande, Copyright ©, 2009.

Shahid Amin, for extract from "Of Many Pasts: Commemorating 1857", published in *Telegraph*, India, July 13, 2006, Copyright © Shahid Amin, 2006.

Transaction Publishers for extract from Katherine Hodgkin and Susannah Radstone, "Introduction: Contested Pasts," from *Memory, History, Nation: Contested Pasts*, edited by Katharine Hodgkin and Susannah Radstone, Copyright ©, 2006.

Duke University Press for extracts from *The Other Side of Silence: Voices from the Partition of India* by Urvashi Butalia; *Goddess and the Nation: Mapping Mother India* by Sumathi Ramaswamy; and Jonathan Hyslop, "Gandhi, Mandela, and the African Modern," from *Johannesburg*, edited by Sarah Nuttall and Achille Mbembe, Copyright ©, 2000, 2011, and 2008 respectively.

India International Centre Quarterly for extract from "The Necessity of Harilal" by Shiv Visvanathan, published by *India International Centre Quarterly*, 34.2, Copyright ©, 2007.

Harvard University Press for extract from *His Majesty's Opponent* by Sugata Bose, Copyright ©, 2011

Introduction

> [T]here is nothing to be gained from the kind of cynicism that Gellner for example uses to designate culture in post-colonial countries. Even if art practice is ostensibly harnessed to the operations of ideology and cultural policy of the new national state, creative practice is heterodox. There is a certain rebellion and also a dissembling radicalism among artists. Quite often there may be utopian formulations or, on the other hand, subversive symbols that have political import.
>
> (Kapur 2000: 202–203)

> Of all the terms used by critics to characterize mainstream Indian cinema, realism defined in the negative or as a systematic absence has undoubtedly had the most currency. Conversely, the achievement of realism in a film becomes a mark of value, a sign of sincerity, and truthfulness on the part of the filmmaker and of "authenticity" of the material presented. This was particularly true during the post-independence period, when such qualities crystallized the hopes of a nation in search of its "true" identity and trying to assign meaning to the complex process of change.
>
> (S. Chakravarty 1993: 80)

Almost four decades since I first saw Shyam Benegal's *Ankur* (The Seedling 1974), it is still possible to recall the intense excitement and admiration it generated among my cohort of friends, acquaintances and family members because of what we registered as its perceptible difference from mainstream Indian cinema. This difference was evident in what we saw as the realism of its *mise-en scène*; the understated and entirely credible performances by its new, mostly FTII (Film and Television Institute of India)-trained actors; the persuasive force of its engagement with the oppression of rural subaltern women and a landless peasantry under feudal social arrangements.[1] Contemporaneous and later assessments of Benegal's films, especially *Ankur*, affirmed his sophisticated sureness of touch, speaking of the "panache and gloss" of a Benegal film "that had never been seen in Indian cinema before" (Krishen 1991: 341), comparing Benegal to Satyajit Ray, possibly India's most well-known filmmaker (Barnouw and Krishnaswamy 1980; Milne 1977), and noting as well that Benegal's "direction showed a sure, subtle control" (Barnouw and Krishnaswamy 1980: 264). Ray himself declared that, "*Ankur* has enough qualities to make one look forward to Benegal's future with keen anticipation" (1976: 103). For many of its viewers, it was the film's sustained engagement with the dynamic of power and powerlessness, domination, and subordination – routed through its representation of feudal relations in rural Andhra Pradesh – that constituted the film's appeal. Representing, more generally, a concern with inequity and injustice and, more particularly, a criticism of what the nation had still not achieved freedom from or left unaddressed, *Ankur* was seen as reflecting Benegal's oppositional politics.

But, originating in a different set of critical assumptions, a significant, theoretically sophisticated strand of writing on New Indian Cinema (henceforth New Cinema), of which Benegal's films are considered exemplary instances, views both this cinema and Benegal's films as active participants in, supporters of, and indeed, as continuous with the (nation-)state's modernizing, developmental agendas (Prasad 1998a and 1998b; Rajadhyaksha 1996 and 2009; and Rajadhyaksha and Willemen 1999).[2] In particular, this strand points to a history, since India's independence, of the Indian state's intervention in the film industry to ensure what it considered good (that is, socially relevant, narrative-centered, realist) cinema as opposed to popular Indian cinema, which it considered to be unrealistic and melodramatic, whose "anti-rationalist ethos … undercut the rational, critical outlook required for the development of a just, dynamic, and independent nation" (Vasudevan 2011: 105). State intervention is also viewed as a sign of considerable anxiety regarding an immensely popular cultural form whose powerful hold on the masses was seen to compete with the hegemony the state sought for itself.[3] State intervention, thus, is perceived as an effort to contain, if not altogether control, popular Indian cinema and the industry that produces it. Not all manifestations of New Cinema, which was funded for the most part by the state-supported Film Finance Corporation (FFC) that was later incorporated within the National Film Development Corporation (NFDC) and designed to address the inadequacies of popular Indian cinema, are seen as continuous with or co-opted by statist imperatives. Benegal's films, however, are. Perceived as incorporated within, and as part of, the logic of state intervention, his films' "realism" is securely tied to the developmental thrust of statist ideologies, which are considered reformist, when not simply predatory and repressive in their aims. The fact that Benegal's early films were privately and not state financed has not stood in the way of their being considered exemplary instances of New Cinema, signaling, as an important theorist of this strand puts it, this cinema's "moment of arrival" (Prasad 1998a: 189);[4] while yet others remark that *Ankur* "consolidated the New Cinema movement" (Rajadhyaksha and Willemen 1999: 415).

Howsoever one glosses the relationship between the (nation-)state and Benegal – as completely, partially or minimally co-opted by statist interests – the (nation-)state has figured importantly in his professional life and political beliefs. His feature and documentary films on national figures like Nehru, Gandhi and Bose, and narratives of national self-definition like Nehru's *Discovery of India* could, arguably, be considered apt illustrations of this interest. Responding to a question I raised regarding his relationship to the (nation-)state, Benegal remarked, "Of course my films reflect my interest in ongoing national debates; issues relating to what defines us as Indians are an important – seminal – point of reference for my films" (interview, March 16, 2006). In the same interview, he noted that "The idea of India" he endorses, is the Nehruvian one[5] – an "idea," fuelled by a liberal mind-set that, from its inaugural moment of India's independence in 1947 to Jawaharlal Nehru's death in 1964, sought to establish "a constitutional style of governance" and committed itself to "secular principles, economic programmes of centralised planning," whose "strategies for peaceful social revolution moderated the fundamental tension between the strong state and representative democracy" (Frankel 2002: 8). In this effort, an activist and interventionist state was considered crucial because it was perceived as central to achieving the social reform projects that anti-colonial nationalism had mapped, within which women's emancipation and the establishment of a casteless society were especially highlighted – projects that Benegal's films often address both explicitly and implicitly.[6]

That Benegal's films, from *Ankur* onwards, have been embraced and rewarded by the (nation-)state is also undisputable. Both his feature and his documentary films have received several National Film awards and have been frequently selected to represent India at international venues and film festivals. Benegal himself has received some of the nation's most significant honors – Padma Shree (1976), Padma Bhushan (1991), the Indira Gandhi Award for National Integration (2004), and the Dada Saheb Phalke Award (2005). From 2006 to 2012, he was more directly connected with the state as a member of the Rajya Sabha. Arguably, then, his films represent a set of concerns whose ideological investments the state welcomes and/or wishes to call its own. Whether this constitutes a species of collusion with statist agendas and ideologies is open to question; more important, whether statist agendas and ideologies are amenable only to singular, unambiguously negative assessments, or whether the state can in fact be considered monolithic or unitary in its operations, is also open to question.[7]

In recognition of Benegal's own representation of the interests informing his films, and somewhat like the critics of his films I reference above, I situate Benegal's films in the debates central to India's self-definition in its formative years and within several of the imperatives associated with New Cinema, which his work exemplifies. Some of these debates still resonate in the current historical moment, albeit inflected by changed historical circumstances. A significant assumption informing my analysis is that, emerging from and straddling the period of crisis – actually, several crises – that followed Nehru's death in 1964 and the Declaration of Emergency in 1975 by the then Prime Minister Indira Gandhi, Benegal's films attempt to craft national selves animated by the idea of a return to the possibilities articulated at the time of India's independence.[8] Focusing on equality, justice and progress, these possibilities, in principle if not in actual practice, sought to address the need for women's emancipation, a casteless society, an end to feudal relationships and the enfranchisement of *all* subjects as citizens, and were all part of the modernizing imperatives to which the new nation had committed itself. Benegal's vision, one could say, is a recuperative one,[9] and an intervention in the politics of both the period of crisis and a present defined by the Emergency when the idealism and promise of the first two decades following independence seemed to be in considerable disrepair, when "that which we took for granted with the constitution of a new India," says Geeti Sen, was opened up for radical questioning (1996: 11).

But Benegal's recuperation of these possibilities is not uncritical; it is accompanied, instead, by an interrogation that asks difficult questions: Did these possibilities cease to be meaningful or were they deliberately deprived of their meaningfulness over time? Were the visions they embodied ever seriously adopted in the first place? If not, was this due to a lack of commitment on the part of the state or were the means devised for implementing them inadequate to the task? The films also raise the question of whether the ways in which the possibilities were defined, were adequate to the promise of transformation they implied. Such questions invite reflection on the state's integrity and/or ability to deliver on its promises, questions that Benegal's films engage to develop a critical, but not entirely negative or dismissive, assessment of nationalist/statist agendas and self-definitions.[10]

The 1970s, which included the Emergency (which for many came to emblematize the period of crisis that eroded the Indian state's legitimacy) are also a significant point of departure for critics of Benegal who view his films as uncritical instantiations of statist agendas. Their understanding of the importance of these years for Benegal's films, however, is different from mine: They view the years leading up to and following the Emergency as a predictable, even organic outgrowth of Nehruvian statist agendas, which view, in turn, affects (in fairly over-determined ways) their assessment of both the state under Nehru and Benegal's statist alignments. In this view, Indira Gandhi's claims regarding the need for a stepped up socialist agenda and program of modernization during the Emergency years are continuous with, even identical to, Nehru's efforts to render India a modern, secular nation organized by socialist values and principles, with developmental agendas at its center.[11] I, on the other hand, understand the place of these years of crisis (including the Emergency) in Benegal's *oeuvre* as a catalyst for articulating what, in the words of one of my reviewers, I see as his "critically minded national project." In keeping with this difference, I view Benegal's relationship to statist agendas, and indeed the (nation-)state's self-understanding of these agendas, in somewhat less restricted and impoverished ways. To that end, I attend to the heterogeneity of, and contradictions within, both. Furthermore, I assume not just diversely situated viewers but also, therefore, differentiated viewing practices. Thus, while privileging a specific interest in Benegal's films in my analysis – one that takes the (nation-)state at a particular historical conjuncture as its primary frame of reference – through the films I select for close examination (each reflecting a different engagement with its specific historical context) and through the deployment of divergent theoretical and also cultural, social, and political frameworks that serve as points of departure for my analysis of these films, I render the interest I privilege in flexible, multiply-inflected ways.

In addition to showing Benegal's films' complex, sometimes oppositional, engagement with the national/statist ideologies and agendas that he in large part also agrees with and/or values, I make much of Benegal's preference for fictional (or "feature") films as the site of dialogical, multiple-voiced interaction where critical and/or opposing views can be articulated in conversation with, or occupying the same space as, the more conventionally statist ones without the latter's merits or demerits being preordained and rendered predictable. Fictional engagements, furthermore, provide Benegal with a freedom from facticity and thus space for working out (and encouraging his viewers to work out) the meaning and truth of contested events and controversial subjects.

Before outlining the specific attributes of my analysis of individual Benegal films I have selected, in what follows I provide a fairly extended excursus on New Cinema's contexts, addressing in particular those discussions that focus on the role of the state in its conception and development and on the crucial place of a realist aesthetic in the latter.[12] The arguments I isolate for analysis are selected from a much larger corpus of writing on these subjects. As with all selections, mine is self-interested to the extent that I only cover those arguments that have a bearing on my analysis of Benegal and his films, particularly as they reveal his complicated relationship with – his simultaneous embrace and critical assessment of – the modernizing imperatives of the (Nehruvian) state.

Apart from some disparities in emphases and/or details mustered in discussions of New Cinema, there is little dispute regarding factors that made this cinema possible. Primary among these is the crucial role of state intervention and the central place allotted to a realist aesthetic in this intervention. This aesthetic is valorized or critiqued, moreover, in direct proportion to a conception of its absence in the Indian film industry's mainstream product. There is broad agreement as well about the subjects/themes said to define New Cinema: the encounter of modernity with tradition, feudal relationships foregrounding the oppression of women and peasants, landless laborers, bonded labor, and rural locations. Benegal features prominently in all these discussions – his films are considered as a virtual embodiment of qualities that distinguish this cinema – much as Satyajit Ray is considered "the father figure," a proto-New Cinema filmmaker, whose films are both representative and works of individual genius (Das Gupta 1980: 36).[13] What distinguishes supporters of this cinema from its critics has to do, for the most part, with whether or not one views the state as a benevolent or repressive entity, through which lens respective assessments of New Cinema, the factors influencing its birth, its commitment to a realist aesthetic, its choice and treatment of subjects/themes and its most prominent practitioners is filtered. These divergent, often diametrically opposed views of the state proceed from the divergent, diametrically opposed assessments of the historical moment from which New Cinema emerges – a moment when the (nation-)state confronted and sought to resolve several crises that called its legitimacy into question.

Thus, most accounts of the elements that contributed to New Cinema begin by recounting the post-independence state's efforts to reform the film industry, not least in recognition of cinema's powerful hold on people's imagination. They note how the state constituted a Film Enquiry Commission, chaired by S.K. Patil and then, intermittently and over a period of several years, launched international film festivals (the first was held in 1952), instituted National Awards (starting in 1954), set up the Film Finance Corporation (1960), the Film Institute (1961) and the National Film Archive (1964) to aid the development of what it considered good cinema (Vasudev 1986: 2–3, 32–35; Binford 1987: 150; Barnouw and Krishnaswamy 1980: 250–252; Thorval 2000: 157–166). Whereas most supporters of New Cinema laud these efforts by the state at reforming cinema, its critics highlight the "combination of indifference … hostility … restrictive measures … and a prophylactic deployment of instructional films produced by the state" through which the latter interacted with, and intervened in, the film industry (Prasad 1998b: 129–130; Rajadhyksha 1996: 678–679).

Vasudevan notes another set of efforts aligned with, albeit not directly part of, the state when he addresses the contributions of "an intelligentsia promoting the development of art practices through film societies and journals." Highlighting especially "a tradition of criticism associated with Satyajit Ray and the Calcutta Film society in the 1950s" (both Ray and Benegal themselves started and were strong advocates of film societies), Vasudevan remarks that, while for "this emergent art cinema public discourse" Ray's "model of naturalism, psychological realism, and narrative integration provided a pertinent aspirational ideal," popular Indian cinema appeared "immature," "infantile," and "bereft of the rationalist imperative required for the Nehru era's project of national reconstruction." A strong "developmentalist … component," in other words, underwrites this tradition of criticism (2011: 8, 105).

A more proximate cause of New Cinema's birth was an appreciably more active FFC, which until then had provided financial assistance to a handful of directors positioned within both "art" and mainstream Indian cinema – Satyajit Ray, Chetan Anand, V. Shataram, and Bimal Roy. In 1964, however, while Indira Gandhi was Minister of Information and Broadcasting (under which FFC was located) and R.K. Karanjia was Chair of FFC, "the decision to support newcomers wishing to make small budget films" was taken. The "objective" was to "encourage 'artistic' films, not merely 'the usual type of films which may be a commercial success'" (Vasudev 1986: 34). The refashioned FFC extended loans to Mrinal Sen for *Bhuvan Shome* (1969); Basu Chatterjee for *Sara Akash* (1969) and Mani Kaul for *Uski Roti* (1969). Accounts of New Cinema distinguish Mrinal Sen, whose *Bhuvan Shome* is considered by many to be the inaugural film of New Cinema, from Mani Kaul, who along with Kumar Shahani is seen to represent New Cinema's avant-garde. Students of, and mentored at the Film Institute by Ritwik Ghatak (whose work, in turn, is counterposed to Ray's), Kaul and Shahani are lauded by critics of the dominant strand in New Cinema exemplified by Sen and Benegal for representing an alternative, minority strand that could, arguably, have led to a genuinely transformative movement. For Rajadhyaksha, for example, "New Cinema … is effectively chronicled, depending on two retrospective histories, as having begun with Mrinal Sen's *Bhuvan Shome* … or Mani Kaul's intensely formalist black and white experiment *Uski Roti*." "The example of Mrinal Sen," he adds, "was followed by Shyam Benegal" (1996: 684–685). Given that the dominant view of New Cinema centers Sen's film as its beginning and privileges Benegal's early films as exemplars of this cinema while locating its primary influence in Ray as the "fountainhead of new cinema, its point of reference even in opposition" (Dasgupta 1983: 42), it's possible to discern in remarks like Rajadhyaksha's a critique of New Cinema as it came to be defined based not only on the sense of a road not taken, but also on the one that should have been.

Rajadhyaksha's (and also Prasad's) strong brief against New Cinema, despite his support for Kaul and Shahani's work, derives substantially from its state sponsorship; his anti-statist position, as I have already suggested, is strongly inflected by the depredations, violence and radically undemocratic character of the Emergency, which in turn is projected backwards to include the Nehruvian state within its purview. Thus, he argues for the Emergency's "complicated presence" in "the New Cinema movement": "[T]here may indeed be a connection between the state support for independent cinema and the vicious disciplining of the mainstream film industry: a *national* project around media control gone badly wrong" (2009: 232–33; original emphasis). Both Rajadhyaksha and Prasad view Benegal's (and Ray's) films from this period as conforming with what Rajadhyaksha calls the "Aesthetics of State Control," not least because of their embrace of the "conventions of *objectivity* and *realism*" (2009: 231; 247).[14]

Those who evaluate New Cinema favorably de-link it from the state's activities during the Emergency and see it, instead, as participating in "the disenchantment of people with established institutions whose validity got deeply eroded in the seventies." For them "the new Indian cinema attempted to come to terms with aspects of the emerging social reality," which included a decade of social and political strife "leading to a critical re-evaluation of the country's most fundamental institutions, traditions, and values" (Vasudev and Lenglet 1983: 16).

What an over-determined focus on the coercive and entirely self-interested character and functioning of the state is unable to do is account for the inconsistencies and contradictions, which are often part of the necessity of having to appeal to different, often mutually exclusive or antagonistic constituencies, that affect the state's ability to specify and achieve singularly defined agendas. For instance, contesting the belief that the Nehruvian state was "based upon a consensus," Kaviraj suggests that, "it is more accurate to state that in the Nehruvian state there was a historic convergence of radically different expectations. The upper classes saw it as an instrument of economic growth primarily for themselves" whereas the "[l]ower strata were drawn to it by the promise of social dignity, an end of the caste system, and a distant dream of economic uplift."[15] "The two dreams," Kaviraj adds, "and their divergent justifications were equally real for the relevant groups to repose their faith in common in the modern-nation-state." Despite all its failures, contradictions, and inconsistencies, therefore, Kaviraj finds that, "its powerful, distinctive presence as a regulatory idea is unmistakable. It is implicitly invoked in every demand for justice, equality, dignity, assistance – because all such demands can be made only in its name" (2011: 41). Elsewhere arguing for "the special case of India" as a "[p]ostcolonial state," Kaviraj finds that the role of the state "from the middle of the nineteenth century" in India "has been absolutely central in the passage of social change" (2009: n.p.).

Much as an exclusive emphasis on the coercive and unitary aspect of the state tends to demarcate the nation from the state (see note 2), so too it demarcates society from state to vest all insurgent and democratic energy in the former. But, arguing that "the state-system in India is profoundly penetrated or influenced by the social forces," Fuller and Harriss find that "[e]mpirically … the boundary between state and society is in reality unclear, blurred, porous, mobile, and ordinary people widely recognize that this is so" (2000: 10). Similarly, Sharma and Gupta, drawing on Mitchell, urge us to "conceptualize 'the state' *within* (and not automatically distinct from) other institutional forms through which social relations are lived, such as family, civil society, and the economy," since "the boundary between state and civil society is itself an effect of power" – "disciplinary practices that help shape both everyday understandings of what 'the state' is and what 'it' does as well as influence the practice of agents" (2006: 9, 8)

When we consider the intermittent and lackadaisical way in which the Indian state pursued a policy for reforming the film industry and for setting up state-sponsored avenues for the development of films that would presumably forward its ideological agendas, the picture that emerges, in the accounts of both supporters and critics, is hardly that of a purposeful, ideologically unified effort. Several essays collected in the short-lived journal, *Cinema Vision* (India), attest to what D'Monte in his contribution characterizes as "the confused quest for good cinema" (1980: 64; see also, Dharkar 1980: 18–19; Zaidi 1980: 22; and Masud 1980: 83, 88). Within a decade (by the 1980s, that is), the New Cinema movement was, for all practical purposes, over as crucial elements for supporting it – for example, distribution (the "chain of art theatres" promised) – never materialized and the money for loans dried up as the state changed its policies (Rizvi and Amladi 1980: 4). Binford connects the lack of structures for distributing New Cinema films with ambivalence on the part of the state regarding these films' wider dissemination. She argues that, on the one hand, the FFC financed films "were among the cutting edge of social criticism," including criticism of the state, which made them problematic for the state. On the other, however, "New Cinema also proved useful to the state": Internationally, it helped the state demonstrate "the nation's progressive commitment and modern cultural stance," while domestically, "by allowing a degree of critical expression … the state [could] increase its capacity to contain criticism within manageable limits" (1983: 51; 1987: 150, 164). Arguably, the most persuasive argument for a more flexible understanding of the relationship between New Cinema and the state can be surmised from segments excised from the passage that constitutes my first epigraph from Kapur, but which were part of the earlier version: Addressing the "core of creative practice," she argues that this core may contain not only "an episodic intransigence," but also "subversive symbols that have direct political import" which are likely to "confound" generalizations about "politics and culture" (1992: 18).

Defining itself as a democratic republic, subject to "electoral politics and public opinion," the Indian (nation-)state, to the extent it had (and has) to rule through consensus and meet the expectations of different constituencies, is better characterized as hegemonic, rather than simply repressive.[16] This is not to suggest that the state cannot, or does not, deploy repressive measures, but that insofar as hegemony requires the consent of those subjected to it, the ruling class must persuade those they rule that their ideas make sense, that they are natural, and even possibly in the interests of the ruled. According to Vasudevan, this class must also persuade itself. Thus, while addressing "ideological operations and their contradictions" as these pertain to "the forms of authority" through which the (Indian) state operates, he encourages us to "examine its moments of self-persuasion" for "ruling forces have to convince themselves as much as their subjects of the capacity to adapt to new conditions" (2000b: 24). Any given hegemony, it is rightly argued, is thus always open to contest, struggle, mutation and defeats.

Chakravarty's comment about the significance of realism, and its "systematic absence" in "mainstream Indian cinema" "particularly during the post-independence period" (1993: 80; see epigraph), is suggestive with regard to its importance for the hegemonic ambitions of the post-independence Indian (nation-)state in its task of self-presentation: Faced, on the one hand, with the task of bringing together a heterogeneous and diverse peoples with often radically disparate identifications and investments and, on the other, with their own, preferred investments and identifications that they believed (whether opportunistically or not) were especially geared to transcending the sheer heterogeneity and diversity of the peoples and their agendas, the national ruling élite found in realism an immensely important ally. For realism, along with a series of cognate terms like "sincerity," "truthfulness," and "authenticity" incorporated within and/or used interchangeably with it, could be and was mobilized by this élite to naturalize (i.e., declare as self-evidently true and authentic) and thereby render authoritative their conception of the nation and its most salient interests. (Analogously, Vasudevan notes that "humanist realist cinema sprang from the ideology of the domestic context: that of the Nehruvian state with its emphasis on economic transformation and a critically founded individualism" [2011: 79–80].) In this regard, realism, while tied explicitly to rendering the truth of the Indian nation and society, actually sought to present a "specific relationship" that "project[ed] not what Indian society was, but what it *should be*"; thus, Mufti rightly labels this realism "national realism" (Mufti 2007: 183; Chakravarty 1993: 81).[17] Additionally, realism, which Chakravarty considers "marginal," even inimical to Indian philosophical and aesthetic traditions, was, she suggests, deployed to mediate "the ambivalence of social attitude to change" – from a pre-colonial and colonial *past* to a *future* marked by (colonial) modernity, for which the cultivation of a scientific/objective/empirical attitude mattered (1993: 81; on this see also, Vasudevan 1997: 153).

Arguably, critiques of New Cinema that include or are themselves based on a brief against realism that the Indian state considered indispensable to "good" cinema, proceed in large part from realism's intimate relationship with such hegemonic ambitions of the (nation-)state. Part of a larger historical and intellectual conjuncture, and similar to the anti-statist critiques, these critiques of realism and its correlate (a realist aesthetic) also derive substantially from post-structuralist theory(ies) as well as from the Marxist tradition of ideological critique, both of which, to borrow a phrase from Nichols, "had realism under siege" (1991: 175), with the Marxist critique insistently identifying the strategies through which realism works as an ideological (a term that rarely carries a positive valence) instrument. Thus, "accused" by these critics of being "an inherently conservative mode of representation," a realist aesthetic's recourse to "recognition" of and "identification" with what's "familiar" is often seen to proceed from dominant ideologies that have been naturalized and thereby rendered invisible (Hallam and Marshment 2000: xii; see also Grodal 2002): "a world that is seen without giving itself to be seen" is how Prasad puts it (1998a: 72), while for MacCabe, "[t]he real is not articulated, it is" (1980: 157). A realist aesthetic, it is argued, is co-extensive with, indeed, reproduces, bourgeois ideology, interpellating the (reading/viewing) subject through a single/singular point of view and a coherent representation of the world, a coherence that derives from the effacement or displacement of contradictions. In contrast, strategies that produce (Brechtian) forms of estrangement and critical distance, and/or display "anti-realist excess" are lauded for being politically progressive (Gledhill 1987: 8–9; Prasad 1998a: 58; MacCabe 1980: 153–157)

In the extensive, heterogeneous and rich scholarship on realism and a realist aesthetic, however, both are subjects of considerable contention, their varied definitions and presumed effects are recalcitrant, for the most part, to monolithic, generalizing formulations. Thus, Christopher Williams, arguing for "the survival and necessity of realism" declares: "Realism is not a single or univocal style. It is not a homogeneous or finished effect." He counters MacCabe's claim regarding the continuity between the "metalanguage" or unmarked discourse of the nineteenth-century realist novel and the realist aesthetic in cinema, both of which presume to present reality transparently, and Bordwell and his colleagues' definition of a monolithically conceived "Classical Hollywood Cinema" that, in turn, identifies a delimited set of cinematic strategies through which this cinema produces its realist effects, to argue that, while "[d]ifferent generic conventions may well make their own versions of realism,… realism itself does not emerge out of a work conforming with generic norms to 'produce the illusion of realism.'" He concludes, therefore, that realism cannot be "meaningfully divided into two distinct, antagonistic entities—illusionist realism on the one end, and intellectual consciousness raising anti-realism on the other" (1994: 289).

Locating realism's beginnings in "changed attitudes toward reality," Raymond Williams subordinates form or technique to an epistemological shift to foreground realism and naturalism's emphasis on the contemporaneous, the secular (i.e., "conceived and worked through in solely human terms") and the "socially extended" (i.e., designed "to include the lives of all men [*sic*]"). Far from being conservative, realism's political importance (for Williams) resides in its attempt to include hitherto marginalized or unknown groups, experiences and attitudes. Furthermore, though initially linked with the bourgeoisie's attempts at self-definition and authorization, realism "was at once shared and taken further by the new opponents of the bourgeoisie in the working class and socialist movements" (1991: 121–123).

Analogously powerful arguments have been made by writers and cultural theorists from colonized/oppressed groups that decry not only the realism claimed by and for dominant modalities of representation, but also postmodernism's radical contestation of the real, or reality, to claim realism, and the strategies through which it is rendered, for themselves. Their understanding and deployment of realism is crucial, they argue, for disclosing their oppression; realism is also crucial to their effort to render the truth of their lived experience and ideological and other commitments.[18] Arguably, this can be viewed as an attempt to put in place, even if only contingently, an alternative way of comprehending realism to the one that dominant ideologies and their representations seek to naturalize.

"Whose reality does realism narrate?" queries a recent call for contributions to a special issue of *South Asian Review* dedicated to "Transnational Realism in South Asian Literature and Culture." The call invites contributors to address the many divergent uses to which realism has been put, or occasions on which a realist aesthetic has been deployed, particularly among the "categories troubled by the South Asian writer" while negotiating the nineteenth-century realism of the European bourgeoisie: the dismantling of the opposition between realism and myth; the difference of written realisms from those of oral story-telling; social realism from magic realism and so on. The contributions to the issue, while reflecting on the diverse uses to which realism is put and/or enacted, often speak of a "realism that awakens the critical faculty" (Bhatnagar and Kaur 2011: 22).

The concept of identification, which constitutes one of the significant affects through which the persuasive force of realism is secured, has been similarly complicated by those who refuse, or find inadequate, the Brechtian call for estrangement or suspicion of identification, which is co-extensive with his critique of realism. Mutually productive of each other, both realism and identification, according to Brecht, "obfuscate" or "prevent" a critical take on dominant ways of viewing the world and thereby block genuine social transformation which would flow from "the possibility of seeing undesirable outcomes as contingent and socially determined, not inescapable, natural necessities" (Smith 1995: 3; 1996: 130). Smith, who finds that characters are an important means through which identification is secured in a realist text, notes that, "character structures are perhaps the major way by which narrative texts solicit our assent for particular values, practices and ideologies" (1995: 4).[19] Insisting, however, that virtually no practitioner or critic committed to a realist aesthetic misreads characters in fiction as real, but rather as "lifelike" depending on the "impression of 'roundness,' of depth and complexity of emotion," he also insists that "identification may function in a variety of ways with respect to ideology having the potential both to reinforce and to question norms." Spectators too, he says, should be seen as responding "more flexibl[y] … neither deceived with respect to the status of representations, nor entirely caught within the cultural assumptions of those representations." Rendering the spectator an active, even critical participant in accessing (rather than simply a passive recipient of) dominant representations, Smith makes a strong case for the imaginative potential of a text to re-envision dominant ideologies: "Traffic between world and text, then, runs in both directions: we need our experience of the world to 'get into' the text, but the text itself may transform the way we understand and experience the world." "Fictions," he says, "prompt and enrich our 'quasi-experience' … our efforts to grasp, through mental hypotheses, situations, persons, and values which are alien to us" (1995: 35, 10, 41, 54, 74).

As my analysis of a substantial, albeit not exhaustive, selection of Benegal's *oeuvre* demonstrates, realism is not a unitary, closed category in his films, nor is the realist aesthetic made up of, or directed toward, unitary ends. Analogously, identification, far from being mobilized only on behalf of statist agendas is more often mobilized, to mention but a couple of instances, on behalf of characters and positionalities, whose legitimate needs the state has thus far been unable, or unwilling, to address (see Chapter one on *Ankur* and *Nishant*), or has actively repressed and/or bypassed in the interests of what it takes to be the claims of modernity (see Chapter two on performing women). Furthermore, insofar as my selection of films includes those which focus on a diversity of interests, subject positions and genres, my analysis is able to address a range of realist practices and strategies that give flesh, as it were, to these interests and subject positions and genres, including not least realism's traffic with myth, melodrama, utopian formulations and historical fiction and fact.

My study is divided into three parts: "The nation *as* its women"; "The nation's alternative and self-authorized biographies"; and "The nation and its ideologies of development." These parts are neither self-contained nor separated from each other through hard, impermeable boundaries. Indeed, they overlap considerably in terms of subject positions. Women continue to occupy a prominent place in virtually all Benegal films, their life-worlds and perspectives constituting significant lenses through which the films represent their investments. Similarly, a concern with social justice, the importance of accessing minority perspectives, and the hope for social transformation animate all his films. The part headings and the titles of chapters do, however, flag the foregrounding concerns for a given part and chapter, including the generic categories and philosophical questions through which viewers are invited to access them. Additionally, the part headings and the films included under them exist in a reciprocal relationship with each other: At the same time, as the former invoke and thereby help activate specific theoretical, cultural, political, and social positions, the individual films, while drawing on and accruing intellectual heft from these positions contribute to, and even transform them via their own thematic and formal properties.

Part one considers the much-lauded, but thus far comprehensively underexamined, claim regarding Benegal's investment in, and focus on, women. It frames its discussion of five women-centered films via Benegal's subtle, and for the most part implicit, critical engagement with what is a virtual truism of Indian nationalism: women's centrality to the (nation-)state's negotiation of/with modernity. By doing so, this section also counters Prasad's claim regarding the spectatorial position elicited by Benegal's "developmental realism," which he aligns with that of the (nation-)state. I argue, instead, for the viewer's identification with the female protagonists, who far from being the (nation)-state's beneficiaries, are often its inarticulate victims and also, eventually, its resisting subjects. To make its case, this part draws on many different kinds of feminist and postcolonial scholarship: the richly diverse literature on a subject's social location and experience that then comprises the gendered (and class and caste) dimensions of this subject's vision; discussions in film studies that address the modalities of female spectatorship; and, finally, the scholarship that emerged from the conjuncture in India of an active and energized women's movement and a scholarly focus on feminist concerns. Exploring the intersections between gender, female (and male) sexualities, caste, class, and hegemonic forms of national self-definition, this conjuncture in some instances preceded, while in others instances followed, certain Benegal films, thereby situating these films as active, even sometimes initiating players in the debates this conjuncture spawned.

The first chapter, on *Ankur* and *Nishant*, highlights the complicated tortuous route to female emancipation – a presumed goal of modernity – that must contend with patriarchal constraints, sometimes internalized as an aspect of the female psyche itself. Invested in the utopian possibilities of the (nation-)state, if a "female protagonist and subject" were to be centered categorically and authoritatively, as Gabriel puts it in a different context (2004: 286), these two films, I argue, address the deeply felt need for, if not the actual availability of, new structures and spaces through which such possibilities can be enacted. In doing so, the two films also point to the sustained ideological labor that such a transformation requires.

The *nachne ganewalis* (singing-dancing ladies) or performing women of *Bhumika*, *Mandi* (Marketplace; 1983) and the eponymous *Sardari Begum* (1996), who are the foci of Chapter two, have a different relation with modernizing agendas of the (nation-)state than the rural subaltern and middle-class protagonists of *Ankur* and *Nishant*: Not just dispossessed, forgotten or ignored subjects, but also women representing professions, identities, and cultural repertoires that flourished under, and were indelibly associated with a feudal order, they inhabit subject positions that were delegitimized, marginalized, and even excised from the self-definitions and constitutive narratives of the new Indian nation on its way to modernity. While the careers of these performing women allow Benegal to interrogate and re-envision what nationalist ideologies normalize as acceptable forms of social control, and licit and illicit forms of women's sexuality, and while, for Benegal, women's emancipation is underwritten by their access to a sexuality that is free(er) from the patriarchal injunctions that these women exemplify, the films do not romanticize their life-worlds or identities. For their relative autonomy as performing women – with access to their own sources of money and power – does not free them completely from their embeddedness within the logic of patrilineal and patriarchal relationships; after all, they depend for their autonomy on male patrons and a feudal patriarchy.

Part two recognizes the centrality that Benegal accords to history – its little known, contested, as well as iconic events and figures – in crafting national culture and identities. To that end, it deals with both fictional and objective or positivist engagements with history, focusing on the former in Chapter three and on the latter in Chapter four. In the process, this section draws upon and addresses the scholarship that deals – pro and con – with the relationship of historical film and fiction with "historian's history" (Pandey's resonant phrase), as well as with the scholarship – pro and con – that deals with history's and documentary film's referential ambitions to disclose the truth or what really happened. On the one hand, this section focuses on historical films' potential, through their intersection with fiction and recourse to imaginative reconstruction, for destabilizing an untroubled relationship with the past to articulate in its place alternative, even dissident versions of official or dominant history. On the other hand, it focuses on historical documentary's (including biopics about national leaders) embrace of official or dominant history. Benegal himself tends to maintain a strict demarcation between these two forms of articulating history, separating the fictional from the documentary, asserting most recently, "the pull of a certain kind of historical truth [about which] you cannot be a revisionist for reasons of narrative and drama" (interview with me, July 31, 2012).

Freed from the constraints of history as fact, and engaging history instead, via fictional narratives of contested and/or marginalized events and subject positions, Chapter three on *Junoon* (Obsession; 1978), the eponymous *Mammo* (1994), and *Trikaal* (Past, Present, Future; 1985) gives its viewers access to a history the nation has failed or refused to write about itself. With the 1857 uprising, the partition of the South Asian subcontinent, and the departure of the Portuguese and Indian takeover of Goa as their historical contexts, the specific choices Benegal makes to represent these historical events (fictionalizing "true" stories, foregrounding the minority perspectives of these stories' protagonists, and centering women's life-worlds and interiorized domestic spaces) can be seen as efforts to inflect our understanding of how these events appear in national(ist) history. As such, these films constitute Benegal's participation in the debates that circulate around the meaning of these events and their historical import. My analysis thus situates Benegal's efforts within the substantial body of scholarship on these events and on historical films and analyses that address the intersections between literature/cinema and history.

On the other hand Chapter four, on Benegal's documentaries on Nehru's biography and Nehru's *The Discovery of India*, as well as his biopics (the latter term is George Custen's) on two other "heroes" of the "national pantheon" – Gandhi and Bose – marks a change of register and perspective in terms of both the cinematic representation of, and traffic with, the dominant content and forms of national history. And this despite Benegal's focus on ostensibly lesser known or forgotten subjects: Gandhi's South African years and "the forgotten hero," Bose. I argue that these films' close alignment with dominant versions of India's national history is at least as much a product of their choice of protagonists, who are considered national heroes, as it is of the forms – documentary and biopic – in which they are cast; in fact, the form and the content exist in a symbiotic relationship with one another. In support of my argument, I engage extensively with the literature on documentary's preferred modes of representation as well as with histories of the state-sponsored Indian documentary, which are tied to statist agendas for unifying a diverse multicultural and multi-religious polity and to familiarizing this polity's citizens with India's vast territory and disparate cultural forms.

Whereas Chapter four seems to confirm an unproblematic view of Benegal's statist alignments – keying his films about Nehru, Gandhi and Bose into those aspects of the dominant national narrative that render their lives "heroic" in somewhat one-dimensional ways – the last section, comprised of only one chapter on a selection of films – *Manthan* (The Churning; 1976), *Samar* (Conflict; 2000) and *Hari Bhari* (Fertility; 2000) – complicates them. Dealing overtly with the developmental agendas of the state, it argues for a nuanced understanding of not only Benegal's engagement with these agendas, but also, following from and/or supporting this assessment, a more nuanced understanding of development in general. Ostensibly devoted to specific "causes" (the importance of setting up a milk co-operative; a critique of caste discrimination; and the politics of family planning), these films, rather than simply illustrating and thereby endorsing preferred statist solutions, in fact complicate them by activating a variety of positions – pro and con – on them and employing representational strategies – like the film-within-a-film – that impede the articulation of monolithic positions.

Although there is little doubt that all Benegal films – in as much as they are films devoted to the modalities of social transformation – are "cause" related films, they are seldom didactic films in the sense of being "cause" promoting films.[20] Committed to the value of telling a story well, in which the characters and their lived experiences unfold themselves with considerable psychological plausibility, these films must, perhaps inevitably, engage with the contradictions and incoherence that are part of such efforts. This does not allow for the kind of homogeneous intent or effect ascribed to his films when they are viewed simply as extensions of, or as consolidating, state imperatives.

Part I

The nation *as* its women

1 "The places occupied by women"

Gender, subalternity, and the (nation-) state in *Ankur* and *Nishant*

> The question we are left with is what form of [national] narrative, action, resolution, and identity would emerge from a categorical and authoritative foregrounding of a female protagonist and subject?
>
> (Gabriel 2004: 286)

> From the perspective of feminism … whose task is not simply that of liberating women but rather one of liberating the human need to control and exploit others in the way men have traditionally controlled and exploited women, reading these … films would mean delineating in them the possibilities of emancipation without losing sight of their complicity in patriarchal culture. The places occupied by women in these films is crucial in this consideration.
>
> (Chow 1995: 44)

Most commentators on Shyam Benegal concur that his first three films – *Ankur* (The Seedling; 1973), *Nishant* (Night's End; 1975), and *Manthan* (The Churning; 1976) – comprise a trilogy – an "emblematic trilogy" of New Indian Cinema, no less (Thorval 2000: 157); as such, these three films are viewed as constituting interconnected projects dealing with the lives of the rural poor and the exploited and oppressed members of this segment of Indian society (Datta 2003: 64–99; Dogra 1978: 13; Rao, M. 1998: 9; Surya 1997: 52). Additionally, some of these commentators note that all three films locate these subjects' exploitation in feudal socio-political arrangements and chart what they see as the ensuing confrontation of tradition with modernity via the arrival in the village of an "outsider" from the city. In his more critical treatment of these films, Prasad, while incorporating or assuming these thematic continuities, also frames these three films' interconnections through recourse to an overarching category he labels "developmental aesthetic," which, deploying a realism that presumes the (nation-)state "as its frame of representation," assigns to the three films' spectators a viewing position that "coincides with the point of view of the [nation-] state" (Prasad 1998b:143, 145; 1998a: 25, 61, 161, 196; Rajadhyaksha 2009: 138–141; 51–155). To be sure, Prasad concedes that these films "do not deploy the realist mode of representation in the same way" and so finds it "necessary to examine each of them in some detail to trace both the unique achievements of each and to assess their cumulative cultural significance" (1998a: 196). Nevertheless, the resolutely linear (developmental?) narrative, through which he charts the significant overlaps in these films as evolving steps in their modalities of representation and address, tends to privilege the "cumulative" – or accretive – over the "unique," enforcing these films' firm belonging within the "developmental aesthetic" singularly construed through its most significant correlate, "statist [or developmental] realism: "Speaking of these "first three films [as] … instances of an evolving aesthetic employing statist realism," Prasad notes that "although the developmental narrative comes into its own only in *Manthan* (1976), both *Ankur* (1974) and *Nishant* (1975) contribute to its construction by employing strategies of distancing which produce the peasant/rural poor as an object of study and sympathy" (1998a: 25). With *Manthan* as his point of departure, I contend, he reads back his framework of "developmental aesthetics" into the two earlier films, construing the overlaps between them as binding transitions that make the three films a coherent, continuous whole. Thus, what constitutes the persuasive force of Prasad's argument – how coherently he knits together his analysis of select details from each film with his (pre-given) theoretical framework privileging the three films' conformity with the state's developmental ideologies – also constitutes its limits: The "unique[ness]" of each film remains hostage to the generalizing ambitions of a theoretical framework unable to allocate more than one position that a spectator might occupy vis-à-vis three different films, far less within one film.

My analysis uncouples *Ankur* and *Nishant* from *Manthan*, discussing *Manthan* in a later chapter with other Benegal films dealing with developmental agendas. It considers *Ankur* and *Nishant* in distinct sections of this chapter to demonstrate that, even if we were to stay within the confines of Prasad's conception of the spectator, there is more than one spectatorial position in play in individual films and to suggest that the positions mobilized are as much a function of the viewer's social location and privileging of certain explanatory frameworks over others as they are of the film's strategies of representation.[1] At the same time, I acknowledge that there are significant continuities between *Ankur* and *Nishant* – thematic, political, even, to an extent, representational – that suggest the consolidation of a larger cultural-ideological project, which has the (nation-) state as a significant frame of reference within which a spectator is being invited to situate these two Benegal films. However, as individual and individualized elaborations of particular emphases within this larger project, the films also inscribe their difference from each other, rendering the project more diverse and complex. Thus, while considering the overlaps between the two significant enough to merit their inclusion within the same chapter, I also offer substantial close readings of each film that address their specific and unique articulations of individual concerns. In terms of the films' representational methods, I remark, in particular, on how the strategies of a realist aesthetic are neither "univocal" nor deployed to elicit what C. Williams calls a "homogeneous or finished effect" (1994: 289); furthermore, these strategies are not necessarily deployed towards conservative ends alone, linked, for instance, with the bourgeoisie's attempts at self-definition and authorization, but rather can be, and have been used, as R. Williams notes, to represent hitherto marginalized or unknown groups, experiences, and attitudes (1991: 121–123).[2]

Of particular interest to my analysis of the overlaps in these films is: (1) how both films focus on the brutalizing effects of feudal power against which the viewer's moral and social judgment is mobilized on behalf of the peasants who are at its receiving end; and, more importantly, (2) how the affective force of this judgment is rendered most powerfully through the films' representation of the material and sexual exploitation of women under patriarchies that derive their power from feudal social and political arrangements. These interrelated concerns of the two films resonate powerfully with the social reform projects – dealing, for example, with women's emancipation and the establishment of a casteless society – that anti-colonial nationalism mapped as it sought to negotiate the contradictory and vexed encounter between (Indian) tradition and (colonial) modernity. The question that I engage, then, is why Benegal returns in the mid to late 1970s, almost a quarter of a century later, to social reform projects that were mapped at the start, as it were, of India's career as an independent nation. The answers to this question are found in a significant point of departure for these two early Benegal films: their extended and critical reckoning with the promises – to end social and gender inequalities, poverty, illiteracy, for example – that the Nehruvian state made at the time of India's independence, but failed to deliver on.[3]

The two films emerged from and during a decade-long period of crises both within, and of, the state marked, at one end, by Nehru's death in 1964 and, at the other, by the Emergency proclaimed by then Prime Minister, Indira Gandhi, in June, 1975, through which the state assumed enormous powers, suspending people's civil liberties, repressing dissent, and muzzling the press and other media through severe censorship. The failure to deliver on the promises made in the first flush of (national) independence stood out in stark relief, becoming particularly apparent because this period constituted a decade of considerable upheaval in the Indian polity. This included, among other economic and political crises, a peasant struggle – in fact, an armed insurrection: the Naxalite movement. Starting in the Naxalbari district in Bengal and spreading to other sites including, most prominently, Andhra Pradesh (where the narratives of *Ankur* and *Nishant* are set), the Naxalite movement was a protest against persisting feudal structures and it exemplified conflict along the axes of caste, community, and class. Supported by student uprisings in Calcutta, this movement seriously undermined the legitimacy of the post-independent Indian state, underscoring its failure: its inability or refusal to address the problems apparent at the time of independence relating to the gross inequities in land distribution, secured not least by the persistence of feudal social, cultural, and political arrangements, and the concomitant problems of a landless peasantry and bonded labor (see, in particular, Baxi 1995; Baxi and Parekh 1995; Khilnani 1999; Masselos 2005). As their specific historical and political context, *Ankur* and *Nishant* invoke an earlier peasant struggle, the Telangana People's Struggle (1948–1951), whose concerns and conduct anticipated those that defined the Naxalite movement. The films' invocation of the Telangana

People's Struggle, then, is not without significance, referencing not just its contemporary relevance for what was happening in the mid seventies of the twentieth century in India, but bearing witness also to how much within the nation had remained unchanged with respect to feudal oppressions.

Kannabiran and Lalitha describe the Telangana People's Struggle as "the armed resistance of peasants against the Nizam and Hindu landlords in the Hyderabad state"; it was enabled by the Communist Party in Andhra, and was withdrawn when the Indian army secured the surrender of the Nizam and the Razakars, a paramilitary group, and thereafter turned its might against the peasants; at the same time the Communist Party was banned (Kannabiran and Lalitha 1990: 201–202; Stree Shakti Sanghatana 1989; Sunderayya 1972; Balagopal 1983; and Pavier 1974).[4] That Benegal was cognizant of the contemporary resonance of the Telangana People's Struggle can be ascertained from a comment he made to Datta when she spoke with him for her 2003 book: "Those were times of great ferment … I was deeply influenced by the peasant struggles" (2003: 24). Additionally, in a contentious interview with Narvekar, while responding to the question, "What made you choose an outdated theme like feudal oppression a second time [in *Nishant*]? Is it not irrelevant to our times?" Benegal retorts: "You call it outdated? How have we changed?" and then adds, "The change is merely on paper.… We have only altered the face of the situation, the basic problems remain the same" (1976: 15).[5]

The significance of Benegal's choice of the Telangana People's Struggle as the historical and political context for *Ankur* and *Nishant* is not restricted to this struggle's parallels with the Naxalite movement. It also resonates in especially meaningful ways with the project of women's emancipation that is at the center of *Ankur* and *Nishant*'s critical engagement with the hegemonic narrative that constitutes the Indian nation's definition of itself. My analysis of the two films demonstrates significant continuities between the predicament that Benegal's female protagonists face, regarding their autonomy and freedom, with that confronted by women who participated in the Telangana People's Struggles, which, in turn, mirrors the predicament faced by women who participated in India's anti-colonial nationalist struggle. It takes as its point of departure the many claims made regarding Benegal's investment in, and focus on, women's position and status. Virtually no analyses of Benegal's films, however, have followed up these claims with any sustained account of what such a focus entails or what implications flow from it. In this respect, then, my analysis makes visible and argues for a spectator position that has thus far remained more or less unarticulated and, thus, unexamined. I argue that Benegal's *Ankur* and *Nishant* can be valuably read as offering a sustained exploration of the terrain implied by Gabriel's question raised in a somewhat different context (see first epigraph to this chapter) where she wonders about what sort of national "narrative, action, resolution, and identity would emerge," if "a female protagonist and subject" was centered as the protagonist (2004: 286).[6]

Some scholars note the conjuncture that included an active and energized women's movement and the beginnings of New Cinema in India to explain this cinema's and, more importantly, Benegal's interest in, and commitment to, women's issues (Chakravarty, S. 1999: 290–291; Rao, L. 1989: 452). As will become apparent, the richly diverse scholarship that emerged from and/or addressed the rise of this active and energized women's movement is indispensable to my analysis of *Ankur* and *Nishant*. Exploring the intersections between gender, (women's) sexuality, caste, class, and hegemonic forms of national self-definition, some of this scholarship preceded while some followed the making of *Ankur* and *Nishant*, linking Benegal's own exploration of these intersections in the two films to this body of work.

Ankur

> Gender equality automatically represents massive social change.
>
> (Benegal to van der Heide 2006: 64)

> [W]hen a victim, however timid, comes to regard herself as an object of injustice, she already steps into the role of a critic of the system that victimizes her. And any action that follows from that critique contains the elements of a practice of resistance.
>
> (Ranajit Guha 1987b: 164–165)

Ankur opens with a long shot of a line of villagers silhouetted against a stark landscape (dominated by boulders) as they make their way to a temple. The camera does not seem to move except to foreground Lakshmi via a medium close-up shot, signaling her importance to the story. At the temple, Lakshmi prays for a child ("Mother, I don't want anything; I just want a child": significantly, her prayer is articulated in the locution of desire – "I want" – of which I will say more later) and the camera pans to Kishtaya, her husband, presumably directing the fulfillment of this desire to the likely agent of such fulfillment. Simultaneously, the credits roll on the screen, marking this scene as preceding the narrative proper, which opens with Surya and his friends receiving their exam results. Soon thereafter, the viewer sees Surya arriving home, where his father, an absentee *zamindar* (landlord), is conversing with his mistress and their illegitimate son. Surya brushes off their greeting, thereby angering his father, and goes in to join his long-suffering mother, to whom he seems close. In a succession of briskly executed scenes, Surya's wish to continue his studies is balked by his authoritarian father for whom "the king is one who owns the land." After a hurriedly arranged marriage with a girl too young to accompany him, Surya is dispatched to his ancestral village to oversee land belonging to his family. With the authoritarianism of his father and his apparent attachment to his mother firmly established in the opening scenes, the film initially seems to want to secure the spectator's sympathy for and identification with Surya.

Surya's arrival in the village marks his entry into an unfamiliar, if not altogether alien, environment – a point driven home via a brief comic interlude when his car gets stuck: helpless, because inept at extricating his car, he must depend on a handful of village youngsters whom a partly obsequious, partly contemptuous *patel* (village headman) musters to help Surya. Surya's lack of acknowledgement is evidence of his sense of entitlement to such assistance.

These opening scenes introduce the viewer to the two protagonists, some of the other characters, and several salient thematic strands the film will develop. They also cue the viewer into some aspects of the realist aesthetic deployed by Benegal: ethnographic details focusing on the landscape, particularities of dress and speech, and rituals that are regionally specific. Some of the force of this aesthetic accrues from its sharp contrast with the non-naturalistic and melodramatic representations associated with popular Indian cinema. Some accrues from an equally sharp contrast with what Chabria characterizes as the "special role" the village has played in the "mythology of Indian popular cinema" where it is the site (and bearer) of "the great Indian tradition with its values of harmony, tolerance, proximity to nature, honest labour etc." – a mythology, says Chabria, that was jettisoned, by New Cinema, not least via its investment in a realist aesthetic (1992: 235). Thus, in *Ankur*, the repressions and hypocrisies evident in the city are equally evident in the village, much as feudal arrangements are not restricted to the village, and patriarchal ideologies concerning gender and caste permeate both rural and urban sites.

However, S. Chakravarty suggests that New Cinema developed its own form of mythmaking about the rural and urban divide that, arising from a westernized "intelligentsia's feelings of being alien in their own environment, also centered the village as " 'real' India": " 'If you want to know the real India,' " Chakravarty quotes from Karnad, who was associated with New Cinema in both its regional and national incarnations, " 'you cannot get it from the Indian who lives in the city. It is the village Indian who is the real Indian' " (1993: 85). Arguably, then, Surya being dispatched to the village is part and parcel of an effort to render him a *national* subject by immersing him (*sic*) in this " 'real' India."[7]

At issue also in Surya's (enforced) move to the village is a related pedagogical project, also connected to becoming adequately national – that of social and geographical extension. To this end, he is "uproot[ed]" from the security of his "familial and social moorings" and compelled to engage with subjects from other "class[es], region[s], and socio-religious communit[ies]" (Vasudevan 1994: 93), so as to become a more responsible and responsive national subject.[8]

In as much as the (middle-class) spectator's position is aligned with that of Surya's – the spectator, after all, enters the narrative proper through Surya, and *sees* the inner workings of feudalism in the city and the village through him – the pedagogical project is directed toward the spectator as well. A nominally modern subject, who tries but fails to resist the law of the father, Surya's arrival at the ancestral village at first presages a figure different from his father. He refuses to observe caste and class taboos, asking Lakshmi, who takes care of the landlord's house in the village and is from a lower caste, to make tea for him, as well as turning down the village priest's offer to take his meals with the priest's family. At the same time, he is not averse to asserting his (feudal) caste, class, and gender prerogatives: He refuses to give his illegitimate step-brother access to the water that would irrigate his brother's fields; he constantly monitors attempts by the village women to draw water from his well; he performs no labor, and is shown being pampered – oiled and massaged – dispensing orders, shouting truculently at all and sundry. Once he seduces Lakshmi into sleeping with him, having run off her husband, Kishtaya, for stealing toddy from the trees on his farm, Surya more or less reproduces the relationship his father has with his mistress, albeit with this difference: Whereas his father continues to look after his mistress and the son born out of that liaison, Surya will seek to evade this responsibility.

In his comments on *Ankur*, Ray is mistaken when he notes that, "Benegal makes the mistake of turning the scales too heavily against the hero *towards the end, with nothing in the early part to suggest that he is capable of such monstrosity* [i.e., Surya's brutal beating of Kishtaya in the film's conclusion]" (1976: 102; emphasis added). While not monstrous, Surya from the beginning comes across as spoilt and self-absorbed, his disavowal of caste-related taboos seems self-interested and opportunistic, if not altogether hypocritical. Ray is right, however, in suggesting that, "*Ankur* is not free from melodrama," if we take Ray to mean by this a certain lack of realism and/or plausibility (1976: 102). If it were not for the verisimilitude of the village setting and the characters with whom he interacts, Surya's one-dimensionality – his lack of roundedness, as it were, or psychological depth so prized in a realist aesthetic – would stand out. Surya, in other words, begins to function as a type, and although the "type" or what is "typical" is not inimical to a realist aesthetic, this (deliberate?) one-dimensionality blocks a sympathetic investment in Surya on the spectator's part. Thus, while the (middle-class) spectator's position is cinematographically aligned with that of Surya's, when it comes to evaluating his character and behavior – almost from the beginning[9] – the spectator's simultaneous recoil from him splits the spectator from Surya as well.[10] Prasad views what he considers the deliberate distancing of the spectator from Surya as a means by which "a position of non-complicity with feudal power" is assured for the former (1998a: 200). I view this distancing – a disjunctive but nonetheless clearly apprehended cultivation of critical distance – as proceeding from an effort at auto-critique produced by a member of the middle class, which, in turn, implicates the spectator to the extent that s/he belongs to this class as well. In his interview with van der Heide, for example, Benegal recalls that *Ankur* was "based on an actual incident, which occurred when [he] was 16 or so." This incident pertained to "a friend of mine," who "had a certain amount of city education" before he was sent off "to look after the farm." His father was "very feudal," whereas the friend could be seen as "more part of the middle class" (2006: 56). In the same interview, Benegal returns again and again to what van der Heide takes to be his "very critical perspective of the educated middle class." This class, says Benegal, "hasn't created its own values"; consequently, the "oppressive" and "terrible" values of the "old [feudal] system" have not been "replaced by a new value system" (2006: 61). Given this understanding on Benegal's part of the failure or refusal or, quite simply, incapacity of the middle class(es) to become appropriately national subjects, it is unsurprising that the pedagogical project in which Surya is implicated fails or is deliberately aborted. A disclaimer, however, is in order here: The middle class(es), far from being a monolithic or singular entity is, instead, internally differentiated and stratified.[11] The westernized, urban fraction of this class, which was considered the primary audience of New Cinema and Benegal's films, is not completely co-extensive with the position Surya represents, even as it might share some of his ways of being and behaving and thereby be the object of the critique leveled at Surya.

All along, however, another spectator position has been available. Focused on Lakshmi, with whom and with whose prayer and desire for a child the film opens, it invites viewers not only to enter her world marked by dispossession, powerlessness, and oppression – the structural conditions of her subalternity – but also to participate in the self-education she unwittingly undergoes in order to become the subject she does at the film's conclusion: raining abuses on Surya, declaring "we are not your slaves," and cursing him with infertility and thus the potential inability to reproduce the conditions of domination in which he is implicated directly and indirectly. (Significantly, the pedagogical project associated with Lakshmi's self-education, which also constitutes her self-emancipation, succeeds where the one associated with Surya fails or is aborted.) The spectator, who begins in a position proximate to Surya's, some way into the film, begins to view the village and the feudal, patriarchal relationships that obtain therein through the positions reflected in, and occupied by, Lakshmi. Lakshmi, in other words, is the figure for who the film seeks what Smith defines as the spectator's *"allegiance"*; or whose position, in Vasudevan's terms, the spectator is meant to "incorporate into [her/his] subjectivity" (see note 10).[12] In the process of doing so, we might well ask: is the spectator being asked to consider seriously the possibility of Lakshmi as the more likely agent of the social transformation needed to craft a viable national self? If yes, then: what is the nature of social transformation that is being mapped through her? Concomitantly: what sort of agency is being vested in Lakshmi in bringing about this transformation?[13] Behind these questions are larger considerations regarding the kind or kinds of national identity Benegal's films endorse and its/their relationship with official nationalism's preferred self-image(s). In what follows, I respond to these questions by tracking the transformation Lakshmi herself undergoes, focusing especially on a handful of scenes of learning, including some in which her self-education proceeds from roles/positions she refuses to occupy.

When tracing the arc of Lakshmi's development, one can scarcely ignore, in the early scenes, how the viewer/spectator often sees her through Surya's eyes, as the camera focuses on Surya looking at Lakshmi going about her work – sweeping, pounding chilies, cooking, bathing in the river. Predictably, such *looking* produces Lakshmi as a sexual object and as sexually objectified. While unsurprising in terms of Surya's positioning as a feudal landlord, it is significant that this *looking* constitutes, and is constitutive of, a gaze and an ideology with which Lakshmi's own comprehension of herself – of her gender and class positioning – seems to cohere, even collude. Her awareness of his gaze (and she is often, though not always, aware that he is looking at her) recognizes and seems to acquiesce to his right to view her thus, and thereby concedes a species of *droit du seigneur* to their situation. This is made apparent in a series of related scenes in which Surya comes upon Lakshmi putting a *bindi* on her forehead, soon after he is shown secretively looking at her as she bathes in the river. With Lakshmi looking at him looking at her, he puts his hand on her shoulder signaling both his attraction to her and his sexual intent. Lakshmi holds his glance and then the camera cuts to Lakshmi in her hut, presumably having rejected his advances. But when Surya comes in pursuit, complaining – "Who will make my tea? Who will cook the food? Who will look after the house?" – and instructs her to come to work the following morning, Lakshmi remains silent. As he departs, the camera offers a close-up of her face with a smile full of sensual knowledge that makes clear she grasps the sub-text of his complaints, which has more to do with his sexual needs and expectations regarding their fulfillment than work left unattended. Arguably, Surya's need of her suggests she has some power over him, much as the glance she returns implies a degree of reciprocity, but Lakshmi's smile also suggests her acknowledgment and acceptance of the situation as it exists, and this is a function of his structurally defined (feudal/patriarchal) power and her (subaltern) powerlessness. (In this scene, viewers cannot help but be conscious that its complex psychological effects accrue from a powerful interpretation of her role by Shabana Azmi. Arguably, Benegal's feminist-centered agenda gains exponentially from the excellence of the leading actresses who populate his films as women protagonists.)

Such an acknowledgment and acceptance of her powerlessness is in keeping with Lakshmi's acceptance of her situation generally. For although she is cognizant of some of the material, indeed structural, bases of her oppression – including her low caste marriage to the deaf-mute Kishtaya because of a lack of dowry, and ongoing, relentless poverty because mechanization has rendered Kishtaya's handmade pottery redundant, all of which she confides to Surya after becoming his mistress – she nonetheless cannot imagine herself changing these conditions. Consider her surprise, following presumably from the conventional social taboo against someone from the upper castes consuming food or water even touched by someone from the untouchable or dalit caste, when Surya asks her to make tea for him. The only times she disagrees with Surya is when he criticizes her husband, about whom she is fiercely protective. Despite this, however, when Surya humiliates Kishtaya for stealing, she implicitly accedes to his right to do so (whether or not she considers this humiliation just) through her despairing silence. These early scenes, then, present a Lakshmi who has so internalized the ideology of the position allotted to her in a caste-ridden, gendered feudal society that the oppressive conditions flowing from this position appear to her natural and self-evident.

The actual moment of Lakshmi's change in status from only a servant to a servant who is also Surya's mistress, following soon after the scene analyzed above, is mediated by a set piece – a didactic intrusion – functioning virtually as a tableau, which represents the adjudication by the village *panchayat* (council) of a domestic conflict involving a runaway wife. The entire village has turned out to witness this event, but the camera lingers longest on Lakshmi, signaling this tableau's centrality to the development of her subjectivity, not least because, looking back into her proximate past and forward into her future, it condenses within itself some of the most significant elements of her situation.[14] The narrative enclosed within the tableau involves a woman's transgression: The runaway wife has not only left her husband to live with another man, but this man also, it is suggested, belongs to a lower caste. Her husband's family sees this transgression in terms of a socially unacceptable desire: "What *more* does this woman *want*?" demands one brother-in-law after enumerating all the material benefits she enjoys as part of her husband's family. The wife reframes the ideological valence of her "want" by asserting first that her husband "is not a man" and then that she "wants a child." Although the husband's lack of manliness is linked to his inability to father a child, another explanation for this lack also is insinuated – that he is unable to fulfill her sexual desire, a meaning reinforced by the wife's claim that hunger is more than a material need (*bhook sirf pet ki nahin hoti hai*). Thus the "*more*" that this woman "*wants*" incorporates a desire for both: a child and sexual satisfaction. Lakshmi's prayer for a child in the opening shot, then, retrospectively acquires an analogous resonance.

What interests me in this tableau, both for what it says about Lakshmi and how Benegal wants the spectator to interpret her position and subjectivity, is not just its endorsement of the desirability of desire from a woman's perspective and the rejection, therefore, of the village society's attempts to contain the threat it poses to patriarchal authority, but also the suggestion that this desire, even when explicitly tied to the desire for a child, is resolutely uncoupled from preserving family and dominant social structures, which also are underwritten by patriarchy.[15] In as much as the "intrusion of the tableau," as Vasudevan notes, "is quite significant in terms of the formulation of the spectator's subjectivity" (2000a: 108), one could say that the significance of this tableau is not just restricted to the development of Lakshmi's subjectivity, but incorporates the spectator's as well, rendering it co-extensive with Lakshmi's. This process, in turn, helps secure the spectator's identification with Lakshmi.[16]

Also interesting in this tableau is the prediction by one of the brothers-in-law that "women like you [i.e., the runaway wife] will one day usher in doomsday." Women's desire or, rather, women's effort to fulfill their desire is equated with disorder, with bringing to crisis the solidity and presumed naturalness of dominant social hierarchies and relations. This prediction, when fulfilled by Lakshmi, does indeed bring to crisis the naturalness of such hierarchies and relations.

Lakshmi's transgression, however, is of a somewhat different order than the runaway wife's. After all, by becoming Surya's mistress she is reproducing a socially accepted, if not socially sanctioned, relationship.[17] Instead, her transgression proceeds primarily from her explicit refusal to continue to abide by the rules of such a liaison both when she rejects Surya's demand that she abort the child conceived during the liaison, and when she refuses to entertain the village *patel's* promise to secure her and her child's material well-being by negotiating an arrangement with Surya similar to the one Surya's father has with his mistress and their illegitimate son. However, given that her willingness to enter the liaison in the first place enmeshes her even further in a situation that underscores her subalternity, how does she end up emancipating herself from a consciousness and mindset – her own no less – that keeps her trapped within the status quo? Initially, the lesson she internalizes from the death (by murder or suicide) of the runaway wife is her own vulnerability, which, in turn, makes her accept Surya's opportunistic promise to take care of her at face value:[18] "How long?" she queries; "Forever," he replies. At the same time, as Benegal pointed out to me, acceding to Surya's sexual advances does give her some degree of social mobility, visualized most explicitly through her move from her hut into the landlord's house, and into his bedroom (interview, March 26, 2006). In a handful of scenes, as if only for a brief period, Lakshmi seems genuinely happy and carefree. This brief interlude of happiness is underscored – ironically, by the use of commercial or mainstream Hindi film music in the background – through its juxtaposition with her lonely trek back to her hut soon after Surya's wife arrives, concluding with a close up of Lakshmi, inside the hut, staring vacantly at the ceiling, her eyes and face reflecting her absolute despair.

It's the discovery of her pregnancy by Surya that most visibly marks the change in Lakshmi from dependent, vulnerable subaltern subject to one who can speak for herself and who can represent her own interests. She responds to Surya's demand to abort the child with a combination of silent contempt (when Surya first calls out to her as she is washing herself at the banks of the river, she spits out the water in her mouth as her only acknowledgment of his presence [Figure 1.1]), counter-questions (when he asks, his tone bordering on hysteria,

Figure 1.1 Lakshmi and Surya in *Ankur*.

"Who will bring up the child? Don't you feel any shame?" she replies in a level voice, "Did I ask you to bring up the child?" and then, "Should I be the only one to feel shame?"), and outright refusal, through which she reiterates her desire for a child ("I want to keep this child.")

In his interview with me, Benegal claimed that the movement away from Surya's perspective occurs when Lakshmi becomes pregnant, and that the spectator most fully enters her view of the oppressive conditions she inhabits from this moment on (March 26, 2006). The film, however, tracks a subtler, more extended process of transformation: From the moment she moves into the landlord's house, the film unobtrusively insinuates her agency and point of view by inviting the spectator, in one instance quite explicitly, to view Surya and her situation through her eyes,[19] and elsewhere through the questions she raises about the advisability of their liaison. In arguing for Lakshmi's transformation as a process that occurs over a longer duration, I am, of course, arguing for those psychologically inflected elements that also constitute this film's realist aesthetic, whose effects flow from the spectator witnessing the unfolding complexity (i.e., made up of contradictions and ambiguities) of her motives, behavior and consciousness, and thus from access to her interiority, *her* developing grasp of herself and her situation. This enables and consolidates a process of identification that reconstitutes the spectator's subjectivity, with the deployment of a realist aesthetic performing a crucial mediating function. Thus, where I had earlier argued that Benegal eschews a fully developed realist aesthetic in his representation of Surya to, in fact, distance the spectator from him, in the case of Lakshmi he deploys it precisely to secure the (middle-class) spectator's willingness to imaginatively comprehend, if not be able to altogether inhabit, her life-world. A realist aesthetic, in other words, is mobilized here in the interests of what R. Williams defines as a form of social extension – the effort, that is, to bring within the purview of the spectator's consciousness a hitherto marginalized and repressed subject and consciousness (1991: 121) or, in Smith's terms, "situations, persons, values" hitherto "alien" or of little or no import to the spectator (1995: 74).

Most assessments of whether or not *Ankur* offers a vision of progressive social change focus on the penultimate image of the film – the little boy throwing a stone at a window of the landlord's house; as the window shatters, the screen turns red. For Lukmani, this gesture is "misleading and unjustified" in as much as the film has not earned the right to it because Benegal has not shown himself to be an adequately "committed" filmmaker (1997: 43). In an analogous indictment, Prasad also views this gesture as somewhat hollow because it enables the spectator's vicarious "participati[on] in the peasants' moment of awakening without ever calling into question the spectator's own position" (1998a: 203). My argument thus far has been that the social transformation the film tracks, and seeks to enact, is focalized through Lakshmi – its urgent need secured through the spectator's participation in, and identification with, her developing consciousness. Rather than focusing on the boy's gesture of defiance, then, I would draw attention to Lakshmi's passionate denunciation of Surya as the defining moment of crisis, when she runs from her hut, across the fields, toward the landlord's house to protect Kishtaya from Surya's assault. Calling him "a bastard," she screams, "we are not your slaves" as she lets loose a string of curses at him. Significantly, Surya's assault on Kishtaya becomes most clearly visible through Lakshmi's eyes: It is only as she comes out of her hut, registers that Kishtaya is being lashed, and begins running toward him that the camera, keeping pace with Lakshmi, moves to a close up of Kishtaya on the ground trying to protect himself from being beaten. Lakshmi's verbal abuse has its non-verbal equivalent in the contempt of the handful of villagers who look on, now made visible through close-ups of their faces (the group includes, not accidentally, his illegitimate step-brother). This contempt is then crystallized through the look Surya's wife directs at him as he runs into the house, away from Lakshmi's curses.

That the film presents Lakshmi as the site for, and agent of, social transformation is confirmed by Benegal's comment that bringing about "gender equality automatically represents massive social change. It also represents a massive change in the entire socio-economic structures of the country – even the politics of the country" (see epigraph; van der Heide 2006: 64).[20] However, while "gender equality" might well be the instrument of "massive social change," is such change shown to have taken place in the film? (Here we may want to bear in mind that Lakshmi's subaltern status includes determinants other than her gender – her dispossession because of her class and caste, for instance – which are included in the critique the film launches against gender ideologies; in this respect the critique is analogous to the one Chow cites as proceeding from "the perspective of feminism" – i.e., not just of "liberating women" but rather "liberating the human need to control and exploit others" [see epigraph; 1995: 44].) The film's response to this question is ambiguous. After cursing Surya, Lakshmi (propping up an injured Kishtaya) is shown returning to her hut, the material and psychic site of her unfreedom. Both literally and figuratively it seems like there is nowhere else for her to go, no "new" or "transformed" physical or mental structures available that can accommodate the woman she has become. Yet, as Sunder Rajan has pointed out, "powerful moments of rupture occur" – when presumably the conditions of possibility for change become visible – "when women are dis-accommodated within [dominant or hegemonic] structure[s], and the process of exorbitation ensues" (2000b: 5).[21] Such a process lays bare the necessity for, if not the actual achievement of, social transformation. Benegal makes such a "process of exorbitation" legible via a deeply discomfiting, because excessive, display of emotion by Lakshmi on Kishtaya's sudden return and offer of his earnings to her. As she sobs and sobs for a full minute (long in terms of viewing time), part of the spectator's discomfiture arises from not being able tie her prolonged sobbing to a knowable or familiar category of understanding – that it indexes Lakshmi's sorrow or regret over her liaison with Surya; that it is a therapeutic event and so on. Rather, its sheer excess seems to signal something more, something outside the bounds of what the spectator can comprehend or explain.

The suggestion at the end of *Ankur*, that social and political structures (and spaces) do not exist that can house Lakshmi's transformed consciousness, mirrors the predicament faced by women who participated in the Telangana People's Struggles (which, as previously suggested, provides a significant historical and political context for *Ankur* and *Nishant*) as documented in the collection of *testimonios* recording women's voices brought together by Stree Shakti Sanghatana in *We Were Making History*. The consciousness that emerges from these *testimonios* – erratic, contradictory, compelling, and deeply moving – is shot through with ambiguity. In their analysis of these *testimonios*, Kannabiran and Lalitha note how the "exhort[ation]" by the Communist Party to participate in these struggles opened up "new horizons" for these women, "catapult[ing]" them into the hitherto male-defined public arena of politics and a "realm of possibility" that promised equality between men and women and freedom for both from feudal oppression. Characterizing it as "the magic of that time," one female participant poignantly notes that in making women part of the struggle, the party "made human beings of us." Kannabiran and Lalitha wonder: Why is there evidence in the *testimonios*, then, of an "undertone of harassment," a "note of pain, of a vision betrayed"? After all, along with drawing the women into the public sphere, the party also addressed "issues of social reforms for women" relating to widow remarriage, the problem of child marriage and the possibility of female education. At the same, however, the party leadership continued to be "enmeshed" in the "very structures [and gender ideologies] it attacked," returning women, figuratively and materially, "to the old familiar site of their oppression and their security – the family and the fireside" (1990: 183–198). Nor is the party leadership held entirely responsible for the failure to create new structures (and spaces) within which social and political transformation could flourish and be nurtured. As Kannabiran and Lalitha point out, the women themselves were complicit in the failure to the extent that they too could not entirely escape their subject formation within patriarchal and feudal structures:

> Expressions of power [were] internalized and built not only into the attitudes of men, but even more importantly into the very bodies of women so that their subordination was constantly and subtly reinforced. A subordination so apparently tenuous, yet so pervasive that it was difficult to articulate. (1990: 182)

Having learned and intimately inhabited various modalities of domination and subordination virtually from birth, men and women, *Ankur* and the *testimonios* suggest, would require sustained, long-term effort to unlearn them.

Just as Lakshmi's predicament at the end of *Ankur* mirrors – indeed, allegorizes – the predicament faced by the female participants in the Telangana People's Struggle, so too does the latter's predicament metonymically represent that of the women who were empowered by their participation in the anti-colonial nationalist struggle to which they were incited by leaders like Gandhi, but whose empowerment was also simultaneously constrained, wittingly and unwittingly, through interdictions regarding, not least, a "respectable sexuality."[22] A normatively defined female sexuality, as M. Sinha reminds us in her "Nationalism and

Respectable Sexuality in India," "has often served as a nodal point for the reproduction of various forms of gendered political, economic, and ideological domination" (1995: 51). Analogously, Uberoi notes that it has "underlain and informed much of the agenda of social reform"; most debates about social reform, particularly as they related to the women's question, were, in fact, "contestations over sexuality" in as much as women's sexuality was seen as inextricably linked to maintaining social order and individual, group, and national identity (1996b: xvi). With the female as a key trope in organizing national self-definition and for mediating modernity, under the aegis of even an enlightened or benign patriarchy, real women's sexuality (the possibility, as it were, of their acknowledging and becoming self-aware of their sexuality) became, or came to be viewed as, a troubling aspect of modernity, at odds rather than continuous with "the modernizing project," not least because, as Vasudevan points out, it opened the projects of a desired modernity "to an uncharted terrain of social flux" (1996: 99).

With this in mind, one can see how Benegal's attempt in *Ankur*, and subsequent films, to map the disempowerment and oppression of women, *but also* the resistance to and subversion of these on the terrain of women's sexuality, constitutes a refusal, even a rejection of the effort, on behalf of national and normative social self-definition, to uncouple and thereby contain what Vasudevan calls "those fraught aspects of modernity that derived from transformation in the social position and sexual outlook of women" from the modernizing project the nation undertook before and after its independence. Rendered natural (i.e., naturalized) and denuded of a moralism that specifies licit and illicit relations, normative and deviant sexualities, women's sexuality in *Ankur* (and other Benegal films) is made co-extensive with their emancipation and the (Indian) nation's modernity. In this effort, a realist aesthetic plays an important role in naturalizing what has been rendered unnatural through moralizing interdictions.

However, though *Ankur* can project, through its representation of Lakshmi's situation and developing consciousness, the need for and possible contours of new structures (and spaces), it suggests that the kind of "massive change" gender equality can bring about is crucially dependent on sustained ideological labor because the resistance to it is so entrenched and of such long duration. This labor, moreover, is at least as much the burden of all the members of society as it is of the state that promised radical transformation at its inception. Benegal returns to certain elements of this ideological task again and again in his successive films.

Nishant

> As you mentioned, the *Ramayana* references are very strong in the film, and in a sense what happens is that Sita escapes with Ravana, rather than Ram rejecting Sita because of her supposed unfaithfulness. It really turns the traditional story on its head.
>
> (van der Heide to Benegal 2006: 71)

> The *Rāmāyaṇa* in India is not just a story with a variety of retellings; it is a language with which a host of statements may be made. Women in Andhra Pradesh have long used this language to say what they wish to say, as women.
>
> (Rao, V. N. 1992: 114)

Made within a year of each other, *Ankur* and *Nishant* display significant continuities, which make them part of a similar, if not identical, undertaking: As in *Ankur*, in *Nishant* the Telangana peasants' struggle is the specific, even exemplary, struggle through which the brutalities of feudal power are made evident. But whereas in *Ankur* this struggle functions as a historical backdrop, in *Nishant* it is an overt player and subject within the film itself, which is "based on an event that became the beginning of the revolt" and that took "place very close to where [Benegal] shot the film" (van der Heide 2006: 71).[23] As with *Ankur*, moreover, *Nishant*'s critique of feudal power is made apparent through and from the position of the sexually exploited subaltern woman, although in *Nishant* the primary female figure who is exploited, Sushila, unlike Lakshmi, is from the middle class; she is feisty and vocal from the start in a way that Lakshmi gradually learns to be.[24] *Nishant*'s gender-based critique also includes an understanding not only of the co-implication of patriarchy with feudal power, but also of their co-implication with certain understandings of masculinity with violence. Finally, like *Ankur*, *Nishant* renders ambiguous the possibility of actually achieving social transformation signaled here via the revolt with which the film ends; more significantly, *Nishant* renders the possibility of social change ambiguous by showing the barriers that prevent the comprehensive emancipation of women that both films suggest is an indispensable precondition of such change. But this ambiguity stems not, as in *Ankur*, from the awareness that the new structures and/or spaces required for such change to occur are as yet unavailable. It stems, instead, from the spectator's inability to decide, on the one hand, what to make of a revolt that leaves behind such comprehensive destruction of both the "good" and the "bad," "oppressor" and "oppressed." Does it mean that all efforts at transformation are futile? Or, alternatively, does it represent a cleaning of the stables, as it were, *before* change can occur? On the other hand, and perhaps more significantly, does it stem from the audience's inability to decide whether the female protagonist alone has so internalized patriarchy's dictates that she is unable to free herself comprehensively, or whether the film as well is so handicapped?

A significant divergence of *Nishant* from *Ankur* accrues from the extended parallels it establishes between itself and the Indian epic, the *Ramayana*, such that, as Valicha puts it, "*Nishant* emerges out of *Ramayana* which [in turn] bears a new impress" (1988: 97). This recourse to mythic and epic material in *Nishant* raises interesting questions with regard to Benegal's deployment of a realist aesthetic. For Prasad, the epic and realist narratives represent distinct, even conflicting, aesthetic projects, with the former, furthermore, "enabl[ing] the transformation of feudalism into spectacle … increas[ing] the temporal distance

… by a few thousand years and inscrib[ing] the peasant revolt in the timeless overarching narrative of conflict between élite groups" (1998a: 207–208). Contrarily, I believe that the two narratives are complementary rather than mutually antagonistic. After all, mythological and epic narratives, no less than historical and other kinds of narratives, provide ways of apprehending one's world and its reality, and "frame," as Hansen puts it, "paradigms which assist individuals and groups in defining their identities, inculcating values … and judging the actions of others" (1988: 25). In as much as a realist aesthetic draws upon, and is constituted by, these narratives in its (re-)presentation of reality, such narratives perform a crucial mediating function. Furthermore, as carriers of the ideological and other investments of diverse groups situated within different historical moments, epic and mythological narratives, no less than other kinds of narratives, are dynamic and subject to diverse, historically situated appropriations and reinterpretations. As such, they constitute what Kapur defines as "a living tradition" (1987: 79). For, as Thapar and other scholars have demonstrated, the *Ramayana* embodies just such a "living tradition," "belong[ing] not to any one moment in history *for it has its own history which lies embedded in the many versions* which were woven around the theme at different times and places" to reflect the divergent "social aspirations and ideological concerns" of different groups (Thapar 1989: 72, emphasis added).[25] Benegal's *Nishant*, in turn, adds to this history by foregrounding and renegotiating the narrative strand that deals with Sita's abduction. However, Benegal's critical renegotiation proceeds, as Vaidyanathan suggests, "more from within than without … Benegal makes use of mythological themes to meet tyranny on its own terms so that the social enemy can be fought with its own beliefs" (1996: 83). Subversive of, rather than oppositional to, the ideological structures it challenges, Benegal's renegotiation of the narrative strand dealing with Sita's abduction runs the risk, inevitably perhaps, of reproducing some of these structures.

The film begins not with a reference to the *Ramayana*, but with a dramatization of feudal conditions comparable to those leading to the Telangana People's Struggle. The opening scenes in *Nishant*, most dealing with the robbery of the temple jewels, establish a set of coordinates – not least, the film's representational methods – for *Nishant*'s critical examination of the nature and persistence of feudal power. These entail the juxtaposition of characters and spaces, sometimes within the same scene, other times in successive scenes, that the spectator is invited to view as analogous with each other, thereby revealing feudal power, for the most part, as all-embracing, propped up not only by its perpetrators but also by its victims.[26] I address two such clusters in some detail below.

When the village peasants discover the robbery in the temple, they go to the feudal landlord and patriarch, Anna, instead of the state's representative for law and order, the *patel*, signaling clearly where they believe real power is vested. This allows Anna to conceal the implication of his brothers, Prasad, Anjaiya, and Vishwam, in the crime. He brings in a soothsayer, who performs a ritual "disclosing" a homeless drunk found earlier sleeping on the temple's steps as the thief. The priest and the *patel*, who could be said to represent sources of power independent of the landlord's, accede to his power by remaining silent, letting him scapegoat the homeless drunk even though they know otherwise. The consolidated force of such feudal power, represented by their collusion with the landlord, is reinforced by visually pairing the two as well, rendering them virtually identical to each other despite the differing sources of their authority (religious vs. secular; "traditional" vs. "modern") – on entering the temple, for instance, the policeman squats much like the priest does along the same wall. Nor are the peasants exempt from such collusion: despite their position as victims of the landlord's oppression, which should make them sympathize with the falsely accused homeless drunk, they participate willingly in his scapegoating as they chase him out of the village.

The film suggests some external reasons for the priest and *patel*'s acquiescence to the landlord's scapegoating of the homeless drunk: as he reclaims the gold chain Vishwam has dropped at the scene of the robbery, Anna promises the priest funds to repair the temple, bribing him to secure his silence. Additionally, the *patel*'s self-interest and relative power are demonstrably co-extensive with his collaboration with the landlord in a way that they are not with the villagers' or the homeless drunk's. But the reasons for the peasants' collusion are shown to lie primarily elsewhere. Insofar as they don't benefit from their acquiescence, their collusion, manifest through their silence, proceeds from their having internalized the structures through which feudal power exerts its force on those who bear the brunt of its oppressiveness; these structures include this power's representation of itself as natural and self-evident rather than as constituted by human beings with specific political and social interests that are (or should be) open to interrogation and challenge. Thus, the peasants *know* that the real thieves are their feudal masters, but this knowledge, far from empowering them to act independently of these masters, seems to entrap them further in their servitude. This is made apparent in another set of paired scenes following those dealing with the robbery in the temple.

In the first one, several peasant children playing in a yard outside the feudal mansion get into an argument. In a re-play of the temple robbery and its aftermath, one of the boys accuses his opponent of stealing the jewels from the temple, to which the accused, explicitly articulating a suspicion shared most likely by all the villagers, responds, "So what? I am the landlord. What can you do?" This demonstration that even children are not exempt from the internalization of the power dynamic that underwrites feudal authority is designed to reveal how pervasive such authority is, although, unlike their silent and silenced elders, the children are not averse to explicitly identifying the *real* thief or *speaking* the truth, even though this truth is restricted to the realm of play and play-acting. As the boys chase each other, yelling "Thief, thief," exiting in the bottom right hand corner of the screen, a group of villagers appears from the left hand of the screen in the following scene, chasing the homeless drunk who has been earlier accused of being the thief. Simultaneously, Prasad and Anjaiya, who are the real culprits, appear on their motorbike from the upper right hand corner of the screen; as they cross the villagers chasing the falsely accused man out of the village, he accuses the brothers of being "bloody thieves," spits at them and curses, "May their house burn to ashes." Thus, having dramatized varying degrees of collaboration with feudal power, not least, through the internalization of its dictates, these opening scenes also identify one source of overt defiance through the figure of the homeless drunk, who refuses, quite literally, to be silent in the face of the injustice being perpetrated against him. But he is also a figure on the margins, in the process, furthermore, of being run out of the village. As my research assistant, Max Wolcott, astutely pointed out, however, the film retains the symbolic freight of the homeless drunk's defiance by making it resonate at the end of the film when his beating *by* the landlord at the beginning of the film is mirrored in his enthusiastic participation in the beating *of* the landlord at the end.

Nishant's opening, then, establishes the sheer oppressiveness of feudal power, which proceeds not only from its consolidation in the hands of a few largely undeserving and corrupt people, but also from the sheer routineness of its operations, its habitual and commonplace presence in, and impact on, the lives of its victims. For instance, Prasad and Anjaiya are often shown wandering around the village and countryside "stealing" food and women with equal equanimity to satisfy their appetites. Reduced almost to caricatures, their behavior and actions are often presented in clichéd terms (their drunkenness and use of coarse language and loud laughter mimic the stereotypical attributes of villains in mainstream Hindi cinema) as if to underscore the banality and ordinariness of the evils that feudal power represents. Interestingly, Benegal's recourse to stereotypical and heightened or melodramatic representation, insinuated into a film that has otherwise been seen as an instance of his realist aesthetic, disturbs but does not destroy the plausibility (a hallmark of this aesthetic) of the brothers' behavior. At the same time, while suggesting reasons for why such power persists, the film's opening also displays a degree of pessimism regarding the possibility of social and political change being effected by the victims, a pessimism that extends to the peasant insurrection concluding the film.

For critics of the film this pessimism is deeply problematic, the film's signal failure (attributed by Prasad to "the statist realism of Benegal's aesthetic") being its inability or refusal to elaborate the "complex processes through which movements of resistance are organized by peasants" or by "a modern political force entering the peasant world and organizing them on the basis of a programme of resistance and opposition" (Prasad 1998a: 207). I argue, instead, as the opening scenes make clear, that *Nishant* is less interested in the organizing of the rebellion than in the preconditions of its possibility – a mentally or psychically transformed peasantry that refuses to see feudal power and therefore its own subordinated position within it as natural or self-evident. More importantly, the film is especially invested in tracking the processes through which women achieve their emancipation, implicitly suggesting that women's emancipation is central to overcoming a feudal mentality and its oppressive practices (although with respect to actually achieving such emancipation the film is equivocal, if not altogether pessimistic).[27] Embedded in this decision – i.e., the focus on women as potentially powerful agents of change – is a critique not just of patriarchal structures but, more specifically, of masculinity.

In a striking choice, the feudal household is presented as made up almost entirely of men, except for the youngest brother's wife, Rukmini, and the maid, Pochamma. More to the point, the feudal household is shown as deeply inhospitable to women, as manifested by the sexual violence directed against them. While the viewer is not told anything about Anna's marital status, s/he is told that Anjaiya's wife has run away and Prasad's has committed suicide. In a scene where Anjaiya and Prasad have forced a poor peasant to send his wife to service their sexual needs, we see the peasant woman first with Anna and then in the room where Prasad and Anjaiya await her, the implication being that any woman brought into the household is shared by all brothers; the violence against her, thus, is fourfold, reinforcing the idea that the only position available for women in this household is as a sexual object. At the same time, as Benegal hones in on the peasant woman's consciousness of her violated subjectivity in a point-of-view shot as she faces the brothers, the viewer accesses their brutal behavior through her perspective and silent suffering. Analogously, the male-centered aggression and violence of the household is intermittently interrupted by a focus on a spirited Rukmini who urges her husband, Vishwam, not "to imitate [his] brothers." Alternatives or opposition to the feudal world(-view) are thus vested in women, though not all women automatically embody such alternatives or opposition. Pochamma, for instance, not only seems resigned to the operations of feudal power but also sometimes seems to actively support it under the guise of offering pragmatic advice. "This is their house," she tells Sushila (the newly arrived schoolmaster's wife who is abducted by the two middle brothers ostensibly as a favor to the youngest who is attracted to her) when Sushila shuts the door of her room against possible intrusion from, and further sexual violation by, the brothers. "They can break the door down." On the other hand, Pochamma is aligned with the rebelling peasants in the concluding scenes of the film and participates in the vandalism they unleash.

Nishant's most extended and concentrated examination of the imbrication of feudal power with the violation of women is undertaken through its narrative's focus on the abduction of Sushila. Closely paralleling the abduction of Sita in *Ramayana*, this narrative focus draws substantively on those versions of *Ramayana* that produce an understanding quite different from the one forwarded by the dominant Valmiki version of the text.

Those critics who have commented on *Nishant*'s allegorizing of the Sita episode(s) from *Ramayana* all assume that Benegal's is an oppositional rendition. "It is the exorcism of Sita that is the burden of Ramayana," declares Valicha, "it is the exorcism of Ramayana that is performed by *Nishant*" (1988: 99). Benegal, however, views his deployment of the material from *Ramayana* as drawing upon both dominant and alternative renditions that demonstrate the epic's complexity, its openness to a multiplicity of ideological agendas, thereby bringing his understanding of *Ramayana* closer to the one espoused by Thapar – as a cultural resource that exemplifies, in Kapur's words, "a living tradition." In response to van der Heide's insistence that his use of "traditional stories like the *Ramayana* and the *Mahabharat* … is often much more ironic and much more critical," therefore, Benegal demurs:

> Yes, but there is also a keener understanding of the epics themselves because the epics have a complexity that a lot of us would like not to see. There are social views and attitudes that exist in the epics that are quite extraordinary, apart from the many interpretations and interpolations that have come into those epics. One has to look at them in so many different ways, whether it is for an ironic perspective or to use them as parallels. Whichever way you look at them, they play a very important role in Indian life.
>
> (van der Heide 2006: 71)

The Sita of the hegemonic *Ramayana* narrative, or of what V.N. Rao calls "the public *Rāmāyaṇa*s" that glorify "the accepted values of a male-dominated world" (1992: 129), is the stereotypically ideal image of Indian womanhood – chaste, selfless, passive, and subservient to her husband's wishes – that continues to have a tenacious hold on the Indian imagination. But this Sita, whose absolute devotion and purity are assumed to be central to the ideal marriage, can herself be historically placed as coming into being at a particular moment, in response to particular social, historical, cultural, and political exigencies. According to U. Chakravarty, who undertakes an analysis of "the development of the Sita myth" in order to "get an insight into the conscious process by which feminine identity was being conditioned," Valmiki's *Ramayana* "grafted onto an originally simple story" a Rama possessed of "masculine heroism, valour and honour" and a Sita embodying the attributes associated with ideal womanhood mentioned above (1983: 70–71).

Chakravarty rehearses the plotlines of "the earliest version of the Ramayana available – *Dasaratha Jataka* and a simple story in the *Santiparva* section of the *Mahabharat*" – and a second myth dealing with Ravana to demonstrate how Valmiki combined and expanded these in order to forward specific ideological agendas that were themselves tied to specific socio-political imperatives. Thus, she points out how "in the earliest version Sita was not abducted and was [therefore] not a victim figure who had to prove her chastity." Moreover, in order to produce "negative images of women," Valmiki's story "hinge[s]" on three episodes:

> Kaikeyi's demand that Rama be exiled; … Surpanakha's overtures to Rama, her rebuff at his hands, and her subsequent mutilation by Lakshmana; and … Sita's demand for the deer and her unjust accusations against Lakshmana following his reluctance to leave her alone in the forest.
>
> (Chakravarty 1983: 71)

Each episode is designed to *contain* women's independence and/or open expression of their sexuality (ibid.).[28] This, Chakravarty argues, is tied to "the image of women in the Aryan prototype in contrast to women in tribal society," which was also tied to the transition to an agricultural economy requiring "the destruction of forest culture." Rama is associated with the former, while Ravana is associated with a pre-agricultural society in which women like Surpanakha (Ravan's sister) are "strong and independent individuals" as opposed to the subservient women in societies like that of Ayodhya founded on an agricultural economy, displaying thereby an "inverse relationship between economic development and the position of women: the higher the economic development of a society the lower is the position of its women" (1983: 72). Also related to the imperatives of a developed, agricultural society that constitutes the context for Valmiki's *Ramayana* is a conception of marriage "aim[ed] at the begetting of children of undisputed paternity to inherit the father's wealth as natural heirs" (Chakravarty, U. 1983: 72). Hence the demand for a chaste and subservient Sita in the Valmiki version, which is irrelevant to the society from which the earliest version of *Ramayana, Dasaratha Jataka* emerges.

Chakravarty's essay also references "redeeming versions" of the Sita legend in renditions that lie "outside the classical Hindu tradition." She mentions two in particular in which Sita refuses the humiliation entailed in Rama's demand for her purification, following her abduction, through *agnipariksha* (fire ordeal); the folk version going so far as to "de-recognize" Rama and "give[ing] her sons a matrilineal heritage," thereby scripting for herself what Chakravarty, "for want of a better expression," labels a "deviant depiction of feminine identity" (1983: 74). V.N. Rao, on the other hand, mines "women's oral tradition in Telugu" – a resource closer to home for Benegal who is from, and grew up in, Andhra Pradesh – to "represent a distinctly female way of using the *Rāmāyaṇa* to subvert," albeit not altogether annihilate, "[male] authority" (1992: 114). Focusing primarily on "a group of songs … sung by upper class [Andhra] Brahmin women," Rao notes how these women "do not view Valmiki as authoritative"; instead, he is merely "a person who was involved in the events of Sita's and Rama's lives and who composed an account of those events – but not necessarily the correct account" (1992: 114–115). These songs privilege women's activities and interests and the domestic sphere, in which Rama figures in a secondary role, "controlled and subservient to the demands of women" by virtue of the social space and "women-controlled rituals" in which he is called upon to participate (1992: 119). While "women in these songs never openly defy propriety," in showing "the affections and tensions of a joint family," these songs' "underlying meanings reveal an atmosphere of subdued tensions, hidden sexuality, and frustrated emotions.… No one's character is untainted; no person loves another unconditionally. Even Sita's chastity is open to doubt," with one episode suggesting that "Sita harbours a hidden desire to sleep with Ravana" (1992: 128).

One way Benegal signals his interest in a more dynamic and complex alternative representation of Sita is by establishing, in a succession of economically executed scenes, a "Sita" figure, Sushila, who is not averse to making her own wishes and desires apparent.[29] As the schoolmaster's family makes its way into the village, she forthrightly repeats her objections to the move. In another scene, on a day when she is out shopping for groceries, she registers her anger, about being stared at by Vishwam, openly to her husband. When her husband, the schoolmaster, reminds her that only a few days earlier he had tried to prevent the brothers' prurient interest in her by asking her to close the window so they could not see her, she smartly retorts, "Should I enclose myself in the house? Start wearing a *burqa* [veil]?" To the extent that the viewer agrees that such a restriction is unreasonable and, thus, sides with Sushila rather than the schoolmaster, his conservatism is exposed as an assertion of (patriarchal) authority and a form of containment from which she justifiably wants to free herself.[30]

Furthermore, by demonstrating certain continuities between the "traditional" feudal household and the schoolmaster's "modern" nuclear family set-up, Benegal renders Sushila's provocative and apparently willful behavior understandable – as a form of recalcitrance, if not outright resistance, to traditional gender- and status-based constraints. The scenes that display the relationship between the two couples – Vishwam and Rukmini and Sushila and the schoolmaster – are juxtaposed with each other to map differences, but also similarities, so that the judgments made about the one spill over into those elicited about the other. Thus, in one scene, on a night that Vishwam has been drinking, he enters his room and bed aggressively to join his half-asleep wife; the scene dissolves into one that shows the teacher and his wife waking up the next morning. At first glance the two seem to reflect diametrically opposed elements, with the latter displaying a serene domestic routine as Sushila takes care of their child and gets the morning meal ready for her small family. But in this and other scenes where the schoolmaster and Sushila interact with one another, there is little companionship or agreement, much as there is little companionable interaction between Vishwam and Rukmini. Also, both men exhibit considerable indifference towards their wives. Though Sushila's oft-repeated request for a mirror has been seen as illustrating her narcissism, it can equally and justifiably be interpreted as signaling dissatisfaction with her husband's lack of attention to her, for which she tries to compensate by asserting her attractiveness and, through that, her claim to his attention. Not surprisingly, then, sex in this marriage is based not on desire or love, but functions rather as a commodity, a form of exchange, much like it does in the feudal household. Thus, one night Sushila resists her husband's sexual overtures, only to relent when she secures his promise to purchase the mirror and a sari for her the next day. Even *before* her abduction, then, the Sita figure in *Nishant*, far from being represented as a submissive, passive object of her husband's patriarchal constraint or of Vishwam's male desire is presented instead as a *desiring* subject in her own right. This has significant implications for who she will become *after* her abduction.

In keeping with his investment in female empowerment and emancipation, when depicting Sushila's successive rape by the four brothers, Benegal concentrates entirely on both the subhuman brutality and villainy of the brothers as evidence of the pathologies of feudal (patriarchal) power and on her violated being, made explicit through a close-up of her anguished face and stifled internal and external pain. As with the rape of the peasant woman earlier, Benegal eschews an explicit depiction of the act of rape itself to block the "visual voyeurism" that S.A. Chatterjee contends is the primary incitement for explicit depictions of rape in films:

> Rape in cinema, in any language, in any patriarchal culture, has certain unwritten specific functions … to arouse the males in the audience sexually … [and] to use, to a certain extent, the opportunity of explicit representations of the female anatomy in a physically violent act that has been forced on the very body.
>
> (Chatterjee, S. A. 1997:44)

For Chatterjee, with "cinematic techniques like close-ups, fast editing, slow-motion … [and] the heightening effects of sound and music" at its disposal, cinema more than any other medium, achieves the functions an explicit representation of rape is meant to accomplish (ibid.). Benegal's refusal to deploy these techniques to depict Sushila's successive rapes denudes them of their element of sexual titillation. All the viewer sees is the brothers arriving and leaving; what's more, the camera stays low so that the viewer sees only the bottom half of their torsos clad in pajamas. This depersonalizes them by rendering them faceless, whereas Sushila is granted subjectivity by being personalized through close-ups of her face. In the one instance, we do see Prasad's face as he lies on top of her, but the camera quickly switches to an overhead shot focused on Sushila's agony. By thus emphasizing Sushila's violation – her subjective perception, furthermore, of this violation – *Nishant* renders the subsequent demand for her purification moot, even morally reprehensible. This Sita, like the Sita of the "redeeming versions" U. Chakravarty alludes to, is being positioned, it seems, to refuse her humiliation by Rama.

Initially rendered inert and shell-shocked by her abduction and violent rapes, Sushila paradoxically directs the anger she inevitably feels, not at her violators, but against her husband who, by her reckoning, has failed to rescue her. At first glance a curious displacement of blame that seems to absolve her real violators, her response is rendered somewhat understandable by virtue of its mediation by two scenes that, one, reveal the film's quarrel with the morality that undergirds assessments of the consequences of Sita's abduction forwarded in hegemonic versions of the *Ramayana* and, two, suggest the possibility for female solidarity – albeit brief and extremely fragile – that could potentially have attenuated the male-dominated space of the feudal household. In the first scene, after Pochamma advises Sushila against closing "the door" on her continuing rape by the four brothers, she repeats the alleged moral interdiction that lies at the heart of Sita's predicament in the hegemonic version of the *Ramayana*: "Where will you go?" she asks, "back to your husband? He won't let you near him." What's more, "the whole village will point and spit at you." Pochamma's realistic, but entirely conservative, assessment of Sushila's future were she to return to her husband is based on an understanding of social morality not peculiar to the hegemonic *Ramayana* alone, although the *Ramayana* continues to be used to validate patriarchal strictures regarding women's sexual purity as an indispensable function of their role as potential and actual reproducers of legitimate progeny.[31] In such a context, the responsibility for Sita and Sushila's respective violations is seen to lie with them, not their violators. Sushila's anger against her husband, then, can arguably be construed as anger also – even primarily – directed against a social structure that blames the victim, holding her responsible for her rape.

In the second scene, after Pochamma complains to Rukmini that Sushila is refusing to eat any food sent to her, Rukmini, who has been sending the food from her kitchen, goes to Sushila's room to urge her to eat: "You have been starving yourself," she says, "you must stay alive for your child; don't be stubborn." Persuaded by Rukmini's genuine goodwill, Sushila eats. Briefly, very briefly, Sushila seems to have found someone sympathetic to the horrors of her situation. But this moment of sympathetic interaction between the wife and the mistress is soon destroyed by Vishwam's explicitly articulated preference for Sushila when Sushila demands and gets her own kitchen where she can cook for Vishwam and herself, thereby displacing Rukmini in her role as wife. For Sushila, this demand is tied to her desire to "live with dignity"; for Rukmini it entails a substantial loss of status as wife; for Vishwam, it is integral to Sushila's humanity: "She's human too," he contests Rukmini's protests about giving Sushila her own kitchen, "she must have her place." A variation of the assertion Surya makes when his father berates him for bringing Lakshmi *into* the intimate space of his household and his bedroom, this statement has also been used by Benegal to speak of Lakshmi's and Sushila's rights as *human* beings; thus it carries some extra-contextual, extra-filmic authority (interview with me, March 26, 2006). But what Vishwam's statement (and possibly Benegal's focus on and sympathy for Sushila) cannot and does not address is Rukmini's plangent question: "What'll it [Sushila's change in status] make me?" Must the empowerment of one take place, the viewer of the film has to wonder, on the back of the other?

Sushila's demand for a kitchen, and thus for a status comparable to Vishwam's wife, is itself mediated by the scene of a chance encounter with her husband that propels her into devising an alternative familial arrangement which, in effect, "de-recognize[s]" her husband. (Cinematically this scene confirms their absolute estrangement from each other: there is not one shot when the viewer can see both their faces in the same frame; instead the viewer sees Sushila and the schoolmaster in consecutive shots with the camera positioned behind one or the other's shoulder. This is very different to the early scenes of the film, where despite the tension and minimal interaction between the two, a two shot is often used and evenly distributed throughout the frame to track their interaction with each other.) In response to her husband's query, "How are you?" Sushila launches into a passionate tirade against his failure to rescue her. She rehearses her many humiliations and indignities, berates him for his cowardice and summarily dismisses his account of his efforts to rescue her, demanding, instead, that he should have "set fire to the mansion," "cut the brothers to pieces," destroyed everything associated with her ignominy. "But you would have done all this," she concludes her tirade, "if you had been a man."[32]

Insofar as Benegal's critique of feudal power includes its imbrication with patriarchy, masculinity, and violence such that each defines the other through the integral links that obtain among them, Sushila's demand for a display of masculinity from her husband premised on violence seems to be deeply problematic, confronting the film's viewer with an ambiguity that seems unresolvable: Is this demand Sushila's alone, offered, that is, from her perspective which the film then asks us to evaluate critically? Or, given that the film elicits its audience's sympathy on Sushila's behalf, not least by centering her subjectivity in its project of tracking the processes through which women can empower and emancipate themselves, is this a demand the film shares and asks its audience to accede to? If it's the former, the film seems to be suggesting that Sushila's development as a genuinely emancipated subject has been short-circuited; she has been unable to rid herself altogether of those elements of patriarchal, masculinist ideologies that constrain her. If, however, it's the second, then the contradiction belongs to the film itself. Thus, far from demonstrating the formidable, perhaps insurmountable hurdle a woman like Sushila must overcome – a profound, subconscious because unrecognized, internalization of patriarchal ideologies – in order to emancipate herself and thereby set the forces of social transformation in motion, the film instead exhibits a blind spot proceeding from its equally profound and unrecognized internalization of the ideologies it takes to task. In this regard, Prasad is right, although for reasons quite different from the ones I have alluded to. *Nishant* does, indeed, seem to "offer the spectator a considerably less secure position of contemplation than *Ankur*" (1998a: 205). In doing so, one could also justifiably argue that, contra Prasad's contention that Benegal's first three films stage a developing perspective linked integrally to his "statist realism," *Nishant*, like *Ankur*, offers more than one spectator position from which to view his films, and far from offering a further development in an evolutionary schema, its protagonist, Sushila, unlike Lakshmi, is unable to emancipate herself in substantial ways from patriarchal constraints.

But the concluding scenes of *Nishant* return to, and seem to affirm, the film's earlier critique of violence based on its imbrication with patriarchy and masculinity, thereby suggesting its own position vis-à-vis the peasant rebellion with which the film concludes. Incited by his wife's indictment of his lack of manliness and cowardice, the schoolmaster rouses himself from his (unmanly?) despair to organize the peasants against their feudal masters – an effort in which the priest joins him. This rebellion, when it happens, is characterized by an inchoate and anarchic violence that, while fulfilling Sushila's demand that her husband should have burned the mansion down, "cut the brothers to pieces" to punish them and redress her (and the peasants') oppression, enfolds her and other innocent people like Rukmini as well within its embrace. "Violence," says Benegal in his interview with S. Chatterjee, "creates more problems that it solves" (2003–2004: 24). With one of the final images of *Nishant* being that of a shell-shocked priest observed anxiously by a little boy, following the destruction the rebellion has left in its wake, the film can hardly be seen to offer the rebellion as something that can be construed as, in R. Williams's resonant phrase, a "resource of hope" presaging a successful transition to a changed socio-political order.

Analogously, Sushila's rebellion against the patriarchal order of things is not successful either, not least because, as I have already argued, her grasp of this order is insufficiently critical and self-reflexive. Valicha makes much of the image of "love or emotional intimacy" Vishwam and Sushila display as they try to escape the carnage in the mansion by running off into the arid, mountainous landscape that surrounds it (1988: 95). Constituting "the momentary union of two lovers" as "they cling to each other in an assertion that is fragile, evanescent," this image functions, for Valicha, in direct counterpoint to the morality that underwrites the "socio-cultural ... framework" of the hegemonic *Ramayana*, which is "fundamentally iniquitous to the female": *Nishant* shows that "Sita can seek liberation outside the morally encysted social system" (1988: 96–97). But neither the scene Valicha examines nor the film itself supports such a "utopian" reading, eschewing as it does a (potentially) romantic conclusion to settle instead for a more "realistic" one where things don't, in fact, work out for the two of them. (A realist aesthetic encourages, even demands, ambiguity, and open, if not always tragic, endings are seen to mimic real life.) As Vishwam grabs Sushila's hand and starts running away from the mansion, Sushila worries about Rukmini, who has been left behind. Vishwam callously dismisses her concern, insisting that Rukmini will follow them. (His callousness is driven home through a brief shot of Rukmini lying dead in the mansion even as Vishwam escapes with Sushila.) When they reach the side of the hill where they rest momentarily before being caught by the rampaging villagers, Sushila's thoughts are focused entirely on her son, and while Vishwam rests his head on her shoulder and clings to her, her own glance is turned away from him looking into the distance, thereby underscoring the asymmetry in this relationship: Vishwam's attraction for and need of Sushila clearly exceeds Sushila's for him. Furthermore, the film itself does not develop the relationship between Vishwam and Sushila enough for its audience to consider it the way Valicha does. For Benegal, "One of the main points about the story" is "the fact that [Sushila] recognizes her own sexuality" (van der Heide 2006: 71) – a recognition that emancipates her from an inattentive husband and draws her to Vishwam, who does seem to recognize her "humanity" and attractiveness. But although Vishwam is distinguished from his brothers enough to make him a marginally sympathetic figure, the film only attends to him as the accidental catalyst for Sushila's potential emancipation, which is ironic given his role in her abduction (Prasad and Anjaiya abduct her in the first place because Vishwam is attracted to her). What's more, in a film that reveals how deeply embedded dominant ideological structures are within the psyche of people, not least the psyches of its victims, it's difficult to imagine Vishwam escaping entirely the feudal mentality that has formed him, much as Sushila, as I have shown, does not escape altogether her psychic formation within patriarchy. Hence, it's hard to imagine a socially progressive shape for their relationship had they survived and, following from this, to imagine such a relationship as the basis of meaningful social transformation.

Even Benegal's re-envisioning of the *Ramayana* tradition partakes of some of this pessimism. Despite his focus on Sushila's display of her independence and desire to discover her own sexuality, Sushila, like Sita, dies. In a variation of Lakshmi's predicament in *Ankur* – that there is no social space as yet available to house her emancipated self – there is in *Nishant* no emancipatory space that Sushila, having left her husband, can inhabit within which to nurture a sense of her developing freedom from social constraints. And this despite that, as Benegal puts it in his interview with S. Chatterjee, "there was no condemnation [in *Nishant*] of the choice she made" when she turned her back on her husband (2003–2004: 24).[33]

Nishant is a dark film (its title, which translates as Night's End, is, surely, ironically meant), more pessimistic than *Ankur* in as much as the latter is unequivocal about Lakshmi's development into an emancipated subject, even though the film cannot as yet identify a transformed social space for her to occupy. *Nishant* cannot even offer such a consolation: its protagonist is destroyed before she has succeeded in emancipating herself fully from the imperatives of a patriarchal ideology, and an aroused peasantry reproduces the violence it has been subject to, a violence that Benegal understands, but cannot condone; indeed, such violence has been the object of his critique in a substantial part of the film. In films that are vested in the more substantive "decolonization of the mind" (Ngugi wa Thiongo's phrase) as an indispensable precondition to an externally transformed society, Benegal's *Nishant* and *Ankur* commit themselves to long-range modalities of transformation. In this regard, change in external structures, while undoubtedly necessary, is regarded as insufficient.[34] Hence Benegal's focus again and again on figures like Sushila and Lakshmi, who, by virtue of their gender and caste locations, learn to balk at ideological restrictions the overcoming of which constitutes the possibility of their freedom. Hence, too, his insistent focus on the internalization of oppression by feudal power's victims that requires a long and arduous process of inner, psychic transformation for his subjects to unlearn.

2 "Performing wom[e]n"

The "*Nachne-Ganewalis*" of *Bhumika*, *Mandi*, and *Sardari Begum*

> The figuration of the "performing woman" in the hegemonic discourse on respectability was, however, peculiar. While the "common" woman's marginality emanated from her differential terms of inclusion, the "performing" woman was excluded from middle-class hegemonic discourses through excision. The middle class excised, erased, and thereby negated the creative role of performing women in its quest for a respectable nation. Women performers were kept out of the frame of the nation in the making.
>
> Singh 2007: 94

Unlike the preceding chapter, which examined Benegal's first two films, made within a year of one another, this chapter addresses three films – *Bhumika* (The Role; 1976); *Mandi* (Marketplace; 1983); and the eponymous *Sardari Begum* (1996) – separated from each other by several years, with the last separated from two earliest films by a little over two decades. Nevertheless, a continuity of interests and ideological investments link the latter three films with each other and with the first two, including: each film's focus on a female protagonist and subject; her conscious and unconscious efforts to emancipate herself from the debilitations of her gender, class, and caste oppression; and, finally, for the purposes of my argument, her function as a figure through whom women's relationship to the hegemonic values and ideological agendas of the Indian nation-in-the-making are assessed and interrogated. The nation remains, then, a salient frame of reference for grasping the ideological investments of these Benegal films.

Within this continuity of interests and investments, however, are differences in emphases and critical positioning between the first two and the latter three: The first two – *Ankur* and *Nishant* – are unambiguous, even relentless, in their criticism of feudal power, which they represent as flowing from, and co-extensive with, the violence perpetrated by, and consonant with, patriarchal social, political, and cultural arrangements. Furthermore, despite their interrogation of the (nation-)state and its modernizing agendas' failure to create a space free(er) of the debilitations of patriarchal ideologies for its female and subaltern subjects, these two films' alignment of feudalism with a coercive tradition is more or less of a piece with an alignment assumed by official Indian nationalism, in whose self-definition feudalism is represented as a set of arrangements and ideologies that the fledgling nation-in-the-making must overcome to fully enter a much-desired modernity.

The performing women in the three later films – an actress in *Bhumika*; a group of prostitutes in *Mandi*; a *thumri* singer/courtesan in *Sardari Begum* – on the other hand, represent professions, identities, and cultural repertoires that flourished under, and were indelibly associated with, a feudal order, but which were delegitimized, marginalized, even excised from the self-definitions and constitutive narratives of the new Indian nation. "Women performers," Singh notes, "were kept out of the frame of the nation in the making" (see epigraph; 2007: 94). By focusing on protagonists who belong to professions and identities that are devalued and marginalized in the new Indian nation, these three later films, I argue, "unsettle" (Singh's term) the processes through which the Indian nation constituted itself, thereby also unsettling an unambiguously negative assessment of feudal social and cultural arrangements.[1] Thus, as opposed to the first two films that, through their strong critique of the ongoing presence of feudal/patriarchal structures in the new, putatively modern, nation and the concomitant failure of the (nation-)state to provide a social space hospitable to its female and subaltern subjects, bring attention to what the (nation-)state has failed to accomplish, the three later films undertake a more fundamental interrogation regarding India's nation-formation itself – what the nation deliberately excludes in order to become a nation.[2]

My claims about *Bhumika*, *Mandi*, and *Sardari Begum*'s interrogatory, dissident relationship with a hegemonic understanding of Indian national identity are indebted to, and draw upon, several critical/skeptical analyses of such hegemonic accounts – analyses that are themselves based on critical propositions regarding ideologies that underwrite national narratives in general. Because these films focus on performing women, my argument draws as well upon the richly diverse body of work on the intimate relationship between nation-formation in India and "classicization" (i.e., the production of a canon and/or processes of canonization) of performing arts like music and dance during the years immediately preceding and following India's independence. Critical/skeptical in examining the processes underwriting the classicization of music and dance, this body of work derives its critique from the exclusions these processes generate – of certain kinds and classes of performers, performance venues, and performance repertoires. To that end, with varying degrees of emphasis, it examines, for instance, the disenfranchisement of *devadasis* and *tawaifs* and hereditary musicians; the erosion of the *mehfils* in the courts of princely states and intimate salon gatherings; and the "sanitization and scientific standardization" of the "older forms" to name some (Peterson and Soneji 2008: 4; see also Bakhle 2005: 4–7; Mitra 2006: 71–75; Soneji 2000: 36–44; Srinivasan1989: 175–198). Indeed, this body of scholarship views the relationship between the classicization of the performing arts and national self-definition as a symbiotic one.

The middle class, as initiator and beneficiary, was crucial to the constitution of both processes.[3] The social reforms undertaken to propel India into independence and modernity were "tied," as Sangari and Vaid note, "to the self-definition of the middle class"; "male-initiated," virtually all these reforms positioned women as the object of reform, linking "different versions of female emancipation ... to the idea of national liberation and generation" (1990: 9). Several important consequences flowed from this class's centrality to India's national self-definition, foremost being what Singh categorizes as "the question of 'respectability,'" which "assum[ed] its sharpest form where the issues concerned women" (2007: 93). For this much sought-after respectability had as its referent an obsessive concern with women's sexuality and the sites within which it could flourish or be interdicted.[4] Not surprisingly, the performing woman, who was also a professional/working woman, could not be included in such a definition of the national subject, not only due to "her seemingly excessive mobility in the public sphere" (Singh 2007: 95) – a sphere that the reformed, recast, woman of the middle-class nationalist imaginary could enter only "in a limited way" (Sangari and Vaid 1990: 19) – but also because of her participation, for the most part, in a:

> non-conjugal sexuality ... [which] frustrated [the nationalist] construction of the morally "pure" Indian woman, the good wife, as the custodian and sign of a modern India, as well as [the] conceptualization of the conjugal, patriarchal Indian family as the pure, inner, spiritual realm of self and culture impervious to colonial encroachment.
>
> (Peterson and Soneji 2008: 17)

At the same time that these performing women became casualties of (nationalist) efforts to classicize music and dance, "conditions" were "created ... under which women, albeit middle-class ones, could enter a public cultural sphere without the fear of social disapproval" (Bakhle 2005: 11). Indeed, one could put it more strongly: the performing women were made into casualties precisely so that middle-class women could enter the public sphere in this regard. For example, while tracing an analogous process, the "invention of Bharatnatyam dance in the twentieth century," Peterson and Soneji point out that "the disenfranchisement of the devadasis," on which this "invention" is premised, "*was the necessary precondition for the takeover of the dance by middle-class women*" (2008: 17; emphasis added).[5] "Classicization," then, like national self-definition, of which it was both product and cause, entailed processes of disenfranchisement and enfranchisement underwritten by a species of middle-class morality in which any overt and autonomous deployment of female sexuality to non-conjugal ends was deemed problematic.[6]

Committed to a "revitalisation of Hinduism" this middle class also initiated, "at least some ... reform movements," as Moro notes, and "crafted an aggressive, anti-Muslim as well as anti-British Hindu identity" that makes them "early precursors of the Hindu nationalist movement in India today" (2004: 190).

Analogously, when accounting for the transformation of music from being what Bakhle calls "an unmarked practice in the eighteenth century to being marked as 'classical' in the twentieth century" (2005: 4), scholars document not just a shift in class alignment – "from service professional to bourgeois elite" – but also in communal identity – from Muslim to Hindu (Qureshi 1991: 161–162). This latter shift, in turn, also contributed to the entry of middle-class women into the cultural public sphere, an enabling condition of which was "[D.V.] Paluskar's Bhakti nationalism" that " 'Hinduized' music and sacralized its pedagogy" (Bakhle 2005: 11). Thus, a nexus of class and often communal identification privileging the discourse of, and injunctions regarding, female and familial respectability produced an alignment between gender and hegemonic understandings of the national subject that excluded the performing women of India's pre-independence past. Insofar as women's emancipation for Benegal, as *Ankur* and *Nishant* demonstrate, is crucially underwritten by women's access to a sexuality free(er) from patriarchal interdictions and, following from this, their ability to express it freely and in their own interests, middle-class injunctions regarding female purity as an integral element of a stable and respectable family become, inevitably, objects of interrogation and criticism, and in some respects become the "true" site of oppressive gender definitions. Benegal's focus on performing women follows from this: as bearers of a sexuality that seems to be free(er) from such injunctions, performing women enable him not only to interrogate these injunctions, but also specify alternatives to them – through their lifestyle, for instance, which includes a refusal to organize their households along patrilineal and/or heteronormative lines; and through their questioning of the ideologies of home and/or the domestic sphere.

Bhumika

> She [Hansa Wadkar] had to create a space for herself in an area that was totally male-dominated. So she was, what one might call, an early feminist in the Indian context.
>
> (Benegal to van der Heide 2006: 85–86)

> In fact, if women did not internalize the voices of men and speak like patriarchs themselves, the social order could not be maintained. Coercion and force never ensure the authority of rule as can an internal voice. Hence, we should be sensitive to the manner in which women define their sexuality in accordance with the dominant paradigms of their societies.
>
> (V. Das 1988: 199)

Adapted from the 1930s and 1940s Marathi and Hindi film actress Hansa Wadkar's 1970 autobiography, *Sangtye Aika [Listen, I am Telling You]*, *Bhumika* is a film about Urvashi (aka Usha), who is compelled at a young age, because of her father's debilitation and subsequent demise through alcohol, to become the family breadwinner. Through Keshav Dalvi, her mother's lover and subsequently her own husband, she secures work first as a singer and then as an actress in the Bombay film industry. Focusing particularly on her career as a film actress and her extra-marital relationships with various men, the film also provides the viewer access to her childhood and adolescence and her relationships during this period with her ailing father, her grandmother, and mother through flashbacks shot in sepia tones. In *Bhumika,* we seem to be in familiar Benegal territory, where an exploration of the indisputable necessity of female emancipation is accompanied simultaneously by a clear-eyed awareness of the challenges confronting such emancipation, including, not least, those that follow from the internalization by women of what Das characterizes as the "dominant paradigms of society" (see epigraph; 1988: 199). Thus, through its restless, rebellious female protagonist, *Bhumika* traces the development of a woman's consciousness and search for autonomy that is uneven and unfinished – its trajectory (with its circuitous and recursive quality) is not amenable to a linear, progressive narrative of development. The film visually mimics this trajectory by deploying flashbacks that constantly interrupt the chronological flow of the narrative, forcing its female subject, and the film's viewer, to shuttle back and forth between past and present.

The source of Usha's conflicts derives from her desire, on the one hand, for the security of a domestic sphere defined by marriage, husband, and children, and, on the other, for the freedom to live her life as she chooses. (While these two desires need not be mutually exclusive or mutually excluding, the film represents them as such.) Thus, although her status as a professional woman provides her with some independence, work is not what she most wants. She wants, instead, to assume the role of a housewife, which is ironic given how much houses and the very concept of home – her own and then Vinayak Kale's – enclose and imprison her.[7] (Figure 2.1) Ironic too are the means she chooses to define her autonomy, for her extra-marital relationships, first with a co-star, Rajan, then her director, Sunil, and finally a feudal patron, Vinayak Kale, only enmesh her further in precisely those restricting patriarchal relationships she seems to want to escape.[8] Indeed, the two – her desire for a home and her extra-marital relationships – are entangled with each other to the extent that through the latter she is trying to escape from, but also find a substitute for, the dysfunctional space that is her own home(-life). On the surface, this dysfunction proceeds from her fraught relationship with a possessive, abusive husband, Keshav, *and* her perverse dependence on him such that, despite her many attempts to escape, she always allows, indeed, instigates, Keshav to bring her back. On a deeper, more significant level, Usha perceives her home(-life) as dysfunctional *because* it does not adhere to a normative conception of home, and the gender roles specified therein, by middle-class standards – a class she aspires to, and whose standards, therefore, she seeks to make her own. For this reason, she is deeply disappointed when her marriage to Keshav does not deliver to her the role of housewife and a habitation within the domestic sphere alone. This class-defined aspiration for a normatively defined home and gender role is premised, significantly, on her rejection of, and desire not to replicate, the non-normative household within which she was brought up as the granddaughter of a singer-courtesan who trained her to sing, thereby teaching

Figure 2.1 Usha returning home in *Bhumika.*

Usha a skill securing her entry into the film industry.[9] This aspiration for entry into the middle class and the embrace, therefore, of values and social mores underwriting the self-image of this class, is not unusual at this historical juncture, although it exacts certain costs and demands certain exclusions.[10] But the film is critical of such an aspiration, viewing it as an impediment to the substantive forms of female autonomy that should inform projects of (female) emancipation.

To this end, then, houses, which are the physical embodiments of the ideologies that circulate around the concept of "hearth and home," are presented as confining, even imprisoning. That a home can be undesirable because it blocks female (self-)emancipation is something Usha must learn (and seems to have learned by the end of the film) in order to acquire the freedom she also desires. It is a process of learning, however, marked by several false or aborted starts. As already noted, although she runs away from home several times, she also returns. A little over halfway into the film, she moves into a hotel, having refused to move into Rajan's house, even though in the past she has stayed there after running away from her own. In the ensuing conversation with him, she implicitly registers the possibility that homes, even those not her own, can be imprisoning. For instance, when Rajan informs her that Keshav has contacted him to urge Usha to return home, Usha says, "There is a difference between a home and jail," to which Rajan responds, "Alright, why won't you move into my house?" Without responding directly to his offer, she says, as if speaking in general,

"One should not feel suffocated in one's own house" ("*apne ghar mein dum nahin ghutna chahiye*"), only to render her complaint more specific to her situation: "The woman of the house should have some value. I feel strange saying this, but I would like to be such a woman of the house" ("*gharwali ki koi keemat honi chahiye ... ajeeb lagta hai, per main aisi hi gharwali hona chahati hoon*"). Despite this exchange about the confining potential of homes, a short while later, she succumbs to the desire for home and hearth when she accepts Kale's offer to live with him in his country mansion.

The film's representation of Kale's mansion – before it becomes a place that Usha comes to (rightly) see as a prison – comes closest to visualizing the film's critique about homes as spaces of confinement. As Usha and Kale drive to his country mansion, the spectator first views the vastness and natural beauty of the surrounding countryside through a shot taken from one of its windows; against this is juxtaposed the inside of the mansion, presented via several shots from above which make it look very opulent and grand, but also confined and confining. Thus, whereas the first shot of the outside of the mansion moves out and expands, the second one inside it closes in and restricts – enclosing Usha within the house.[11] The film subsequently deploys fairly conventional shots and metaphors to reinforce her confinement in Kale's mansion through attention to its interiors and the focus on a music/jewelry box that Kale presents her with, which comes to symbolize her captivity in an expensive and beautiful setting. Eventually, through Kale's wife (who is literally bedridden) and through her experience as Kale's mistress-wife, Usha relearns a lesson she had supposedly learned before: that homes can be prisons, and they are prisons because patriarchal injunctions make them so. Instructing Usha to accept her "imprisonment," Kale's wife queries Usha, just as Usha is getting ready to leave Kale, once again having engineered her departure with help from Keshav: "What will change even if you go – your bed? your kitchen? Men don't change; how much more will you suffer [before you grasp this]?"

Nevertheless, the Usha with whom the film ends seems to have internalized some of this "lesson," although in somewhat extreme ways: Having decided to move back into the hotel room she had occupied before she joined Kale's household, she refuses to live with her now married daughter, telling her, instead, that it is imperative that she (Usha) learn to live alone, learn to live, that is, with her "aloneness/loneliness" ("*mere akelepan se mujhe khud hi nibhana hoga*").[12] By the film's conclusion she has also decided not to return to films, signaled by her refusal to answer Rajan's phone call inviting her to do so. She thereby seems to have "resolved" both sources of her conflict by in fact eliminating them for the time being, although her refusal to return to films may have a different resonance as well, more or less parallel to the foregoing critique the film undertakes of normative home(-life) as a site of confinement for the female subject.

For her profession as a film actress also imprisons her within the confines of a restrictive and restricting male desire – a critique that *Bhumika* makes obvious from the start: As the credits roll, the film opens with a dance number, reprised twice in the body of the film, which represents the female subject as performer, spectacle, and object of desire in what turns out to be a film-within-the-film. The camera pans the room to show an audience of men, cutting to one man (wearing a distinctively colorful turban) entering the room. It then pans back to the stage, reinforcing the fact that the audience is composed entirely of men. The gaze within which Usha and her dance are captured, then, is male, whose primary mode of perception is established via the lascivious look the man wearing the colorful turban directs at Usha. Then the movie cameras (within the film) come in from the top, revealing that the viewer has been watching a scene being filmed for a movie. *Bhumika* thus establishes two gazes: the filmic, which is the gaze the film directs at the scene and seeks to inculcate in its viewer, and an intra-diegetic male gaze that is aligned with that of the audience *within* the film. These two gazes do not coincide, the former seeking to establish a distance from the latter through which the films in which Usha appears can be critically evaluated.[13]

In his interview with van der Heide and elsewhere, Benegal has identified his interest in Wadkar's autobiography as proceeding from an interest: (1) in Wadkar herself, the "space" she was forced to "create ... for herself in an area that was totally male-dominated" (see epigraph; 2006: 85–86); and (2) "in how the film industry developed in the country, through the 1930s, the 1940s and the 1950s" – the chronological span, as it were, of Wadkar's film career (2006: 85–86). And while in Usha's dance sequences (like the one described above), Benegal was "tip[ping]" his "hat to this tradition of cinema," he notes that, in reconstructing this tradition, he also was representing "what the prevailing thinking was" (van der Heide 2006: 90, 86), including, as he notes in his interview with Behroz Gandhi, an exploration and interrogation of the gender ideologies that underwrite these representations.[14] By drawing attention in each instance to the frame – the director and personnel engaged in filming these scenes – the film distances its spectator *outside* the film from the viewers *within* the film, to enable a critical assessment of how women were positioned within these films (as when Sunil, directing a song and dance scene, explicitly eroticizes Usha's body by wanting her clothes to be wetter and more transparent).

Not surprisingly, films constitute an important element in the development of Usha's self-awareness regarding her own gender- and class-related investments. In particular, her performances of certain exemplary female mythological characters like Sita and Savitri, who represent, in India's patriarchal cultures, the much-prized qualities of chastity, obedience, and self-sacrifice, stimulate thoughts and self-reflections critical to her slow, uneven understanding of who she is and what she wants to be.[15] They constitute examples of women's roles that she must refuse in order to become an autonomous female subject. Furthermore, in as much as these female characters represent selves and moral qualities constitutive of the middle class's self-image, critically assessing or refusing what they represent opens up for interrogation the ideologies of the class to which Usha aspires.

Like much else in this movie, films occupy a complicated place in *Bhumika*, and are not amenable to singular modes of apprehension or interpretation. For even as the Indian films of the 1930s, 1940s, and 1950s provide negative role models for the female subject that she must refuse in order to be free, they also enable Benegal to recuperate a context through which a different conception of women's roles can be sketched that, in turn, renders visible and interrogates the gender ideologies underwriting national self-definition. One of the professions available to the disenfranchised *tawaif* (courtesan) was as an actress in cinema, a profession not yet considered appropriate in the 1930s and 1940s for the entry of "respectable" middle-and upper-class women.[16] Benegal explicitly draws attention to this transition in a conversation with van der Heide. Elaborating upon his response to van der Heide's characterization of "film actresses [as] the new courtesans of Indian culture," Benegal first corrects him ("they were … but no longer are") and then goes on to note the courtesan's sudden loss of "place in traditional society," at the same time that she was "not necessarily welcome in what one might call decent households" (2006: 89).

Usha comes from a family of courtesan-singers; her grandmother, who is a singer, seeks to teach Usha to sing as well. The film visually establishes the connection between Usha and her grandmother through shots that position them in the same space, while positioning Usha's mother separately from them, thereby differentiating her from them spatially and emotionally. In one exemplary scene, when Usha tells her mother and grandmother that she is pregnant with Keshav's child, she is shown sitting next to her grandmother. The camera switches back and forth between a shot of the two women and one of her solitary mother, cementing Usha's relationship with her grandmother while also conveying the tension in her relationship with her mother. In this scene, soon after the mother and daughter have been urged by the grandmother to reconcile with one another, the grandmother and Usha sing a *raga* (musical mode) that the grandmother had taught Usha as a child and that is repeated several times as background music to Usha's thoughts as she works out the conflicts within herself.[17] Usha's mother, once again, stands in the background, excluded from this community of two singers. As she walks down the hallway, entering a room on her own, rather than follow her, the camera lingers on the hallway as Usha and her grandmother sing in the other room, revealing the house (and home) as a space filled with potential solidarities, but also tension and pain.

It is ironic that Usha's relationship with her mother is so fraught given her mother's virtually identical desire for (and desire to hold on to) middle-class respectability, itself premised on her rejection of her own mother's ostensible lack of it as a courtesan-singer: "I am the first one in our caste/community to have married," she tells Usha, "I did not do so, so that my daughter would become a courtesan-singer" ("*apni jaati me mein pehli hoon jisne shaadi ki; is liye nahin ki meri beti gaanewali bane*"). In another scene, she takes Usha to task for shirking her chores while she practices singing with her grandmother: Whereas the latter would tie Usha back to her grandmother's profession, at least work, Usha's mother avers, may secure her a "good man" and the possibility of marriage. The conflict Usha faces between her desire for home and middle-class respectability and freedom and autonomy are thus re-staged via the conflicting positions her grandmother and mother occupy for Usha. One wonders if Usha's hostility to her mother is a reflection of her subconscious, reflecting a division within the self where an investment in her freedom exerts more power over her than her desire for home and middle-class belonging.[18]

Significantly, the historical moment Benegal seeks to reprise, via his adaptation of Wadkar's autobiography, tracks the courtesan-singer and her place in society *as it is being transformed* under the exigencies of national self-making. Quite apart from what it tells us about the importance of this transformation to the middle-class's construction of who and what belongs, or can be included, within the boundaries of the fledgling nation, it is also a transitional moment in which that which is excluded in the formation of the nation is still available as lived experience; it can be rendered visible so that its projected loss can be made apparent and felt viscerally. The costs entailed by the national self-definition undertaken by the middle class can, therefore, be made clear. Benegal's use of flashbacks – virtually always in sepia color – in which Usha remembers her past as a young girl growing up in her grandmother's household are crucial in this effort. The flashbacks (as flashbacks) invoke a past accessible only through memory; they are also suffused with an aura of sadness that is a function, in part, of nostalgia, but mostly of an inchoate sense of loss, made audible in the film through Benegal's frequent use, as background music, of the *raga* sung by the kirana *gharana* singer as the playback voice for the grandmother. In an early flashback, when a young Usha, practicing this *raga* with her grandmother, becomes impatient ("Enough," she says and runs away), her grandmother, a gentle, graceful figure, demurs, presenting the *raga* and its singing as a resource of hope and resilience in the face of despair: "these notes [this song] keep me from going mad," she says, implying that they might keep Usha also from going mad.

There are other, somewhat more oblique, ways in which the film also registers the costs of the exclusions perpetrated by the middle class's engineering of the national imaginary. Usha's mother, despite claiming to be the first woman from her community to have married and thereby escaped the fate of her own courtesan mother, is represented as a deeply unhappy figure. Her anger and hostility towards Usha, her mother, her husband, even her lover Keshav, is displayed throughout the film. It may be that she is unhappy at not, in fact, having escaped her mother's fate, given her husband's inadequacies. But it may also be that her unhappiness flows from the necessity, in the first place, of the transformation her caste/community must undergo in order to enter the middle class *and then* the recognition that, despite the cost this entails, it might not be enough to secure middle-class belonging.

On the face of it, *Bhumika*'s delineation (via Usha's grandmother's flashbacks, which detail the cost of the loss of the cultural and affective repertoires courtesans represented, combined with Usha's deep emotional attachment to her grandmother) seems to signal a preferred identity and identification that Usha should retrieve and pursue once she has become cognizant of the trap that home and middle-class belonging represent.[19] And, indeed, much is attractive about this identity and identification as instruments of the autonomy and freedom for the female subject Benegal seeks to envisage. Recognizing that "the courtesan has traditionally been the bearer of artistic traditions," Gordon and Feldman find that "in this role courtesans have been among the best educated and freest women of their time" (2006: 7). Along somewhat different lines, V. Rao uncouples the *tawaif* (courtesan) from the prostitute to note – as does A. Srinivasan in terms of the devadasi (see note 5 in this chapter) – "association with a *tawaif* conferred status; it signified the sophistication, wealth, and cultural life-style of the patron" (1996: 278). A professional, public figure who wielded considerable influence, the *tawaif* also generated the need for, and dependence of, "artisans and craftspersons" and "instrumental accompanists (*tabaliyas* and *sarangiyas*), even *gharanedar ustads*" necessary to the performance of her art, thereby producing an entire social and economic network of which she was the center (Rao 1996: 279). Oldenburg considers the courtesan's "life-style" itself as "a form of resistance," "consciously involved in the covert subversion of a male-dominated world" (1990: 260).

On the other hand, addressing the scope for "female agency [and autonomy]" that the *tawaif* represented "within the patriarchy of quasi-feudal productive relations," Qureshi provides a more ambivalent and sobering account, alert to the contradictory ways in which the courtesan's ties to diverse male constituencies, including, not least, male patrons, impinge on this agency.[20] She suggests, first, that "the viability of these 'non-wives,'" and hence their agency, was premised on "the seclusion of respectable elite women to maintain reproductive control over feudal property"; she queries, further, whether or not courtesans could "produce and reproduce themselves as professional performers without the traditional ties of dependence with hereditary male musicians who had the social organization to do both"; finally, apropos the historical moment within which *Bhumika* is set, Qureshi wonders about the "social and musical conditions" that enabled courtesans to "transcend social and gender boundaries creatively," whose (forced?) demise and subsequent absence blocked their continued participation in the nation once "the bourgeois reform of classical music [and dance]" began (Qureshi 2006: 313).

In *Bhumika* (set during times when these performing women's influence was on the way out and their presence being displaced), although attracted to the possibilities "performing women" represent in terms of their (relative) independence and autonomy, their (relative) ability to subvert dominant social and political arrangements, and their abiding connection with artistic traditions, Benegal is unable nevertheless to imagine these women's attributes outside of their embededness within the logic of patrilineal and patriarchal relationships. In other words, these performing women's professional and personal lives, no less than the lives for women envisaged by the middle-class nationalists, are implicated in social and political structures and relationships resulting from patriarchal ideologies. Thus, although the possibilities the performing women represent are the means through which middle-class constructions of national identity are interrogated and criticized, the film seems to argue that they cannot, perhaps should not, be uncritically reproduced at a later, different historical moment in women's attempts to acquire agency and autonomy.

Male domination, if not the primary object of critique in *Bhumika,* is a primary focus, and something Usha must eschew in order to be an emancipated and autonomous self. None of the male figures in *Bhumika* come out particularly well. Even Usha's father, an ostensibly kinder, gentler figure in his relationship with her, has no compunctions about beating his wife and invokes his right to do so by virtue of being her husband. Keshav and Kale direct psychological and physical violence against Usha, while at the same time extracting labor from her: Keshav lives off her money and sexuality; Kale makes her his surrogate "wife," who is called upon to satisfy him in bed and run his household, since his "legitimate" wife is bedridden. Even the more innocuous Rajan (who Usha characterizes as the only person who has "given," not "taken" from her) and Sunil are not particularly appealing, being both narcissistic and self-absorbed in their interactions with Usha. For Benegal, these male characters are "all very much part of the patriarchal society where the world never asks them to prove themselves, whereas a woman needs to prove her credentials in every situation. So that's why they look ridiculous in the process" (van der Heide 2006: 88).

At the film's conclusion, Usha's decision to move back into the hotel room she left to join Kale as his surrogate wife, and her assertion of the necessity of learning to live alone and coming to terms with her loneliness/aloneness is more or less in keeping with this critique of male domination. Having thus far sought to define herself through her relationships with various men, she chooses *being alone* over other potential networks of relationships and identifications. Does this mean that these networks don't as yet exist? Or does it mean that they do, but do not interest Usha? Or, finally, does it mean that her decision to be alone is a first step in self-discovery – a space she must grant herself before she can begin to invest in alternate networks and solidarities and alternate definitions of self?

Mandi

> Traditionally, a brothel was a very important institution within society. Young men were always sent to a bordello to learn social graces. Rukmini [the Madam of the bordello in *Mandi*] sees herself as an influence that helps to refine society.
>
> (Benegal to van der Heide 2006: 125)

> The basic dichotomy, in short, between the wife and the courtesan rests on the opposition between the keeper of the (pure) lineage and the keeper of culture; and this divide seems to describe the bookends of diametrically opposed realms of power open to the Indian female.
>
> (Srinivasan, D. 2006:165)

Mandi is based on a short story, "Aanandi," by Ghulam Abbas, itself "based," according to Benegal, "on an incident that took place in 1929, when Jawaharlal

Nehru [independent India's first Prime Minister] was the chairman of the Municipal Board of Allahabad. The board decided that a brothel," located "at the center of the city" and "next to where Nehru was born," should be "relocated far away" because "the city fathers were offended that this illustrious family lived next to this brothel" (van der Heide 2006: 124). Benegal, along with Satyadev Dubey and Shama Zaidi, amplified the four-page-long story into a film script and relocated its action to Hyderabad. Benegal's "first ensemble film" (van der Heide 2006: 123), *Mandi*'s cast of characters is led by Rukminibai, the madam of a brothel and the women she supervises, mothers, and controls; and her favorite Zeenat, born into the brothel, who turns out to be mayor Agarwal's daughter from his liaison with one of its women. The characters in the brothel also include a deaf-mute woman, Phoolmani, brought there at the film's opening, having been kidnapped and sold into prostitution; Dungrus, an ostensibly emasculated houseboy and servant who looks after the women's needs; and two semi-permanent residents: a photographer who always is lurking around the brothel, observing its lifestyles and photographing the women in provocative poses, and a policeman who is in an ongoing relationship with one of the women, Kamli. Among those from outside the brothel are the businessman, Gupta, who seeks to evict its denizens so he can raze the building and secure the land for commercial development; Shantidevi, a self-righteous social worker also dedicated to driving the denizens of the brothel out of town; and the mayor, Agarwal, whose son, Sushil is engaged to Gupta's daughter, but falls in love with Zeenat.

As in *Bhumika*, one of *Mandi*'s central narrative strands addresses the conflict generated by middle-class morality in its encounter with a way of life that implicitly and explicitly calls it into question. (In fact the suffixes to the names of the two main antagonists identify the two conflicting identities in question: Rukmini*bai* vs. Shanti*devi*, that is, "courtesan/kept woman" vs. "goddess.") However, as a satirical comedy, in which virtually no character occupies or is allowed to occupy the moral high ground, *Mandi* is very different from *Bhumika* in its tone, which, then, affects its, and the spectator's, evaluation of the performing women and their life-worlds. For, although *Bhumika* is unsentimental in its assessment of the soon-to-be-lost-world of the courtesans, it nevertheless registers this world's prospective demise as a loss by registering some of its deeply attractive features through, not least, the film's sympathetic portrait of Usha's grandmother and, through her, its evocation of the cultural and affective repertoires that courtesans represent. *Mandi*, on the other hand, through its all-embracing satire and broad comedy, is engaged in deconstructing the very bases of the "loss" *Bhumika* bears witness to, its performing women are apparently not much different from their "respectable" counterparts and vice versa. This strategy de-sentimentalizes even more so the myths underwriting the representation of "the courtesan as historical and cinematic spectacle" in what S. Chakravarty calls the "courtesan film genre" of mainstream Indian cinema,[21] rendering the allegedly "deviant" or "morally reprehensible" world of the performing women continuous with the world of "respectability" (1993: 269). Despite this, however, the film's primary affective allegiance is with the world inhabited by the courtesans.

Benegal's film establishes the equivalence of these two ostensibly opposing worlds in a variety of ways. The film's title *Mandi* or "Marketplace", for example, is given a more general – and expansive – range of reference than the narrower "notion of prostitution as commodity form" that S. Chakravarty references in her brief reading of this film (1993: 301). For marketplaces, with their accompanying instrumentalities of buying and selling, haggling and negotiating, are evident everywhere,[22] not only in the relationship between the *kotha* (brothel) and its clients, but also among the inhabitants of the *kotha*, including, not least, the *kothewalis* (women of the brothel) themselves;[23] what's more, if the women of the brothel are on sale, so is mayor Agarwal's son, Sushil, whose marriage with the businessman Gupta's daughter has been arranged precisely so that Agarwal can be rescued from his debts. The world outside the *kotha* is thereby shown to be continuous with the world inside the *kotha*, much as the world inside the *kotha* is shown as continuous with the one outside.

Analogously, (the project of) respectability is presented as a mirror image of its ostensible opposite, or other, signified by the brothel and its women. The film visually establishes the mutual imbrication of these ostensibly distinct worlds through a pair of scenes involving characters and agendas otherwise in relentless conflict with each other, but for a brief period forced to occupy the same social and ideological space. In the first one, Dungrus "rescues" a distraught Phoolmani from accompanying her kidnapper and brings her to Rukminibai, who tries to incorporate her into the *kotha* culture by speaking of the villainy of men manifested, for example, in Phoolmani's betrayal by her kidnapper; her own by a man in her past; and, by implication, the betrayal of all women by men: "Never trust a man," she instructs Phoolmani, "all men are rascals and loafers." The second scene, also about rescuing Phoolmani, involves Shantidevi and her flock of female social workers from *Nari Niketan* (Women's Welfare Association), who arrive at the *kotha*'s door to protest the kidnapping of a minor, Phoolmani, whom they now wish to rescue from the clutches of the *kothewalis*. Both scenes circulate around the literal and figurative "rescue" of Phoolmani, with Shantidevi's *Nari Niketan* and Rukminibai's brothel ostensibly functioning as refuges for abandoned or "homeless" women. Both scenes also share structural characteristics – the shot of Shantidevi with two women of her flock as they sit on a sofa facing the camera recalls the composition of the earlier shot with Rukminibai, Zeenat, and Phoolmani. Furthermore, they share the attributes of a staged performance, made evident in Rukminibai's narrative of her own betrayal by a man through the verbal plaudits it earns from Dungrus ("ho!" he says, and then again "ho!" urging her on, signaling as well that this is a frequently repeated performance by Rukminibai), whereas Shantidevi's lecture to the women from the brothel is delivered from a hastily set up, makeshift stage – a chair on which she stands in order to make her (pretence of) distress visible to the crowd. The heightened rhetoric of both Rukminibai and Shantidevi's speeches demarcates these speeches as species of acting, calling into question their sincerity and truth.[24]

However even as an equivalence is set up between the two, they and the social worlds they inhabit are marked off as different in as much as Shantidevi and her cohorts always come off badly, worse off, that is, than Rukminibai and her cohorts. And this is not only because the spectators encounter them first in Rukminibai's space; nor because Rukminibai, in this charged encounter, retains control over the situation by virtue of having invited Shantidevi into the brothel; nor even, more generally, because visual appearances matter and Rukminibai and her *kothewalis*, with their lively demeanor and sartorial splendor, have a definite edge over Shantidevi and her cohorts, who are colorless, buttoned down and humorless. Shantidevi and her cohorts come off badly mostly because of their willful ignorance, blinding them to their class privilege and unwitting collusion with the double standard that class maintains. For example, raising her voice against the *kothewalis*' supposed abjection, in classic (Indian) nationalist terms, Shantidevi enjoins them to put an end to it ("Won't we ever wake up?" she asks, "Will we destroy our over thousand-year civilization?" and then "Women should be worshipped"). The *kothewalis* heckle her with a question that has an immediate bearing on their material reality: "Who will feed us?" To which Shantidevi responds, ignoring the material circumstances of the women and appealing, instead, to a presumed ideal: "Bread/food is not everything in this world." Her interlocutors are given the last clinching word in this encounter, when one of them murmurs, "You must get it [bread/food] free." The more substantive fault of which Shantidevi and her kind are guilty, as representatives of "respectable" society, has to do with what Rukminibai draws attention to, in this scene and on several other occasions: "We exist therefore society exists" ("*Hum hain to samaj hai*"), she says, implying that women like her keep society stable by serving as an outlet for society's ungovernable (sexual) passions. Inveighing against society's double standard that holds women accountable and lets men off the hook, she also asks: "Why don't you keep your men in chains?" "Why blame women?" "Because men buy," she adds, "women sell."

The *kothewalis* come off better than Shantidevi and her cohorts not only in a negative sense, however; the artistry of the performing women constitutes their defense. Against Shantidevi's characterization of her *kotha* as a site of morally degrading business, Rukminibai counter-poses the *kotha* as a site – and training ground – for the courtesans as artists. The opening scenes go some distance in establishing the truth of her claim by showing at least two of the *kothewalis* – Zeenat and Basanti – as artists, constantly engaged in their music and dance practice. After a music and dance performance by Zeenat and Basanti at Gupta's place on the occasion of his daughter's informal engagement to Sushil, Rukminibai reaffirms the role of her women as artists by making an ardent speech about courtesans as transmitters of culture.[25] Rukminibai is correct: "the courtesan singer-dancers (*tawaif*)" were, as Qureshi notes, "at the center of elite entertainment in feudal and mercantile-colonial milieus of India" for the century and a half preceding Indian independence (2006: 312). Arbiters and "preservers" of high (court) culture, the *tawaif* "actively shaped developments in Hindustani music and *kathak* dance styles" (Singh 2007: 99).

That Rukminibai needs to assert this, however, may betray a certain anxiety on her part regarding society's (continuing) recognition and acceptance of this truth. Moreover, the kind of influence and power courtesans of yore are said to have wielded is clearly not available to Rukminibai and her cohorts. (In this regard, consider the film's representation of the kinds of patrons Rukminibai's *kotha* seems to attract; virtually none belong to the classes that courtesans in the past drew their patrons from.) In historical terms, this recognition by the film is accurate. As noted earlier, the years leading up to and following India's independence were marked by a significant erosion, partly in the name of middle-class morality, of the influence and power of these performing women, not least through the dismantling of their performance venues and audiences.[26] The film registers the duality of the courtesans' social roles by, on one hand, having Rukminibai fiercely guard and speak about Zeenat and Basanti's (Zeenat's more so than Basanti's) talent and artistry, and, on the other, having Nadira (who, Rukminibai says, "will be the death of us") transact the "other" business of the brothel, providing partners for the men who turn up there for sex alone. What emerges, then, from the film's layered, seemingly contradictory account of the courtesans' position as it interacts with the exigencies of national self-making, is a complex portrait of performing women caught at an historical moment when their identities and material realities are, and have been for some time, under siege. Strangely, the broad humor and satire directed at Rukminibai and her cohorts – but much more cuttingly at their detractors – enables an assessment of courtesans and their culture that is not uncritical but also not dismissive, moralistic, or patronizing. The film achieves this somewhat difficult balance by at once historicizing their roles and predicament in the face of nationalist self-definition, and situating them, as Qureshi thinks one must for a "culturally appropriate perspective on their … role as courtesans" to emerge, "in the terms of the milieus that grounded courtesans culturally and sustained them socially … free from the bourgeois signification of courtesans as 'fallen women'" (2006: 320).

A rich body of work "retrieving," as Singh puts it, the courtesan's voice and experience from the "margins" of the "nation's narrative" now exists, making their life-worlds visible to urge a more informed assessment and, more significantly, to map through it an alternate set of (nationalist) gender identifications and values. Most of this work dates from the late 1980s, emerging especially from the rise, development, and consolidation of feminist, gender, and subaltern studies scholarship in India. Benegal's *Mandi*, while part of the historical conjuncture that produced this body of work, is an early contribution to it, pre-dating much of it, particularly, on courtesans and their culture. As a cultural form consumed by a larger, more general audience, moreover, films have greater reach and influence. Thus, this film's representation of the lives and activities of these *kothewalis*, which makes them engaging, attractive, but also flawed – exploitative and competitive – *human beings* is a powerful instrument in rescuing them from their "bourgeois signification … as 'fallen women.'"

In identifying those attributes of the courtesans' world particularly hospitable to women's freedom and autonomy, most scholarship on this subject draws attention to how this world centers women, focuses on matrilineal forms of inheritance, and inverts normative male-female power relationships obtaining in society at large. In this world, for instance, the birth of a girl is desirable, while that of a boy is tolerated. The film's narrative builds on some of these features. Thus, Rukminibai instructs the doctor, who has come to supervise the birth of Kamli's child, "Make her give birth to a girl child"; to Kamli she says, "If you give birth to a boy, I will throw you out." When a girl child is born to Kamli, a celebration ensues, and the birth is even interpreted as the cause of the miraculous change in the brothel's fortunes when, deprived at first of their source of income following their relocation to the desolate margins of the town, their business suddenly begins to pick up and flourish.

The film displays the solidarities among the women of the brothel (even as it reveals the conflicts among them) through shots of these women clustered together at various points, exchanging gossip, and trading insults and repartee with the male inhabitants of the brothel. On virtually all the dramatic occasions when one or another conflict arises, the spectator sees Rukminibai with Zeenat huddled together, discussing or addressing the source of the problem even as Rukminibai keeps the initiative for doing so in her hands. Oldenburg, in her essay on the courtesans of Lucknow, makes much of the emotional and sexual self-sufficiency of these women, claiming that "for many of them heterosexuality itself is the ultimate *nakhra* and feigned passion an occupational hallmark" (1990: 277). Although *Mandi*'s women do not seem to subscribe to such a view of heterosexuality, the film does display on more than one occasion the erotic current that runs through the relationship between Rukminibai and Zeenat, where Zeenat's concern about Rukminibai's well-being is often expressed through sensual, tactile gestures. Rukminibai and Zeenat are also shown sleeping together in an entirely routine fashion.

Men enter this women-centered world as patrons and as service providers, and while not altogether denuded of their patriarchal entitlement, by virtue of entering a space resolutely marked as female, they are forced to negotiate a space that may well attenuate their automatic assumption of control. Dungrus's position within the *kotha* exemplifies one kind of role men, including grown-up male children of the *kothewalis*, inhabit as male denizens of the woman-centered *kotha*. Dungrus is called upon to perform all sorts of tasks a servant normally performs, but the *kothewalis* also allow him a degree of intimacy with themselves and their bodies that a servant would not be given access to. One of the *kothewalis*, for example, asks him to wash her back as she is bathing – a potentially emasculating act because it presumes that such a request does not constitute a source of sexual incitement for him. Indeed, Dungrus's presence – including requests for his presence – at otherwise closed and intimate female discussions underscores how unthreatening, because lacking in power, his presence as a male is in the *kotha*.

But the film's representation of the life-world of the *kothewalis* also acknowledges its implication in the (patriarchal) society that surrounds it. To that end, through Dungrus and through the women of the brothel, *Mandi* shows how hierarchies generated by power, or the lack of it, do not simply disappear in a potentially alternative environment peopled, in this instance, by women. Dungrus's extended monologues (when he returns to the *kotha* drunk, and freed, therefore, from his normal reticence and inhibitions) prophesying Rukminibai and her *kotha*'s destruction, articulate an otherwise concealed hostility and resentment against the non-normative set-up at the *kotha*. These monologues thereby reveal how much he has internalized the patriarchal dictates of society at large despite having lived in the *kotha* his entire life. The women of the *kotha*, on the other hand, give voice to their resentment of Rukminibai's overt preference for Zeenat. Finally, *all* the *kothewalis*, including Zeenat, express their resentment of Rukminibai's effort to control them, even though the film expends effort in showing her as *the* person who has produced and nurtured a space within which various versions of female agency can be expressed.[27] Arguably, by representing the women of the *kotha* with their warts and all, Benegal's film denudes them of the romance and idealization associated with them in other films that belong to the genre of the courtesan film. In fact, S. Chakravarty quotes Benegal himself on *Mandi* ("I was interested in creating a whole microcosm of Indian life – the survival instinct, as evident in [Rukminibai's] character, middle-class hypocrisy, the manipulation that goes on constantly, the young poking the old") to suggest how the film constitutes a complete "break with the nostalgia-ridden past" (1993: 301, 304). Such a "break" also establishes these women as unexceptional, even ordinary, which the film accomplishes by tracking the daily routines of the *kotha* – Rukminibai saying her prayers each morning; the women of the brothel standing around gossiping with each other; Zeenat and Basanti performing their daily music and dance practice. The aim here, I think, is to secure the spectators' understanding of, and sympathy for, these women by gesturing towards their normality and ordinariness and, through that, toward the potential continuities between the spectators' and these women's lives.

At the same time, however, against the satire and comedy that establish an equivalence between the world outside the *kotha* and the world within it; against, furthermore, the film's effort to reveal the flawed humanity that the *kothewalis* share with their counterparts in the "respectable" world, the film wants to assert the difference that a courtesan culture can make in the lives of women, including potentially alternate modalities of being women that can and do raise serious questions about gender relations in the "respectable" world. More than two-thirds of the way through the film, when relocation to the margins of the city has changed the dynamics of power between Rukminibai and the women of the brothel, the latter articulate a critique that has a significant bearing on how to think of women's roles in society. With virtually no clients coming to the godforsaken site to which the brothel has been moved, the *kothewalis* are called upon to perform their own domestic chores – like cooking and cleaning. They reject this alternative by aggressively informing Rukminibai: "If we had to do cooking etc. why would we have entered this business?" It is not cooking they are rejecting so much as an ideology that positions women within the domestic sphere, with no power to determine how they should live. D. Srinivasan argues that the courtesan and the wife reference two "diametrically opposed realms of power open to the Indian female" (see epigraph; 2006: 165); in refusing domesticity, arguably, the *kothewalis* also are refusing the role of wives, thereby overtly and covertly refusing their incorporation in a patriarchal hegemony that would exert control over their sexuality so as to retain the purity of its lineage. It's also worth noting here that, in effect, the *kothewalis* are rejecting the ideological valence attached to the concept of home that Usha, in *Bhumika*, is so attracted to and against whose attractions she must struggle in order to be free. *Mandi*, as I have tried to show, is not naive about the constraints faced by women, even in circumstances that allow them a degree of freedom to determine how they want to live. What the *kothewalis* enable the film to articulate, however, is the possibility of having the option to decide how they want to live more available to them than it would be to "respectable" women, including, not least, wives.[28]

The film's concluding scenes articulate several different agendas reflected in the divergent fates the women of the brothel embrace: Zeenat runs away with Agarwal's son Sushil, who has been courting her all along, but whom spectators already know, and she finds out later, is her half-brother; she also runs away from him taking his money, while his attention is diverted by the breakdown of his motorcycle. Basanti leaves with the photographer for Bombay because he has promised her the possibility of an entry into films. Kamli settles for domesticity with the policeman with whom she has had two sons and a daughter. Nadira, Rukminibai's economic and business competitor and antagonist, along with the rest of the women, strikes a deal with the developer and businessman Gupta and goes into business with him, presumably with a view to providing the services of "her" women for his clients. Rukminibai is ousted and, accompanied by Dungrus, leaves her newly relocated *kotha* in a huff. In this way, all that Rukminibai and her women had been fighting against (middle-class morality, capitalist development) overtakes life in the newly relocated *kotha*. From now on the value of the women who remain with Nadira will exist entirely in terms of Gupta's world of cash and markets. With Zeenat and Basanti gone, certainly, the *kothewalis* will no longer be known for their artistry, nor is Nadira capable of functioning as an arbiter of culture. The film provides little or no clue about Zeenat's future beyond the fact of her escape, possibly in order to pursue some form of self-discovery.[29] Basanti's choice to accompany the photographer, on the other hand, signals not just "the opportunity encoded in cinema for a career change to fit the times" that courtesans embraced (Kidwai 2004: 52), but also an active refusal to accept Nadira's business/development-model definition of the courtesan's identity: In an earlier scene, for instance, when a similar discussion takes place among the women about who would better represent their interests in the new environment, Basanti refuses to commit herself to Nadira on the grounds that at least with Rukminibai she is given time to pursue and disseminate her art.

In keeping with Basanti's gesture of refusal is the conclusion of the film that revives hope for a *kotha* run on the old lines, when Phoolmani runs away from *Nari Niketan* where she had been housed after her rescue by Shantidevi and company. The last shot shows her running towards Rukminibai and Dungrus as they rest in a desolate landscape, bemoaning their fate. Her arrival is presented as something miraculous as she arrives just as Rukminibai has been urged by a disembodied voice to pray to Baba Kharak Shah (whose *dargah* happens to be near the new location of the brothel).[30] And Rukminibai does indeed greet Phoolmani's arrival as a miracle, with the film suggesting she is Zeenat's replacement and will enable Rukminibai to re-launch her career as the madam of a new *kotha*. Juxtaposed with the "realism" of the other women's fates is the "magic" of Phoolmani's arrival – signaling the survival of a residual element of the older *kotha* formation – which holds in tension both a clear-eyed recognition of the fate of the courtesans under the new dispensation and the possibility of a renewal of the old dispensation under Rukminibai's aegis now that she has Phoolmani to work with.[31]

Mandi ends up being surprisingly optimistic about the survival of a courtesan culture, even as it shows this culture's mutation into different forms and agendas more in keeping with the politics of a national self-definition committed to displacing or repressing it comprehensively, if not erasing all signs of it. Nor does the optimism seem out of sync with the deconstruction and de-sentimentalization of the courtesans' world that the film's satirical take on it has entailed. Or perhaps it is the satire, with its accompanying comedy, that is able to keep the tone of the film buoyant and lively. *Bhumika* is a somber, even tragic film. Despite its strong critique of male domination, its protagonist provides the film's viewers with little hope about the attenuation or demise of patriarchal ideologies that seem to structure and contain virtually all social space. *Mandi* (and here its form as an ensemble film is significant) does not so much contest this view as disperse the force of patriarchal ideologies by producing several different interactions of differently inclined *kothewalis* with it and by indicating that these are not the last we have seen of such interactions. Phoolmani running away from *Nari Niketan* seems to point to the continuing contestation and struggle not only over how courtesans will be defined and redefined, but also the cycle of decline and renewal to which they have been subjected twice already over the space of the film.

Sardari Begum

> *[Sardari Begum]* turned into a very interesting film because [its eponymous protagonist] was a Thumri singer – Thumri is a North Indian light classical form of singing. It gave me the opportunity to use some very good Thumris in the film.
>
> (Benegal to van der Heide 2006: 172)

> Whereas *ghazal* could distance itself from the courtesan tradition by virtue of its male perspective and its independent role as poetry outside of a musical context, *thumri* had "performance" as well as "femaleness" woven into its basic structure, and could not escape the stigma that came to be attached to women performers.
>
> (du Perron 2002: 186)

Sardari Begum is about a young woman who runs away from her family and home to become a *thumri* singer. It also is about the search for Sardari Begum's story by an investigative journalist, Tehzeeb, who, sent to cover Sardari's accidental death in a communal disturbance, discovers that Sardari was her aunt. And finally it is about Sardari's legacy continuing through her daughter, Sakina, who struggles against her mother's efforts to reproduce herself through her daughter only to become a *thumri* singer after her mother's passing. Along the way, the viewer encounters the people – a husband, a patron and his wife, a brother, a musical accompanist, the manager of a radio station – with whom Sardari interacts and through whom Tehzeeb discovers Sardari's story. As, too, the viewer encounters the mostly Muslim milieu within which Sardari's story unfolds.

Sardari Begum is considered part of a trilogy: van der Heide labels it "the Khalid Mohamed trilogy" (2006: 172) and Datta "the trilogy on Muslim women" (2003: 11).[32] Uncoupling it from *Mammo* and *Zubeida*, with which it is typically linked, and attaching it instead to *Bhumika* and *Mandi* privileges the film's focus on a performing woman, a *thumri* singer in this case, thereby bringing it within the ambit of the subject matter and issues that animate this chapter. In fact, Benegal himself seems to privilege such a focus when, in conversation with van der Heide, he notes that the film is "interesting ... *because* [Sardari] was a Thumri singer" (see epigraph; van der Heide 2006: 172; emphasis added). "This gave me the opportunity to use some very good Thumris in the film," he continues, and, he added in a conversation with me, "the opportunity to reconstruct a lost tradition and the world to which it belongs" (March 28, 2006). The film does, indeed, include several melodious *thumris*; during the scenes in which Sardari and Iddanbai, her teacher, perform, the camera, in addition to focusing on the faces and gestures of the performing women, also focuses on the accompanying (*sarangi* and *tabla* players) musicians' hands and fingers to display their skills as well. Arguably, such a focus constitutes an attempt to visually recall, record, and also reaffirm, specific performative features of *thumri*. (Figure 2.2)

Thumris and *thumri* singers represent not so much a lost art as one whose role underwent significant changes in independent India when, as Manuel puts it, "Thumri moved from the *kotha*, courtesan's salon, to the public concert hall" accompanied by changes in both performers and performance styles entailing, in particular, the diminution, even erasure, of the erotic and sensuous (Manuel 1989: 81). In several important respects, changes in style that affected *thumris* and *thumri* singers are similar to the changes that hereditary music and dance repertoires and their performances underwent in the process of being sanitized and sanskritized in order to be deemed classical, national, and modern.

In her historical reconstruction of *thumri* and its marginal(ized) place in the classical music canon, du Perron notes how its contemporary status as "a light song form whose primary function is to provide some diversion at the end of a serious *khyāl* concert" is "reductionist" and at odds with its "original function as a vehicle for dance [*bandish thumri*]" and, soon thereafter, its "role as a primary avenue for emotional expression in songstress-courtesan (*tavāyaf*) performance

Figure 2.2 Sardari performing in *Sardari Begum.*

[*bol banāv thumri*]."[33] Like Manuel, she finds that "*Thumri* was integral to the courtesan tradition" and "courtesan life has affected its musical and its textual shape" (du Perron 2007: 2). Both du Perron and V. Rao draw attention to the changes in *thumri* and its singers as proceeding from an "ambivalence regarding the erotic and regarding aspects of our [Indian] culture and history that have been seen as problematic" (Rao 1990: WS-31). This ambivalence extends to, perhaps is even based on, British colonial and, thereafter, Indian nationalist assessments of one of its most enthusiastic proponents and patrons, Wajid Ali Shah, the last Nawab of Awadh, whose name is indelibly associated with *thumris*. The British, who forcibly terminated Wajid Ali Shah's decade-long rule in 1856 and exiled him to Matiya Burj in Calcutta, viewed him as debauched and effeminate, and condemned the *nawabi* culture in which *thumri* flourished as decadent. Furthermore, as du Perron notes, colonial British propaganda also represented "dance itself ... in the context of courtesan performance" as "debauched," thereby rendering *bandish thumri*, the older form of the genre to which dance was central, problematic. This colonial denigration of an indigenous musical form and culture was embraced by the Western-educated Indian middle classes, whose values, shaped by English education, came to determine what counted as India's national culture. Thus, to survive, *thumri* that had emerged from, and flourished in, feudal relations and culture was forced to change since these were seen as thoroughly incompatible with the "modern"

India envisioned by the middle class (du Perron 2007: 3, 5, 20, 52; see also Rao, V. 1990): *Bol banāv thumri*, says du Perron, "emerged in a climate which supported the reconstruction of arts to confirm the notion of the 'great Indian cultural heritage,' a movement cultivated by reformists and educationists such as Hariscandra Bhārtendu" (2002: 178).[34] As *thumri* was detached from courtesan (and *nawabi*) culture and became the domain, particularly since India's independence, of "middle class respectable women and men alike," among other changes she notes was a "loosening of the relationship between performer and protagonist"; additionally, the "tension between secular and devotional" that had been "a component of many *thumrīs*," was " 'disambiguated' " whereby "the predominantly secular context of *thumrī*" was re-envisioned and recast in the devotional mold either through simple reinterpretation or through an actual change in words (2002: 188, 183, 189–192). Thus, the trajectory of *thumri* du Perron traces is akin to the one Bakhle traces in her account of the classicization of Indian music whereby "a whole generation of courtesans (*baijis*)" was "replaced by upper-caste women performers" and music was "sacralized" by the "bhakti nationalists" through which endeavor, then, it could be "envisioned as the instrument of Hindu proselytizing" (Bakhle 2005: 5–6).

Benegal's invocation of *thumri* as what drew him to the story of Sardari Begum, therefore, explicitly and implicitly articulates with the cluster of thematic and explanatory frameworks pursued in my analysis of *Bhumika* and *Mandi*. Not least, the focus on performing women enables him to explore issues surrounding women's empowerment in the context, particularly, of Indian nationalism – the bases, in other words, for their autonomy and freedom in a society whose hegemonic (patriarchal) worldviews seeks to contain, even repress these altogether. This entails, as my analysis of each film discussed thus far demonstrates, a concomitant substantive engagement with its inverse: issues relating to women's disempowerment, including the various obstacles that haunt women's attempts at autonomy and freedom, including the internalization by women of oppressive patriarchal interdictions.

Of particular interest is what some of *thumri*'s contemporary exponents and analysts like V. Rao, characterize as its "feminine [for du Perron female] voice." In making her case for *thumri* as an instance of "feminine voice," V. Rao disavows some stereotypical assumptions regarding such a "voice," while affirming others, *before* specifying why it should be seen as such: "It is the 'feminine' voice in music *not* because of its evident identification with women" nor because "the poetic text articulates female desire (albeit constructed in the male gaze)."[35] Rather, *thumri* is "feminine" *because* it is "interrogative/subversive": *Thumri* constitutes the "limited space of women in the world of classical music" that they "extend," she elaborates, *not by* "rejecting or evacuating" the "physically or ideologically" confining space patriarchy constructs for women, *but by* "exploring and working within it with unexpected richness" (1990: WS-31). Through a series of inversions that transvalue hegemonically defined concepts – *thumri* is "a fine cameo form"; it is "light and attractive, but lacking in majesty"; it is "*desi* (regional, roughly 'folk')"; it is an "open" rather than "closed" form that allows "otherness" to be "introduced into the body of [a] *raga* (musical mode)" – V. Rao establishes *thumri*'s "relentlessly questioning" modality that, while constituting the " 'other' voice in music," produces its critique from within hegemonic (patriarchal) structures, undermining but not destroying them, not least because its own position and ostensible power is implicated in them (1990: WS-31; WS-35). Thus, what for du Perron represents a form of disempowerment – "a [female] voice that locates women's expression of feeling in the realm of excitement for men" (2002: 192) – can, arguably, following V. Rao, be viewed as a simultaneously empowering and disempowering form of ("feminine"/ "female") expression, much like the women with whom *thumri* is indelibly linked:

> *Thumri* and *tawaifs* ... does one read them as politically powerful – as women who were able to speak (sing) freely of their sexuality, take lovers, influence kings, earn money, hold land in their own names, read, write, compose poetry and music...? Or does one "read" them as unfortunate victims of a patriarchal society, objects of elite male lust,... of both class and gender oppression – as women needing to be rescued...?
>
> (Rao, V. 1990: WS-32)

The film's complicated formal structure that compels a non-linear narration and apprehension of Sardari's story in some ways allegorizes the positioning of *thumri* as "feminine voice," as elaborated by V. Rao. On the one hand, in Sardari, Benegal seems to have found a female subject who refuses to accept, and thus seems to be free of, obstacles thrown up by society, especially its male figures – her father and brother, for example – in her pursuit of a career in music. In fact, she willingly gives up her family and becomes Hemraj's mistress to do so, in the process refusing as well incorporation within, and definition through, normative relationships (such as through marriage, etc.).[36] On the face of it, Sardari seems either not to have accepted society's valuation of the role of women or, if she has, not to have accepted its validity for her own conduct. On the other hand, her story is (re)presented through a formal structure that embeds it in the discourse of (patriarchal) others. The film's viewer is not given direct access to Sardari's consciousness and thus to her own valuation of her life; instead, her views and emotions are represented through memories/recollections of a host of people – mostly men – related to or associated with her: her brother, Jabbar; her husband, Sadiq; the manager of the radio station she contracts with, Sen; her primary accompanist, the *sarangi* player; a young male fan, Amod. Of all the kin and associates who recall Sardari's life only two are women: Sardari's patron Hemraj's wife and Sardari's daughter, Sakina. Each recollection is inflected, to varying degrees, by the recollector's own interests specifically and by patriarchal interests more generally, and this is true of the women's recollections as well. Nevertheless, Sardari's striking independence from social mores and valuations comes through (albeit as stubbornness or willfulness in some recollections), existing in a finely wrought tension with more conventional valuations. This is so, I believe, mostly because these recollections are organized and mobilized by her niece, Tehzeeb, who is a lot like her aunt, especially with respect to her independence from conventional social mores.[37] In this respect, the formal strategy of the film suggests that, in addition to being represented from a variety of perspectives, Sardari (who has deliberately eschewed conventional family relationships in pursuit of her music)[38] finds, in her death, a family member well positioned to represent her, insofar as this is possible, on her own terms.[39]

Before she discovers the familial link, Tehzeeb (and the film's viewer) first encounters Sardari through the discourse of the (nation-)state, regarding communal relations between Hindus and Muslims. The policeman, whom Tehzeeb queries about Sardari's accidental death ("*kaun marā?*" ["Who died?"]), launches into an explanation about the cause of the communal riot that led to the death, blaming electioneering and opportunistic politicians who use these communal disturbances to consolidate their vote bank; as for the identity of the person who died, he says dismissively: "*Arre, koi nachne ganewali thī*" ("Oh, she was a songstress-courtesan"). Thereafter, several of Sardari's mostly Muslim neighbors proceed to memorialize Sardari as an iconic figure by stressing her "national" identification ("She was a fine example of Indian civilization/culture [*Bharatiya sabhyata*]," says one) while also using her death to decry the communal disturbance as an instance of Muslim beleaguerment in predominantly Hindu India ("Those who started the disturbance," says another, "don't want the well-being and prosperity of our people/community/nation [*qaum*]"; yet another presents the communal disturbance as an attack on "the [secular] fabric of this nation"). In this outermost, most general frame, articulating the discourse of the (nation-)state, the narrative strategy is fairly straightforward and represents Sardari simply as an instrument of political agendas mapped by her public memorialists. Although Tehzeeb does not dismiss this discourse, she nonetheless refuses her editor's request to place Sardari's narrative within this explanatory framework ("If there is a communal angle," he says, "then it will be interesting," implying that he might then let her write Sardari's story for the paper).[40] She is much more interested in the story of Sardari's rebellion; the story, that is, of her aunt, the singer of *thumri*s ("What should we do to keep her memory alive?" she asks Sardari's daughter and her cousin, Sakina, who refuses to oblige by staying resolutely silent at first). This is the story she wants to tell.

The more complicated – non-linear – strategy of the rest of the film follows from Tehzeeb's desire to piece together such a story, which she seeks to do by interviewing intimates and associates for their recollections of Sardari. The complications entailed in this task, which also disrupt a strictly chronological or linear telling, are a product, first, of different people having access to different moments in Sardari's life and, second, of the different ways in which individuals remember, not least because of their different ideological orientations.[41] For example, Sardari's brother and Tehzeeb's father, Jabbar, in response to his daughter's question about why she was never told about the existence of her aunt, begins his recollection with the altercation between Sardari and their father following the latter's discovery of Sardari's participation in a *mehfil* or salon gathering ("Did I let you learn music so you could become a *baiji*?" ["*gana sikhaya to baiji ban jaogi?*"], her father angrily questions her). This altercation leads to Sardari's running away from home. For Jabbar, Sardari's disobedience and subsequent loss of "respectability" (because she became a member of her patron's household, thereby also becoming a kept woman [*rakhel*]) constitutes a sound justification for his silence about his sister ("How could we have kept contact with her?"). When Tehzeeb invokes her aunt's reputation as "a well-known *thumri* singer," Jabbar again has swift recourse to conventional social mores: "girls from respectable houses don't sing [in public forums]" ("*sharif ghar ki ladkiyan gana nahin gaati*"); and then again, "all I know is that she brought disrepute to our house/family."

Later, the viewer finds out details about the *mehfil*, which so alienates Sardari from her family, from the reminiscence of the *sarangi* player who accompanies her at her performances. Significantly (and perhaps pertinently), in his reminiscence, Sardari's participation in the *mehfil* has a quite different resonance: It is her exceptional talent as a singer that he recalls from the *mehfil*. Because the *sarangi* player was the accompanist of Sardari's teacher, Iddanbai, also a songstress-courtesan herself, he finds Sardari's participation in a *mehfil* an unremarkable event in terms of (its presumed lack of) social respectability. In the interview with Tehzeeb, the *sarangi* player comes across as very protective of Sardari; additionally, in the interview, as well as in other people's recollections, he is represented as someone deeply appreciative of Sardari's talent as a singer and loves her almost like a daughter. His representation of Sardari, therefore, is one of the more supportive and complimentary ones, open to her positive qualities, gentle and understanding about her negative ones.

There is one set of events – dealing with money Jabbar borrows from Sardari for Tehzeeb's education – at which Jabbar, the *sarangi* player, and Sardari's daughter, Sakina, all are present, but which each recalls quite differently. (This scene is reprised three times in the film, each emphasizing different aspects of the transaction, with the camera focusing on different combinations and different details of the three subjects involved in the transaction.) The brother's recollection, seemingly in response to Tehzeeb's query about whether or not he loved Sardari, circulates around the time he had gone to return the money he borrowed from her. When Sardari refused to take it back insisting that it was never meant as a loan ("There is no such thing as a loan between brother and sister" ["*Bhai behen mein koi len den nahi hoti*"]), adding pointedly as well that the money is not contaminated by sexual commerce ("I have earned it by singing, not by selling my body" ["*gana gaake paisa kamaya hai, badan bech ke nahin*"]), he departed in anger, swearing never to visit her again, and leaving the money behind. His account of the incident represents his sister as headstrong, highly-strung and febrile. When Tehzeeb goes on to admiringly point out what she sees as Sardari's independence and sense of autonomy ("she lived her life as she wanted to") Jabbar responds by underscoring Sardari's lack of realism ("she wanted the sky and stars" ["*woh aasmaan aur sitare chahati thi*"]).

The *sarangi* player's recollection, focusing on Sardari's generosity, on the other hand, circulates primarily around the first part of the transaction – when Jabbar came to borrow money. He recalls how Sardari was astute enough to know that Jabbar's visit was a self-interested one, so she asked Sakina to bring her *batua* (purse) before her shame-faced brother could even articulate his demand; how Sardari gave him double the amount he asked for, and asked him to bring his daughter to meet her aunt. He recalls the other end of the transaction – when Sardari angrily flung the money Jabbar had left behind across the room where the *sarangi* player was seated – primarily to suggest that her anger stemmed from her grasp of a possible sub-text in Jabbar's refusal to accept the money as anything other than a loan: It would mean that he (Jabbar) was implicitly conceding Sardari some claim – of filial affection and association, say – over his daughter.

Sardari's daughter, Sakina, recollects the event as well – in bitterness and anger against her mother – providing yet another perspective on Sardari and the ideological sub-texts that inflect it. For Sakina, her *mamu's* (uncle/mother's brother) departure in anger is a sign of her mother's inability to maintain any ongoing relationships with her kin and associates. More pejoratively, for Sakina it is a sign of her mother's selfishness ("*khudgarzi*"), such that she is unable to comprehend and certainly never attempts to meet Sakina's deeply felt need for family and kin, and for a life other than the one her mother has embraced. Sakina frames her conversation with Tehzeeb by remarking on how "the Sardari Begum people knew wasn't the one I knew," and then goes on to reprise for Tehzeeb the altercation she had with her mother after Jabbar left in anger: She recalls a series of accusations she directed against her mother about not letting her (Sakina) receive a proper education,[42] and estranging her from her father (whom she takes to be Sadiq) and her uncle. When Sardari demurs that she has given her daughter everything in her life, Sakina levels her most serious accusation: Sardari never let Sakina address her as "mother" ("*mujhe tumne amma kabhi nahin kehene diya*") because that would have revealed how old she (Sardari) was. "After this [altercation]," she tells Tehzeeb, "I stopped singing and stopped talking with my mother." She concludes by remarking on how "lucky" Tehzeeb is to "have come from a loving household," even though this contention seems to fly in the face of Tehzeeb's remarks about Jabbar's efforts to repress her independent spirit. Sakina's view is more like Jabbar's than Tehzeeb's; she seems to want, like Usha in *Bhumika*, to inhabit a more conventional world, marked by middle-class values.

By presenting the same set of events from three different perspectives, the film sets out to build a psychologically complex, realistic, three-dimensional portrait of Sardari displaying both positive and negative aspects of her character. But these portrayals of Sardari are not, as already noted, without their own biases. Premised on the self-interest and ideological standpoints of their representers, they tell us something as well about the people who represent Sardari; more than that, they tell us something about the socio-cultural values with which these representations of Sardari are imbued. Sardari's brother and father are identified with, and speak, the discourse of (middle-class) respectability and conformity – they both emphasize the importance of social norms and constraints – whereas Sardari and Tehzeeb are identified by their resistance to such conformity: Tehzeeb describes her aunt as "colorful" ("*kafi rangeen hasti ki thi*") and sarcastically dismisses her father's wish for an obedient, pure daughter. But lest the spectator view such resistance to social norms as an integral dimension of women's way of inhabiting their social world, there is Sakina, who, despite, or perhaps because of, her unconventional upbringing, seems to desire a socially conformist and conventional upbringing and environment to live and grow up within, the lack of which constitutes the basis for her alienation from her mother. The *sarangi* player, on the other hand, in his respect and admiration of Sardari's talent and palpable affection for her, neither appeals to, nor exemplifies a discourse of respectability and conformity in his recollection, focusing almost entirely on the world of music and singing that he and Sardari occupy. When Sardari's patron Hemraj's wife is dismissive of what she sees as Sardari's real intentions ("She expected him [i.e., Hemraj] to marry her; what did she have [that he should have done so]?") and accuses Sardari of running away with the family jewels, the *sarangi* player contests and corrects her version of the events: Hemraj "could not satisfy her [Sardari]," he says, "because [while] he may have been attracted to her, he did not her appreciate her [talent in] singing."[43] Furthermore, he notes that the jewels that Sardari is accused of stealing were, in fact, forced on her as gifts by Hemraj.

In *Sardari Begum*, as in *Bhumika* and *Mandi*, the discourse and world-view of patriarchy, with its investment in a middle-class respectability that seeks to contain women's autonomy and independence through interdictions against their sexuality, is opposed to the world inhabited by the performing women, who evade, if not altogether escape, patriarchal constraints by virtue of their (public) professions, premised on and enabled by their non-conformity and non-conjugal sexuality. But *Sardari Begum*, no less than *Bhumika* and *Mandi*, shows how neither patriarchal ideologies nor resistance against, or evasion of, them constitute monolithic terrains of action and desire, not least because their female subjects' independence and, therefore, ability to resist patriarchal constraints paradoxically depends on men who create the opportunities allowing these women to become independent: After running away from home to resist her father's authoritarian dictates, Sardari finds refuge in Hemraj's household by becoming his mistress; it is through Sadiq, who marries her when she is pregnant with Hemraj's child and introduces her to a broader constituency of listeners, via her appearance on radio programs and in music conferences (*sangeet sammelan*), that she acquires a professional career, which enables and supports her independence.

Against the singularity and resoluteness of Sardari's brother's and father's disapproval of her, moreover, the film displays the approval, even admiration of the *sarangi* player and, more significantly, of Sen, the radio station manager, who loves Sardari and wants to marry her. But, despite his love and unequivocal rejection of Sardari's unconventional profession and social location as a potential impediment to their marriage, he balks at accepting Sakina and including her in his household, thereby displaying a residual, if not full-fledged, resistance to Sardari's identity as a courtesan-songstress.[44] Along somewhat different lines, Sadiq, Sardari's husband, who takes all credit for fashioning her into a well-known singer, is more than comfortable with her public profile and independence, but mostly because both bring in the money that sustains their lifestyle. In this regard, Sadiq is like Dalvi in *Bhumika,* but unlike Dalvi, he is neither haunted by jealousy nor, as Dalvi seems to be, damaged by a sense of his inadequacy (on this, see Benegal's comments to van der Heide 2006: 88). In his interview with Tehzeeb, Sadiq acknowledges that things turned sour between him and Sardari once she determined that his self-interest, which was not consonant with her interests, always came first.[45]

In addition, Sakina and Tehzeeb are not represented as monolithically conforming or resisting subjects respectively. At the film's conclusion Sakina, who has thus far resisted incorporation into Sardari's profession and vociferously decried the value of her matrilineal inheritance, is shown performing exactly the same *thumri* with which the film opens, except that, in the film's opening, it is Sardari performing it before she is accidentally killed: Represented, in Sardari's dying words, as the only inheritance Sardari can confer on Sakina, *thumri* singing seems to be willingly embraced by the latter. Sakina also recalls a Sardari, who, as she is dying, strangely, wants to be recognized as a "good" mother. To this Sakina accedes, not just to Sardari (whereby it could be seen as an interested falsehood – giving in, that is, to the demands of her dying mother) but also to Tehzeeb, undermining thereby both her earlier accusations and the portrait of a Sardari free from normative, middle-class notions of motherhood. When Tehzeeb reminds her about her (earlier) harsh accusations against Sardari, including her vow never to be like her mother, and asks, "When you said yes to *phupijaan* [paternal aunt], were you not lying?" Sakina responds, "No, I was telling the truth." Concomitantly, Tehzeeb, whose refusal to abide by middle-class notions of respectability is a source of considerable tension and conflict between her socially conformist father and herself, assures the latter that she will never give him any reason for such disapproval from hereon. She follows this by breaking off her relationship with her boss. (The latter act, however, could be viewed as a bid for independence in as much as the relationship entails things staying the same, with her lover married to someone else.)

What is the viewer to make of these "reversals" – Sakina's concluding gesture accepting the mantle of her mother's career? Tehzeeb's turning her back on her lover and thus on the unconventional relationship that in some ways linked her to her aunt, Sardari, and drove, as it were, her effort to remember Sardari's story? More specifically, how do these "reversals" speak to the changed position of the songstress-courtesan the film sketches as a significant contextual framework through which it seeks to map the continuing relevance, or not, of this position for women's autonomy and emancipation? As in *Bhumika* and *Mandi*, *thumri* and *thumri* singers in *Sardari Begum* are caught in a moment of transition: Although the *sarangi* player recalls performances (by Iddanbai and the young Sardari) that include those presented in intimate *mehfils* organized by

Hemraj, the film (via Sadiq's and Sen's recollections) locates Sardari's performances mostly through her career as a radio artist and performer in large public concerts (*samelans*), thereby marking *thumri* and its singers' passage from a "feudal" to a "modern" performance space. Sardari initially makes this transition successfully, becoming both famous and rich in the process (Sadiq recalls her as the "rising new star" in the firmament of music *samelans*). Her resistance, however, to singing popular, romantic *thumri*s and *ghazal*s for a now more heterogeneous and unevenly informed and engaged audience, combined with her estrangement from first Sadiq and then Sen, leads to the diminishment and decay of her position (in words that mimic Sadiq's earlier, Sen recalls her as "a broken star" once she withdraws from public life in anger against the changed performance venues and audiences). Toward the end, as Sakina recalls, Sardari was reduced to arranging marriages in the neighborhood to keep her household going.

If the "decay" of Sardari's career can be considered exemplary of the radically changed situation that songstress-courtesans like her face in the new nation, then is invoking her independence and considerable freedom from middle-class (patriarchal) ideologies, which are such powerful elements in all their varied representations and tied as well to her profession, simply an exercise in nostalgia, an anachronism that serves no particularly useful purpose? It seems to me that through Tehzeeb and Sakina, as the film's conclusion represents them, Benegal both acknowledges the power/hegemony of the transformed social landscape of the "modern" nation into which a songstress-courtesan cannot simply be inserted unchanged *and* retains the figuration of the performing woman as carrier of certain counter-hegemonic possibilities, not least for the historical imaginary that has excluded her. Tehzeeb, despite her real affinity with Sardari, cannot in fact be or become Sardari. Neither can Sakina, despite her embrace, finally, of a Sardari-like position, be or become her mother. But in both cases, Sardari and the world she stands for exert a powerful pressure by providing a prior model of female autonomy and independence with which they can interact in order to work out their own specific forms of autonomy and freedom. (Along somewhat different lines, I find it instructive that Tehzeeb and Sakina both begin at opposite ends of the spectrum in terms of their reaction to their social worlds and end up occupying the exact opposite of where each began; in the process, they end up almost mirroring each other's starting point: Does this mean that the film is suggesting that each must accept, indeed, learn from those social positions and realities which she at first rejects or excludes?) Performing women, *Bhumika, Mandi*, and *Sardari Begum* suggest, can and should be made to exert such pressure on the national imaginary that excludes them, and to this end, Benegal retrieves this figure for more extensive dissemination. But the figure of the performing women he retrieves is a complex one, particularly in its relationship to patriarchal society at large.

In her "explor[ation]" of "how women were used/deployed/perceived" in "nationalist historiography" that she characterizes as a "predominantly masculinist project," Mukherjee nevertheless cautions her readers that "how [women] were presented in the dominant discourse of the time" and "how they represented themselves in the[ir] personal narratives" may not be amenable to a "binary opposition," not least because their self-representation, via autobiographies, was a product of their education that was itself initiated by men: Not only was "women's education," in general, "very much part of the agenda of nineteenth-century enlightenment in Bengal," but, specifically, "the impetus for education came almost invariably from their husbands who would sometimes teach them the alphabet in the secrecy of their bedrooms, away from the prying eyes of the extended family." She also notes that there are many analogous instances to be found in "Marathi women's autobiographies of the same period" (1996: 110). But given "the idea of mastery" associated with authorship – the "pen is an instrument of power that provides an entry into public space conferring on the author attributes of authority" – "female authorship" was, by definition, "subversive," "unsettling to domestic structure and hence to social order" (1996: 123). Benegal's *Bhumika, Mandi*, and *Saardari Begum* offer portraits of performing women who partake of and exemplify the contradictions and paradoxes Mukherjee identifies with women writing. Retrieving them in their full complexity for a national narrative that thus far has sought to exclude them brings attention not only to the repressions and elisions of this narrative, but also refuses its simplifications and singularities.

Part II

The nation's alternative and self-authorized biographies

3 Fictional engagements with (national) history

Junoon, *Mammo*, and *Trikaal*

> Historicizing has a played a key role in consolidating notions of national, gendered, ethnic, and racial identities, presenting deterministic and essentialist conceptions of times and human action.... Versions of history thus play a powerful role in determining how individuals and groups inherit and understand their social and cultural milieu. History and memory have also played a part in destabilizing conceptions of the nation.
>
> (Landy 2001b: 2)

> [O]ur dissatisfaction with the Hindustani [popular Hindi cinema] historical stems from its inability to transcend the boundaries established by modern elitist historiography. The reason why this cinema is [not], and cannot be, revolutionary is located in its selection of historical facts ... reducing history to the march of patriarchal orders of the past.
>
> (Deshpande 2009: 91)

Benegal's "realism" self-consciously locates his cinematic narratives, including their characters and the social situations and predicaments they encounter, in specific historical moments and particular geographical settings. As such *all* his films can be said to conform with what historian Natalie Davis calls "history films," by which she means "those having as their central plot documentable events, such as a person's life or a war or a revolution," as well as "those with a fictional plot but with a historical setting intrinsic to the action" (1987: 459).[1] Thus the five films examined so far (and the three that are the subject of this chapter) can be incorporated, with varying degrees of accuracy, within one or the other, and sometimes both, definition(s) provided by Davis. Analogously, the preoccupations of the five films discussed thus far, including the preconditions for women's emancipation and the necessity of women's and subaltern people's empowerment, are also concerns in the three films covered by this chapter. Nevertheless, by assigning prominence to "(national) history" in the title of this chapter, much as "women" are assigned prominence in the titles of the previous chapters, I am flagging an emphasis in the subjects Benegal addresses in these three films, including thereby the generic categories and philosophical questions through which the viewers are invited to access them. This emphasis recognizes the centrality that Benegal accords to history in crafting national culture and identities. Nor is Benegal an exception in this regard. For the belief that a nation is defined via "the constructions of its histories" is shared by other cultural producers from former colonial formations (see Rosen 2004: 267, 265–300).[2] Addressing the integral role of history in defining a postcolonial Indian national identity and culture, Prakash notes how "the assumption that India was an undivided subject" was "common to [Indian] nationalism as a whole"; as such, this nationalism assumed that India "possessed a unitary self and a singular will that arose from its essence and was capable of autonomy and sovereignty." He adds, "*It was the task of History to unleash this subjectivity from colonial control; and historiography was obliged to represent this unleashing*" (1990: 389; emphasis added). Analogously, Bhattacharya observes: "the writing [or production] of history in a sense became tied to the elaboration of the democratic, liberal, socialist, humanist vision of Nehruvian India" (Bhattacharya 2003: n.p.).

This chapter focuses on three films, *Junoon* (Obsession, 1978), the eponymous *Mammo* (1994), and *Trikaal* (Past, Present, Future, 1985), separated from each other by several years, each of which engages via fictional narratives with an historical event – the 1857 uprising; the Partition of South Asia; Goa's "independence" from the Portuguese and incorporation within the Indian Union – that is a site of contention and controversy, or repression and silence, or marginalization and elision in the official biographies of the Indian nation.[3] As sites of contention and contradiction, the events labeled "1857" and "Partition" have (in particular) been open to constant re-writing and reframing by successive generations and by individuals and groups with diverse investments within and across these generations. Thus, these events, historicized anew at various critical and temporal junctures, provide particularly rich examples of the processes that go into the construction of national histories.

As *Junoon*, *Mammo*, and *Trikaal* demonstrate, the "(national) history" alluded to in the title of this chapter pertains not only to those narratives the Indian (nation-)state has purposively written about itself, but also to those it has failed or refused to write about itself because of the nature of the historical event and/or protagonists involved. The three films' protagonists, as Eurasians (Anglo-Indians),[4] Muslims,[5] or Goan Catholics of mixed Portuguese and Indian ancestry, along with their kin networks and identifications, belong to minority communities, even though (in the historical moment in which their stories are situated) some are from the ruling class.[6] Furthermore, in a signature move, all three films privilege the predicaments of female protagonists and their responses to their world, even when, as in *Junoon*, the ostensible focus of the narrative is on a male figure – played by one of Hindi cinema's most handsome and charismatic actors, Shashi Kapoor – and his romantic obsession with a young Anglo-Indian woman. Indeed, we could plausibly view the focus of these three films as a response to the question Butalia poses about the revisionary histor(ies) of Partition: "How does 'history' look when seen through the eyes of women?" (2000: 16). Through this focus Benegal sidesteps and displaces official histories' centering of (only) male protagonists and their world of heroic public action. Unlike, therefore, the "Hindustani historicals" that Deshpande excoriates for their "inability to transcend the boundaries established by modern elitist [or official] historiography" (see epigraph; 2009: 91), these three films' relationship to the official narratives of the nation can be seen as skewed or off-centered, even when they sometimes uncritically reproduce some component elements of official or dominant national narratives.

Although there is no necessary connection between cinema and alternative, even dissident, versions of official or dominant history, cinema's potential for producing such alternatives or dissidence is often touted and seen to derive from qualities that it shares with narratives in general and the novel in particular.[7] Ferro, for example, notes that, with "popular memory and oral traditions" as her/his instruments, "the historian-filmmaker can give back to a society a history it has been deprived of by the institution of History" (1988: 19). For novelist and historian Slotkin, the novel's (and arguably cinema's) imaginative recuperation of "a past time" enables "writer and reader [or filmmaker and spectator] to explore those alternative possibilities for belief, action, and political change unrealized by history." "In doing so," Slotkin adds, "the novelist [or filmmaker] may restore, as imaginable possibilities, the ideas, movements, and values defeated or discarded in the struggles that produced the modern state" (2005: 221). At minimum, both fictional and cinematic narratives are seen to possess the ability "to render," as Rosenstone, invoking Raack, puts it, "the fullness of the complex, multidimensional world in which humans live" (1988: 1176). For Slotkin, as for Raack, "novelizing an [historical] event is to see it from within, from the limited and contingent perspective of those who are caught up in the action" (2005: 255); and as "empathetic reconstruction[s]" that are able "to convey how historical people witnessed, understood, and lived their lives," historical films and fiction are well positioned to "recover all the past's liveliness" (Raack, quoted in Rosenstone 1988: 1176). Cinema and fiction, it is implied, because of their recourse to the resources of imagination, can paradoxically deliver a more "real" past, a deeper "truth" than, presumably, history can.

Cook, arguing that cinema "bring[s] spectators closer to the past, to produce a kind of second-hand testimony that includes the audience as witness to reconstructed events" (2005: 2), assigns to "popular historical films" and "the historical costume drama" a somewhat different capability: the potential for creating a critically alert spectator who, through her/his participation as witness learns to recognize that history is *made, actively constructed,* not simply *given.* With "their proclivity for putting on display an array of period artefacts, [as] in a museum," these kinds of films, she suggests, render visible "the process of historical reconstruction," thereby drawing their spectators "into a complex and self-conscious engagement with history" (2005: 201, 226). Rosen also underscores the historical film's ability to produce a self-conscious engagement with history on the part of the spectator. Noting the "complex play in spectatorial apprehension of every image in a historical film," he goes on to specify how:

> the conversion of document into narrationally positioned diegetic detail … and then – if we understand the pictured objects as appropriately or reasonably "authentic" reconstructions … – a conversion back from the diegetic to the quasi-document … results in spectatorial comprehension that might be summed up as follows: "Oh that's what it looked like…." What we see, then, is not what actually *was*, but what it would have looked like.
>
> (2004: 181–182)

As the scholarship on the Partition of South Asia, which articulates with trauma studies and scholarship on the Holocaust, tells us, literature and cinema, more than providing opportunities for alternative or dissident versions of history to emerge, are sometimes the only sites within which certain kinds of cataclysmic historical events can find "life" and embodiment. However, in his critical analysis of what he calls the "historian's history" of the Partition, Pandey, while granting the structural inability of "the language of historical discourse" to represent the large-scale "pain and suffering" of otherwise ordinary people who lived through a cataclysmic event like the Partition, argues that these limits proceed mostly from a disciplinary identity and ideology that official or historian's history has wittingly and purposefully embraced and/or crafted. "The historian seeking to represent violence in history," Pandey acknowledges:

> faces the problem of language (how, for example, does one describe pain and suffering?), of analytical stance (how can one be "objective" and express suffering at the same time?), and of evidence (for does not large-scale violence destroy much of its most direct evidence?).
>
> (Pandey 1994:193)

But the self-constituted limits of historian's history that most concern Pandey have to do with this history's "adopti[on]" of "the point of view of the … [nation-]state" (ibid.). Historian's history, he suggests suppresses or removes all signs of struggle and contention so that the truth or facticity of the history offered by the hegemonic structures and institutions of the (nation-)state can appear natural and self-evident (1994: 190–193). For Pandey, then, it is not what literature and cinema can do, and history cannot, that is the problem; rather, it is the limits the latter has embraced *as a disciplining force* that is at issue. Literature and cinema are thus invoked as resources for alternate, even oppositional, constructions of history as evinced by Pandey's focus on Manto's "Toba Tek Singh" and Kidwai's memoir *Azadi Ki Chaon Mein* (*In the Shadow of Freedom*) (1994: 215ff.; Bhalla 1999; Kidwai 2004).

The ensuing analysis of *Junoon*, *Mammo*, and *Trikaal* focuses on Benegal's strategies of representation as these articulate (or not) with the rich historical scholarship that has been produced on the historical contexts these films evoke; it considers as well the diverse body of work on historical films and analyses that address the conjuncture of literature/cinema and history. Particularly extensive and wide ranging on the 1857 uprising and the Partition, some of the most interesting and provocative instances of the former scholarship are contemporaneous with Benegal's cinematic rendition of these events (as in *Mammo*), while some follow it (as in *Junoon*). The choices Benegal makes to represent these events – fictional(izing) "true" stories, adopting minority perspectives, and centering women's life-worlds and interiorized domestic spaces – can be seen as attempts to inflect, with somewhat different emphases, the understanding of events otherwise seen, particularly in nationalist histories, to belong to a (masculine) public sphere of heroic action. By doing so, these three films also attempt something else: In their ruminations on "the question of national cinema," Vitali and Willemen describe "history … as an unstable terrain that is always contended over by dominant and non-dominant forces at play in specific historical formations." Addressing the role of cinema in this context, they add that:

> it is precisely as discursive terrains for struggle between dominant and non-dominant forces over the power to fix the meaning of a given narrative stock that films can be seen not to "reflect" but to "stage" the historical conditions that constitute the national.
>
> (2006b: 8)

Junoon and *Mammo*, by "staging" (national) events through perspectives and identifications that disturb the presumed coherence and authority of dominant narratives of the nation, become part of the ongoing struggle to determine the meaning of these events. While the end of Portuguese colonialism in India has never been viewed as a "national" event, *Trikaal*'s meditation on the value of minority identity and identifications is a crucial element in Benegal's engagement with national history. *Trikaal* also provides us with instances of memory's interactions with history, particularly, memory as an indispensable feature of historical thinking, as well as the different instrumentalities for recovering the past.

Junoon

> I was always intrigued with the idea of making a period film and with reconstructing a period. I did a bit of this in *Bhumika* but *Junoon* provided the opportunity to create a whole environment, a whole different world.
>
> (Benegal in interview with me, February 19, 2011)

> Commemoration is too serious (or political) a business to be left to historians: poets, publicists, politicians, playwrights [and filmmakers?] all must contribute.… To hang the story of the Ghadar by a single thread would amount to hanging its myriad rebels twice over.
>
> (Amin 2006: n.p.)

Produced by popular mainstream Hindi cinema star turned producer, Shashi Kapoor, Benegal's *Junoon* is adapted from a short story, *A Flight of Pigeons*, by

Anglo-Indian writer, Ruskin Bond. It is the story of the Labadoor family – particularly of Ruth and her mother, Mariam, and grandmother – who at the onset of the 1857 uprising are rendered homeless, literally, when their home is set on fire and, metaphorically, when Tom, Ruth's father and Mariam's husband, a minor functionary in the colonial administration, is killed at a church massacre, from which Ruth escapes. As people identified with the English colonizers, they go into hiding. Provided refuge, first, by a Hindu loyalist, Lala Ramjimal, they are then forcibly moved by Javed Khan (obsessed with Ruth, whom he also wants to marry) to his residence. Mariam balks at the proposal (as does Javed's wife), but finally suggests a compromise: Javed can marry Ruth if the British lose Delhi to the rebels, but he must forsake her if the reverse happens. Although *Junoon*'s opening locates its action within the world of the 1857 uprising, with the text on the screen alluding to significant landmarks in the uprising's progress, the film for the most part is set in interior domestic spaces, representing primarily the world of women. The 1857 uprising is tracked via the intermittent appearances of Javed's brother-in-law, Sarfraz, a fiery, committed rebel who tries to rouse Javed from his apathy and decadence. Delhi falls to the British; Mariam holds Javed to his promise to forsake Ruth; and a disillusioned Javed rides away to battle English forces, his conversion to the cause of the rebels having begun with the death of his cousin, Hafiz.

Bond and Benegal both locate the short story's (and film's) origins in an incident that "actually happened" (Benegal to Tejani 1979: 27) during the 1857 uprising, underscoring their allegiance to normative conceptions of the historical real. In presenting the incident, of course, they draw on the technologies of fiction, particularly those pertaining to the narrative/cinematic point of view, through which they represent the "truth" of history. In their remarks on, and development of, this historically verifiable incident, however, they point to different sources and methods of authentication: Bond suggests that he is merely transcribing events from Ruth's diary;[8] Benegal references the archival research he carried out in the National Archives in Delhi, in the church at Shahjahanpur in which the massacre took place and where Tom was killed, and in the Victoria and Albert Museum and the National Army Museum in Great Britain (Tejani 1979: 28). In his interview with me, after asserting the meticulous research that went into this "period film, based on a factual event," he spoke about the help he received from a "Lucknow lecturer," who provided him with historical materials on the Rohilkhand Pathans, of whom Javed is one (February 19, 2011).[9] Benegal's comments to me also suggest the brevity of the short story called forth his research efforts. The net effect of his remarks is striking: they imply that he is producing an independent account of the events for which Bond's story serves merely as one source. Moreover, another consequence of his remarks is to locate "historical fact" within the uncertain – albeit richly generative – terrain of contingency and flux, dependent, not least, on the social location and ideological investments of the writer/filmmaker. For Bond and Benegal also ascribe different reasons for their interest in the incident and produce narratives whose emphases diverge sufficiently from one another to foreground significantly distinct ideological investments. Tacking between the two, then, allows one not only to grasp the centrality of re-presentation (in both senses of the word – as description and as a speaking on behalf of a specific position and constituency) in producing historical "truth," but also historical "truth" as itself a site of struggle and contention.

Bond's interest in Ruth Labadoor's diary, which *A Flight of Pigeons* ostensibly *transcribes* "in as factual a manner as possible," stems from its being "the recorded experiences of a 14-year old girl of mixed blood," whose "special position as an individual of different racial strains made it possible for her to witness the reactions of people from different communities – Hindu, Christian, and Muslim – who were involved in the terror and drama of that year." In addition to her perspective potentially conforming to Bond's ("my own family background was similar to that of Ruth Labadoor," he says), hers also is distinct from that of "Englishmen" who have been the primary producers of "books on the Indian Mutiny, or War of Independence of 1857." Bond also makes much of the movement of Ruth and her mother between the "three different worlds" of "European, Hindu, and Pathan" households, which allows them "to experience the common humanity of people from completely different backgrounds" (Bond 1980: 7–8). Indeed, Bond's representation of Ruth's memoir of this period in her life underscores the ease with which Ruth and her mother and grandmother inhabit the various "native" households in which they take refuge, becoming virtual insiders – speaking Urdu with ease, taking up "native" names, eating "native" foods, and wearing "native" clothes (Bond 1980: 39–40).[10]

"Bond saw the events from an Anglo-Indian perspective," said Benegal during my interview with him. "I saw them differently" (February 19, 2011). Bond does, indeed, adopt an Anglo-Indian perspective – Ruth's to be precise – on the events: Told in first person by Ruth, the narrative of *A Flight of Pigeons* is restricted to her take on the world around her, focusing on her family's experiences and their part in interactions with others. Benegal's film, on the other hand, eschews a single narrative point of view. Although it includes Ruth and her family in most of the film's frames and does indeed focus on their story, it does so from the perspective of, as Vaidynathan puts it, "their successive [Hindu and Muslim] hosts" (1996: 121). Vaidyanathan is also right in claiming that Benegal's film "presents the revolt entirely from the Indian point of view" (1996: 121) – although I would substitute the word "substantially" for "entirely," and, for the sake of precision, characterize this point of view as "Muslim-Indian." For, from the opening scene, with the *qawwali* (a form of Muslim devotional singing) being performed, as the titles roll, through the Labadoors' residence in Javed and his *chachi's* (paternal aunt's) households, Benegal's film focuses almost entirely on a Muslim-Indian milieu, excepting, of course, the brief time the Labadoors spend at Lala Ramjimal's and the one scene devoted to their household. Moreover, with Sarfraz as the primary advocate for, informant about, and participant in the 1857 revolt, the film's viewers *hear* about and *see* the revolt substantially through him. His views are deeply anti-colonial, focusing on the "heavy chains" and extensive brutalities with which the English have bound

Indians (at one point he confronts a startled Mariam with what are familiar details in Indian accounts of the uprising, involving rebels being shot out of the mouths of cannons or being hung on trees as evidence of colonial power [on this see, Lakshmi 2007: 1747]), and he is bitterly dismissive of their presumed humanity and civilization: "You English are priceless" ("*Jawab nahin tum firangiyon ka*"), he marvels sarcastically, "The question of humanity only arises when an English person dies" ("*Insaniyat ka sawal uthta hain jab angrez mare jate hain*"). His version of the causes for the revolt and the revolt itself is countered by both Javed (who, in the opening scene tells Sarfraz, "The nawabs who are helping you are doing so because they don't want to lose their luxuries" ["*woh nawab jo tumhari madad kar rahen hain apne aish nahin khona chahate*"]) and Mariam (who reminds him of the brutality with which he killed Tom). But they are shown as less credible, because self-interested, and so Sarfraz's views are supported, to some extent, by the film.

However, in speaking of his interest in this particular historical context and story, Benegal underscores "the ambiguity, which has always been there, of our relationship with the British ... a very strange kind of love-hate relationship," even "when the Nationalist movement was active" (van der Heide 2006: 96). Javed, obsessed with Ruth, as Benegal conceives him, presents an opportunity to explore this ambivalence and, potentially, the modalities of its transcendence.[11] (I say "as Benegal conceives him" because this characterization is Benegal's alone; in Bond's story Javed is a huckster – a rough, aggressive fellow, represented as already opportunistically among the party of rebels. Benegal's reconceptualization, I believe, speaks to a different ideological agenda than Bond's.)

To van der Heide, Benegal presents "Javed's desire for Ruth" as "linked to the historical situation": "getting Ruth," says Benegal, "would be equal to the sepoys beating the British" (2006: 100). Such a claim, however, presumes that Javed is invested in the sepoys' success in a way that the film does not evidence. Chaudhry and Khattak offer a different and, to my mind, more persuasive reading of the link "to the historical situation" as the film portrays it. Viewing it as a *bildungsroman* that tracks the moral development of Javed, they note:

> In *Junoon*, the central conflict of the plot mirrors the internal dilemma of Javed Khan,... who is [as] obsessed with Ruth ... as he is with his pigeons. Both obsessions are presented as barriers to be surmounted in his progression towards a transcendent state of nationalistic fervor.
>
> (1994: 19)

Whether or not they are right to see "nationalistic fervor" (rather than simply a commitment to national self-determination) as the film's desired end for Javed's progress, they are right in linking Ruth with the pigeons – and with the English – and in noting how the film seems to endorse Javed's forsaking of both as necessary to his development from a state of colonial dependence *as well as nawabi* decadence. For, if the pigeons are associated with Ruth and with the English, as the *fakir* in the opening scenes makes explicit, they also are associated with feudal decadence. Alluding to the culture of "pigeon fanciers" in Uttar Pradesh in which Javed participates, Benegal notes how Sarfraz finds this to be "an aspect of Javed's decadence, of his unwillingness to make the kind of commitment [to the national cause?] Sarfraz sees as necessary" (van der Heide 2006: 102). Benegal is drawing here on those accounts of 1857 that locate the causes for the uprising not only in the "historical processes ranging from the British policy of conquest and expansion to the colonial exploitation of India," but also in what scholars consider as "the beginnings of a process that interrogated and critiqued the internal feudal order"; thus, "the 1857 rebellion represents possibly one of the most powerful and dramatic anti-colonial movements that *also* questioned internal exploitation" (Pati 2007b: xiii, xvi; original emphasis).

Nevertheless the anti-colonial, anti-English critique remains a strong, if not over-determining, one in *Junoon*, aligning Benegal's film with many Indian representations of the uprising. Rajadhyaksha and Willemen's characterization of *Junoon* as a "colonial sexual fantasy" that "sidesteps any engagement with the issues underpinning what is described as the first war of independence" [1999: 407], therefore, seems somewhat perverse to me. For one thing, there is an asymmetry in the representation of spaces allotted to Mariam and Ruth's Anglo-Indian habitats versus those allotted to the Indian Muslim and Hindu habitats, in which Ruth and Mariam are often seen as troublesome intruders. For another, Benegal's film significantly re-conceptualizes Ruth's and Mariam's roles, making the latter, in particular, the bearer of the colonizer's identity – keeping her sense of difference, superiority, and entitlement sufficiently intact even when she moves into Ramjimal and Javed's households so as to undermine Bond's claims regarding the value (objectivity or impartiality by virtue of its hybridity) of an Anglo-Indian perspective when it comes to presenting the events of 1857.

The film devotes only two scenes at the beginning to Anglo-Indian habitats. And although it meticulously recreates these habitats, confirming Benegal's investment in recreating "a whole environment, a whole different world" (see epigraph to this section), the film also signals its intention to leave the Anglo-Indian world behind fairly quickly. (The shutting of the gate, as Tom and Ruth leave for church, is made to symbolize the act of shutting off – bringing to an end, that is – that part of their lives.) Once Mariam and Ruth go into hiding, they are shown only in indigenous habitats: Ramjimal's and then Javed's residences, with two brief stays at Javed's *chachi's* place. At Ramjimal's and Javed's, they are the recipients of considerable resentment and hostility – at Ramjimal's because his mother and wife fear for the well-being of their family for giving shelter to "enemies"; at Javed's because his wife, in particular, correctly registers the threat Ruth poses even before Javed has articulated his intention to marry her. Ruth and Mariam are also presented as disruptions in the enclosed domestic spaces that are overseen by women – disruptions associated with the world of their men and with the public world of politics and war: "Where have you brought these burdens/afflictions from?" ("*Yeh kahan se balain leh aye*?"), queries Javed's wife. Insofar as viewers understand, even sympathize with, the predicament of the women in Ramjimal and Javed's families, they see the Anglo-Indians as an intrusive, alien presence in the two households and withhold their sympathy from Ruth and Mariam.[12] At the same time, however, the film also registers the claustrophobia and anxiety the Labadoor women feel, hiding from frequent knocks on the door, and enclosed in small rooms, fearful for their lives. (Figure 3.1) The film, thus, gives the viewer some access to their mental world.

Only in the Labadoor women's interactions with Javed's *chachi* and her family do the film's viewers come close to a representation of the potential for the inter-racial connections and harmony touted by Bond and Fanthorne in their iterations of Ruth's and Mariam's stories.[13] Once the Labadoors have been moved to the *chachi*'s residence, not only does the film display camaraderie and affection between women belonging to otherwise mutually opposed communities – even the death of Hafiz (the son of the house), in the battle with the British, seems not to shake their affection for the Labadoor women – but it also removes the Labadoors from a claustrophobic "inside" within which they have been "hidden" thus far from the outside world, among swings hung from a mango tree and songs celebrating the onset of the monsoons. Strikingly, however, this movement from hostility and resentment to harmony, from the inside to the outside, is presented as an idyll – a utopian moment enclosed within a larger structure defined by discord and resentment – that is self-conscious of its status

Figure 3.1 Labadoor women in hiding in *Junoon.*

as an idyll (on this, see Benegal in van der Heide 2006: 100). Thus, inter-racial harmony, particularly in the interactions between women, which is such an important part of both Bond's and Fanthorne's narratives, is presented in *Junoon* as an idealized, mostly unreachable, possibility. Here Benegal seems to be working against the grain of not only Bond's and Fanthorne's texts, but also the "Mutiny" novel,[14] whose "strategic importance," says I. Sen, "lay in its efforts to reinforce colonial power in the context of post-Rebellion uncertainties and insecurities," and to that end devised several narrative strategies that countered any legitimate bases for the Rebellion (2010: 111). Bond's and Fanthorne's texts, on the other hand, share some of the aspects of the "Mutiny" novel, while departing from, and/or resisting others.

Contra Bond, when Benegal eschews Ruth's perspective as the organizing one through which *all* the events, characters, and interactions among them are made available to the viewer, he is, in effect, eschewing also the disposition of her narrative: the emphases she selects and the evaluations she elicits, implicitly and explicitly, from her readers, of events and characters (including her own), and interactions among them. In "her own words" (Bond 1980: 7) she comes across as a sober, thoughtful person, a daughter whose mother, Mariam, is to be admired as a courageous, forthright woman, and for being particularly protective of her family, especially Ruth. In "her own words," furthermore, she presents her mother, Mariam, as a model of inter-racial accommodation and integration. In the film, however, Ruth comes across as a hysterical, inarticulate, dependent young woman, whose nightmares, while justified given the massacre she witnessed in which her father was killed, are also the stuff of "gothic" colonial fantasies: Javed, a dark, predatory figure on a horse usually rides through these nightmares.[15] To be sure, this figure in some ways mirrors the Javed who, in her waking hours, is shown watching her. But her insistent question – "Papa, who is this Pathan who keeps watching me?" – resonates with both a sense of outrage stemming from a sense of her own (superior) status that is at odds with her presumed hybridity (which is supposed to make her sensitive to everyone's humanity) and with a sexual *frisson* that is at odds with her presumed lack of sexual interest in Javed ("I don't want to marry him, Mamma" she pouts and protests to Mariam). Quite apart from rendering Ruth a somewhat implausible object of Javed's obsession, a significant consequence of eschewing her perspective as the organizing one results in the (re)definition of role that Mariam comes to play in, or is assigned by, the film.

In *Junoon*, Mariam is presented as a virtual stand-in for the English, the "battle of wills" between her and Javed "epitomiz[ing]," says Benegal, "the British-Indian relationship" (van der Heide 2006: 101). Thus, even her otherwise admirable attributes of courage and forthrightness and her fierce protectiveness toward her family get actualized through the lens of her positioning as "British." Far from seeing her as comfortably integrated within the native households, viewers are made to notice her and Ruth's "difference" from the others, not only due their hostility, resentment, and discomfort with Mariam and Ruth and the disruption they have caused, but also because the two (Mariam more so than

Ruth) hold themselves apart. In a polished, nuanced performance, Jennifer Kendall (who makes even her estranging English accent function as a marker of difference when she speaks Hindustani in a high pitched sing-song fashion) portrays Mariam as someone, who, even under threat and exhausted and frightened by their ordeal on the run, never loses her sense of entitlement, which Javed, in one of his more prescient moments, correctly labels a species of arrogance – *akad.* Admittedly, she does not display the same arrogance with Ramjimal, but that might well be because he is a loyalist, "who was gaining from the British at that time … somebody who dealt with them on a business level" (Benegal to van der Heide 2006: 98); he, therefore, needs no such display to understand his place. "Pathans," on the other hand, of whom Javed is one, "had nothing to do with [the British]" (Benegal to van der Heide 2006: 98). Ramjimal's family, however, is not entirely exempt from Mariam's sense of her own superiority. In one scene, she brings a bundle of jewelry to Ramjimal to sell for much needed funds (Ramjimal's business, dependent as it is on the British, has run into trouble). While perfectly circumspect with him, she exchanges what can only be described as a sweetly venomous look with his mother, who is watching them and who has been the most articulate opponent of the Labadoors' continued residence in Ramjimal's household: "Not only can we pay our own way," the look seems to say, "we can also pay for yours!" Nevertheless, Mariam, despite her *akad* and the hostility and resentment she generates, remains a compelling figure.

Arguably this is due to Kendall's acting talents; equally, and perhaps more significantly, however, it is due to how Benegal envisages his female protagonists – excepting Ruth, but including Javed's wife and *chachi* and Ramjimal's wife and mother, even in their very brief appearances – as complex, multifaceted characters, alternately kind towards, and resentful of, the Labadoors, capable of raising the spectator's ire, and/or sympathy, and/or fascination. The same claim is more difficult to make for the film's male protagonists. Javed's passion for Ruth, for example, is presented as an asserted, not embodied truth, so that his comment about being smitten – "this girl has cast such a spell on me" ("*yeh ladki ne kya jadoo kiya hain mujhpe*") – comes across as altogether unpersuasive, a peg, simply, to hang the film's preoccupations on. Sarfraz is also one dimensional, called upon to articulate not much more than his anger and contempt against the British and display his heroic dedication to the uprising.

Mariam's perception of her *difference*, of the need for having and maintaining it, reflects, to an extent, the historical moment within which her story unfolds. G. Chakravarty, for example, remarks on how "from the first quarter of the nineteenth century … insularity and exclusion functioned at once as the modalities of colonial power and as a means of articulating a differential relationship with the indigenous" along the axes of "national, racial, and religious" identities. "Anglo-Indian identity," thus, "was as much a matter of exile from Britain, as it was of self-imposed exile from the immediacy of India" whereby it "remained more decidedly un-Indian than it was ever un-British" (2005: 103). Mariam's summary refusal of Javed's proposal is of a piece with this perception of "Anglo-India's un-Indian[ness]" as a marker of "colonial power," which her "compromise" then makes explicit: ("If the rebels win Delhi, then Ruth is yours," says Mariam to Javed; "if the English reassert their control over it, then Ruth will not be yours" ("*Dilli apki to Ruth bhi apki*; *Angrezon ka kabza ho gaya to Ruth apki nahin*"). But it is also, to an extent, an accurate understanding of the relationships between colonizer and colonized that were established once the 1857 uprising was crushed. Thus Lakshmi points out how "an inter-racial marriage," while "accepted in the early nineteenth century, was virtually anathema post-Mutiny" (2007: 1747). Remarking on the causes for such a shift, Stoler points out how:

> racist ideology, fear of the other, preoccupation with white prestige, and obsession with protecting European women from assault by Asian and black males were not simply justifications for continued European rule and white supremacy. They were [also] part of a critical class-based logic.
>
> (2002: 25)

In other words, stereotypes of "indigenous subversives," but also a means for keeping "potentially recalcitrant white colonials in line" (ibid.) As a possible source for, and exemplification of, such recalcitrance on the part of white colonials, inter-racial marriage and relationships were redefined as potential sources of danger in urgent need of redress. "Following the great rebellion in India," says Stoler, "moral reforms stipulated new codes of conduct that emphasized respectability, domesticity, and a more carefully segregated use of space" (2002: 77).

Although *Junoon* offers a strong anti-colonial, anti-English critique, it does not, therefore, mean that it simply regurgitates the dominant nationalist narrative of which this critique is a staple feature. Arguably, Benegal's very choice of a narrative focusing on Anglo-Indian and Muslim protagonists and their particular ideological alignments prevents such a regurgitation, presenting Benegal with different or alternative opportunities for understanding the 1857 uprising as a moment in the constitution of an Indian identity. In his review of *Junoon*, Milne's formulation of the film's procedures suggests what I take to be Benegal's particular investments: "The real fascination of the film," he says, is "the skill (and exemplary impartiality) with which it unravels the complexities behind what appears to the characters themselves as a simple conflict of opposites." According to Milne, "the whole central section is designed as a thread on which a tangled profusion of attitudes can be strung and examined at leisure" (1980: 7). Setting aside for the moment Milne's claim about *Junoon*'s "exemplary impartiality" – for, as my analysis has demonstrated, the film does take sides, and elicits the viewer's sympathy for select characters and events – what his comment grasps quite precisely is the film's investment, made apparent via its forsaking of a single narrative perspective, in disseminating many different (albeit interconnected) narrative strands in conversation, even contestation, with each other in its account of 1857. For example, we have Javed's narrative, but then we also have Mariam's and Ruth's and Javed's wife's, which interact with, and inflect (as they are inflected by) his; alternatively, we have Mariam's narrative, which in turn interacts with, inflects, and is inflected by, her hosts' – Javed and Ramjimal's, and also those of the women in their families. In a different register, we have narratives of oppositional relationships between the colonizers and colonized, conceptualized along the axes of difference, and a narrative of solidarity, exemplified, admittedly, through an idyll, but operating nonetheless as a counterpoint to the hostility and resentment displayed on both sides. Consequently, although it may be possible to discern where Benegal's sympathies lie, it is not possible to treat these sympathies as themselves not amenable to critical assessment. In offering more than one narrative strand and perspective, Benegal's account of 1857 refuses a singular, essentialist conception of an event that is considered significant in the nation's autobiography.

Mammo

> It's Mammo who he [Riyaz] wishes to *recover*.
>
> (Benegal to van der Heide 2006: 175, emphasis added)

> Is there such a thing, then, as a gendered telling of Partition? I learnt to recognize this in the way women located, almost immediately, this major event in the minor keys of their lives…, while for the most part men spoke of the relations between communities, the broad political realities.
>
> (Butalia 2000: 12)

If, as D. Chakrabarty remarks, "1857 came to be codified into a general form of insurrection … an incitement to popular politics" (2007: 1694), then the Partition in much recent scholarship has become, as Pandey notes, "a metaphor for the kind of extraordinary genocidal violence that was not witnessed again in India, perhaps until 1984," when Indira Gandhi's assassination by her Sikh body guards resulted in the horrific anti-Sikh pogrom (2001: 92).[16] And yet, as the work by Pandey and others has amply demonstrated, this was not always the case. With its focus almost entirely on the imperatives of national definition, "the violence of 1947" had, in its earlier renditions, "been treated as someone else's history" thereby installing a "wide chasm between historians' apprehension of 1947 and what we might call a more popular survivors' account of it" (Pandey 2001: 6). Elsewhere, interestingly, averring that "historian's history is forever in danger of adopting the point of view of the … state," Pandey "illustrates" this history's procedures – i.e., deciding "what is to be remembered and what forgotten" – by comparing "Indian nationalist writings on the Partition" with "British colonialist writings on 1857." In both, "the crisis of the nation" – India and Pakistan with respect to the former, Britain with respect to the latter – and of its ruling class or leadership are accorded center-stage, while "the history of the lives and experiences of the people who lived through the time" or the " 'native' rebel … the generally faceless men, women and children of the subcontinent," respectively, are relegated to the margins, even consigned to oblivion (1994: 193–194). Literature – fictional and non-fictional – and, one might add, cinema, are assigned, or take on, the representational task of "other ways of constructing the memory of Partition," resurrecting "themes [and subject positions] that have been suppressed and … forgotten" (Pandey 1994: 215), not least because of what is viewed as their ability "to articulate the inarticulable" (Saint 2010: 3).

Made and exhibited in 1994, Benegal's *Mammo* belongs to, even emerges from, the historical conjuncture that produced a substantive rethinking and radical interrogation of national(ist) histories of Partition that had restricted themselves, for the most part, to its "political" dimensions, whereby it was "generally seen," Menon and Bhasin note, "as the unfortunate outcome of sectarian and separatist politics, and as a tragic accompaniment to the exhilaration and promise of a freedom fought with courage and valour" (1998: 3).[17] As Pandey, among others, has noted, this interrogation, furthermore, was itself a product of "a set of far-reaching political and historiographical [re]considerations" of "the beginning of the end of the Nehruvian vision of a modern, secular, welfare state" and the "new consolidation of a right-wing, religious-community based politics" (2001: 6). To these we might add, on the positive side, the efflorescence of feminist scholarship triggered by a reinvigorated feminist movement in India, and of Subaltern Studies projects that, in challenging the élite orientation of conventional (nationalist) historiography, sought to bring within the purview of history "the stories," as Butalia puts it, "of the smaller, often invisible players: ordinary people, women, children, scheduled classes, [and peasants]" (2000: 9; see also Saint 2010: 182–185). Such interrogation drew attention not only to the violence – "genocidal," "horrific," "collective," "large-scale" and "communal," "sexual(ized)," and "gendered" – that accompanied the forced mass migrations, dislocations, and dispossessions of Partition, but also extensively and self-reflexively addressed the representational means through which such violence could be accessed or be made accessible. In producing new ways of thinking about Partition, furthermore, this interrogation highlighted the creation of new subjectivities and subject positions.

Several features/motifs of this revised, critical accounting of Partition – the recovery of "small voices" (Ranajit Guha's phrase), the focus on women's experience and subject positions, the privileging of literary and cultural texts, the centering of the attendant anguish of forced migration and displacement from "home/nation" – resonate in *Mammo*. Sometimes, however, they do so in unpredictable, even subversive ways, suggesting some of the potential limits of this revised discourse on Partition.

Mammo is a story about the unexpected and not entirely welcome arrival from Lahore, Pakistan, of the eponymous protagonist, Mahmooda Begum (aka Mammo) on the doorstep of her sister (Fayyazi) in Bombay, India. Her grandnephew, Riyaz, an orphan brought up by his grandmother, is particularly resentful of Mammo's sudden descent on their small household: "Grandma some woman has come" ("*Naani koi ayee hai*"), he says inhospitably and disrespectfully when announcing Mammo's arrival. Mammo is a lively but disruptive presence, not averse to imposing her views and "occupying" the house (or so it seems to Fayyazi and Riyaz on various occasions). Her positioning within Riyaz and Fayyazi's household as a formerly Indian subject (now Pakistani citizen) visiting her kinfolk in India, enables Benegal to address, in subtle, suggestive ways, not only what P. Kumar defines as "the ambivalent and liminal position occupied by Muslims in post-Partition India" (2008: xv),[18] but also the tragic absurdities of a relationship between two rival, but deeply interconnected, nations that compel people with attachments to, and belonging within both, to procure a visa to visit what is in effect one's own "home." Through Mammo, then, the film addresses both the inflexibility and potential flexibility or porousness of borders for subjects whose affective (and kinship) belongings straddle what have been defined as two separate nations, even while their citizenship consigns them to one or the other: Mammo is deported when she "violates" the terms of her three-month visa, but "returns" twenty years later, this time without a visa (circumventing thereby the need for renewing it) but only by declaring herself dead (and thus giving up any claim on India as a citizen-subject).[19]

Although what happens to Mammo and what she makes happen constitute the central narrative strand of the film, her story is recounted by Riyaz, whose narrative also incorporates his development into a subject and subject position that, I believe, the spectator of the film is invited to occupy. Riyaz is initially deeply resentful of what he views as Mammo's disruptive arrival and presence in his household. He describes her as a "stranger" to his friends at first and complains about having to give up his bed and not being able to study or listen to his selection of Western classical music. Even Mammo's sister (and Riyaz's grandmother) Fayyazi, is ambivalent about Mammo's assumption of belonging within her family and household. She worries whether there is enough space or resources to house Mammo indefinitely; she speaks angrily of Mammo's "occupation" of her home; she reminds Mammo during a quarrel that Mammo is only a guest in her house, not a resident, at which point Mammo queries: "I am a guest in my sister's house?" Through Riyaz and Fayyazi's initial response, the film suggestively allegorizes the way in which Muslims have been positioned in India as not (quite) belonging to the (national) family, as not (quite) welcome in the home (that is India). But between Mammo's two arrivals at the beginning and the end of the film – as a young widow and then twenty years later, after her deportation, as an old woman – Riyaz and Fayyazi learn to *live with*, even develop a strong attachment to Mammo, which renders their initial hostility and ambivalence moot. The change in Riyaz (and Fayyazi) is in part a function of his beginning to view Mammo not as a burden, as someone he is forced to take care of, but as someone with whom he can share certain activities (like secretly smoking, or going to see films – an activity he is passionately interested in). Similarly, Fayyazi has to learn to allow Mammo to help her out and share her burdens. *Living with*, in other words, means interaction on a quotidian level and reciprocal basis.[20]

One of the striking features of *Mammo* is the virtual absence of any direct depiction of violence, given that violence – as motif and fact – as Pandey and others have argued, is central to the revised understanding of Partition, but which nationalist accounts have treated as an aberration, or as not part of "our history."

In part, this absence can be explained via the film's choice of a narrator too young to know about Partition and the violence accompanying it. But it is equally a choice with which the film as a whole seems to concur, as its representational strategies make clear. For the film settles on highly mediated versions of Partition violence, privileging literary and cinematic renditions over others, but does so, paradoxically, by denuding these renditions of the affective charge that is considered to be their special terrain of operation.[21] This privileging is made plausible by having a narrator who is also an aspiring writer and a film buff. Indeed, Mammo and Riyaz bond over their mutual love of cinema and literature; and here, too, Riyaz learns from Mammo when she redirects his admiration for Khalil Gibran towards Saadat Hasan Manto and Faiz Ahmad Faiz, who are her favorite writers and, possibly, two of the most powerful chroniclers of Partition and its viscerally felt discontents. However, although Mammo invokes the idea and image of "hell" in conjunction with Manto's work, her characterization of his work also seems to domesticate the ferocious ironies and melodramatic excess through which Manto renders his fictions of Partition unbearably haunting and Partition's violence vividly palpable. In response to Riyaz's comment that he wants to write about what he *sees* and what he *experiences*, Mammo says, "So you want to write like Manto? He too wrote about what he saw," suggesting thereby a species of ethnographic realism as Manto's métier. She follows her remarks on Manto with a representation of the "hell" of Partition through a set piece (a story about a woman escaping from the depredations of Partition violence with her two children; rendered crazy by the death of one, she throws the live one into the river instead) recalled in a ruminative fashion that virtually leaches the story of most of its immediacy and, thus, horror, and this despite the fact that her "recall" is actualized in the film through shots of people running from the violence within which they are caught.[22]

Benegal's reticence about representing violence through and in all its excess and horror is of a piece with his "realism" that, in opposition to the melodramatic mode embraced by popular Hindi cinema, relies on, indeed cultivates, low-key and understated images and sound for its effects. His reticence also partakes of a larger discussion regarding the representation of violence, not least when such violence constitutes a kind of limit-experience. A decade or more of writing on this subject has rendered it familiar and almost predictable, but *Mammo*, as noted, emerged at the historical conjuncture when "new" scholarship on Partition began to radically question national(ist) silences, particularly pertaining to the violence through which the two nations of the subcontinent came into being. Highlighting this violence as central to what should constitute a revised understanding of Partition, this scholarship resorts to words that seek to capture its extremity. And yet, such recourse to excess itself becomes a sign of language's inability to adequately represent such extremity, triggering the search for alternate forms of representation, including, though not limited to, literary and cinematic figuration.

Amitav Ghosh raises some interesting questions about the status of such figuration in a 1995 (the year *Mammo* was made) essay that deals with the anti-Sikh pogrom following the assassination of Prime Minister Indira Gandhi in 1984, an event or set of events, that helped trigger the "new," revisionary scholarship on Partition. He invokes Bosnian writer Dzevad Karahasan's essay "Literature and War" to interrogate the aestheticization of violence that exists as a possibility in literary figurations of it. Such aestheticization, Ghosh suggests, drawing on Karahasan, inures the world against violence, makes it "indifferent" to it: "When I went back to my desk in November 1984" (that is, after witnessing the violence of the anti-Sikh pogrom), says Ghosh,

> I found myself confronting decisions about writing that I had never faced before. How was I to write about what I had seen [during the anti-Sikh pogrom] without reducing it to mere spectacle? My next novel [*The Shadow Lines*] was bound to be influenced by my experiences but I could see no way of writing directly about those events without creating them as a panorama of violence – "an aesthetic phenomenon," as Karahasan was to call it.
> (2002: 48–49)

Arguably, a similar discomfort with representing violence informs Benegal's choice of a narrative that is primarily about what constitutes "home" and "(national) belonging" for subjects, like Mammo, "forced" to emigrate, for family and other reasons, with kinfolk and other affective attachments left behind in a country to which they wish to return.[23] The formidable barriers created by the partitioned (nation-)states strenuously guarding the territorial "borders and boundaries" that prevented such returns also constitute a form of violence, but one that can be rendered in an unspectacular way. The particulars of Benegal's inter-textual deployment of M.S. Sathyu's *Garam Hawa* is of a piece with such a representational strategy and confirms his preferences.

Many view *Garam Hawa* (1973) as the first film to address the predicament of Muslims in post-Partition India. Sarkar captures this predicament via a quote from the September 1948 issue of *Film India* describing the Muslims who stayed behind as "the living dead," and "orphans in their own land" (2009: 190). The story (primarily) of Salim Mirza, who unlike his brother, and (subsequently) other family members including his elder son, refuses to emigrate to Pakistan, *Garam Hawa* traces the losses he accrues – of his family business, home, and daughter – as anti-Muslim discrimination spearheaded by communal forces intensifies. Sathyu is not averse to showing the violence resulting from Partition – both outside the confines of Mirza's home in communal street riots and within, on the body of his daughter who commits suicide by slitting her wrists when deserted by her second fiancé who opportunistically leaves for Pakistan. Instructively, *Mammo* draws attention to *Garam Hawa*'s focus to highlight its own – Riyaz tells Mammo, "this new film is about Partition" – and takes its subject from the only extended scene it replays from *Garam Hawa*: the one in which Mirza's mother is "returned," just before she dies, to the home to which she was brought as a bride, but which Mirza lost because the property was in his brother's name and thus declared evacuee property on the brother's departure for

Pakistan. In a film not averse to deploying melodrama to achieve heightened emotional effects, this scene is resolutely understated, quiet, and unspectacular, but also deeply moving, resonating with Mammo's comment to Riyaz on an earlier occasion: Walking around a not-so-clean-and-neat Bombay, Mammo praises Lahore's streets, its greenery, its order and cleanliness ("Oh if only you had seen Lahore!" she exclaims) only to concede cheerfully,"one's earth/land is always one's own earth/land" ("*apni mitti, apni mitti hoti hai*"). Mammo also explicitly articulates the parallels between her condition and the grandmother's in *Garam Hawa*: While watching the scene of the grandmother's return to her "own" house, Mammo exclaims, "This is just like my story."

As Benegal's "borrowing" from *Garam Hawa* makes clear, his film's engagement with Partition discourse is primarily vested in those aspects that address questions of "home" and "(national) belonging." However, what neither *Garam Hawa* and *Mammo* address, but what feminist scholarship on Partition has been particularly intent on bringing to light is that both "home" and "(national) belonging" are equally amenable, especially in hegemonic national(ist) formulations, to becoming sites of coercion and violence, as evinced, for example, in the discourse that informed the recovery of abducted women. Butalia, for instance, points out how, inundated with ever-increasing complaints about "missing women," the then prime ministers of India and Pakistan, at a September 1947 meeting in Lahore, issued a joint declaration ("given executive strength through an Inter-Dominion Treaty" on December 6, 1947), which mandated the restoration of "women and girls who had been abducted to their families" (2000: 110). Butalia (and Menon and Bhasin) specifies the ideological underpinnings of this operation with respect to India by noting how "the question of gender became a crucial one for the fragile Indian state in its quest for legitimacy." The "massive and sustained 'recovery' operation which lasted nine years after Partition" was underwritten by what the Indian state saw as its "'family' and, more specifically,… patriarch[al]" responsibility (2002: 129). Butalia also draws attention to how "homes" were construed as "the place of [the women's] religion"; hence the paradox: whereas India defined itself as secular, "women, [who were] theoretically equal citizens of this nation, could only be defined in terms of their religious identity"; and whereas, "[t]heoretically, at Partition, every citizen had a choice in the nation he/she wished to belonged to … [i]f a woman had the misfortune of being abducted,… she did not have such a choice" (2000: 111). Many women resisted – because the "disruptive times" had allowed them "to marry men of their choice outside their own communities" or because "they had forged a new (albeit fragmented) existence with their abductors" (Kumar 2008: 147–148) – but often with little success.

As with the concepts of "home" and "(national) belonging," "recovery" is also a double-edged term/concept, underwriting both patriarchal national(ist) efforts to restore women to their "rightful homes" (and religions) and dissident feminist efforts to render audible and visible the silenced and suppressed narratives and presence of women's lived experience of the Partition. Benegal's film draws on both sets of meaning in unexpected ways and thereby re-conceptualizes them. Almost as if in reference to the latter (i.e., the dissident feminist) effort, Benegal characterizes Riyaz's narrative of Mammo as an effort to "recover" her. Thus, for example, he responds to van der Heide's statement that one doesn't get to know much about the adult writer, Riyaz, with the remark that it is "Mammo whom he wishes to *recover*" (see epigraph; 2006: 175; emphasis added). Indeed, that is precisely what Riyaz does, in some ways, quite literally, remembering (Mammo's query to Riyaz as a young boy, when he opens the door to her as a young woman, is: "so you have forgotten me?") and writing her into her "return" to Bombay twenty years after she had been deported. The film begins with the adult Riyaz, having dreamt of Mammo, sitting down at his desk to go over what he had written earlier, which is presumably about Mammo since the viewer sees and hears him next asking his grandmother about Mammo's whereabouts ("where is grandma Mammo now?" ["*Mammo naani kahan hain?*"]) and whether she is dead or alive. Fayyazi mentions letters Mammo wrote her to which she did not respond; Riyaz asks for the letters and is perusing them when the doorbell rings and he opens the door to a younger Mammo recalled from the time he was a young boy, only to be shown again opening the door at the conclusion of the film – this time in response to the arrival in real time, or the film's present, of a considerably older Mammo, whose lively "voice" takes over the narrative. "The move between the past and present is done very simply by means of a doorbell," van der Heide remarks to Benegal (2006: 174). Conflating the two arrivals, separated by twenty years, of Mammo on Fayyazi's doorstep, signaling, on the one hand, the beginnings of Riyaz's development into an adult who learns to *live with* and grow attached to the "stranger" who is Mammo and, on the other, a species of wish fulfillment triggered by Riyaz's recall of Mammo, suggests that the conditions for Mammo's "return" must include a re-formed, more hospitable Riyaz.

"Recovering" Mammo in the film is also coterminous with repatriating her, as it were, to her natal and "national" family – and here the former (i.e., nationalist) effort is being referenced – except that Mammo is a Muslim subject (who had been taken to Pakistan by her husband) being "recovered" and "returned" to India. (Significantly, in this case, Mammo is the agent of her own "recovery" or repatriation.) One need read only the many stories/case histories Zamindar analyzes (2007: 198–200, 209–214) to realize the virtual impossibility of this happening, not only because of what she characterizes as "Muslim Difference" (for the most part, only "'Pakistani nationals belonging to minority communit[ies]' … could be registered as Indian citizens" [2007: 198]), but also because "women were not entitled to autonomous citizenship because … their 'domicile' was vested in that of their father or husband" (2007: 209). Mammo's recovery/repatriation thus constitutes a subversion, at many different levels, of the "official" recovery operations otherwise undertaken by the Indian state; arguably, however, the subversion here entails a shadowy existence situated outside the purview of the (nation-)state: Mammo must declare herself dead in order to continue to live in India.

P. Kumar characterizes Mammo's "return" (and thus her recovery of, and by, her natal home) as a "radical disruption of state authority through a manifest act of subaltern agency," a claim she then goes on to rightly qualify by recognizing that "even as we may validate Mammo's successful defiance of the state's juridical regime, we also realize that she must 'die' to the state in order to be able to lay claim to the Indian nation" (2008: 227). Nevertheless "acts of subaltern agency" through which she constantly "lay[s] claim to the nation" virtually define Mammo as she is represented in the entirety of the film. Mammo is a resilient subject – her resilience rendered particularly apparent by Fayazzi's lack of it – who, while cognizant of the suffering and tragedy of Partition, including her own, consistently demonstrates her ability to withstand these, not least through her ingenious overcoming of obstacles. From the start, she treats all Indians she meets in Bombay as her "family": While registering her arrival at the police station, for example, she unsettles its bureaucratic space by asking the inspector who is noting her details about his wife and children, his earnings and so on. She subjects the taxi driver taking her back to Fayyazi's flat to the same questions. The only time the viewer sees her as desperate and unable to control her circumstances is when she is being deported, which condition she proceeds to overcome in her own inimitable way, albeit after a substantial length of time. "Mammo," as Benegal puts it, "lightens the whole thing up, since she has no such inhibitions" (van der Heide 2006: 174).

Benegal's focus on a figure like Mammo, like his reticence regarding the overt representation of Partition violence, tells us a great deal about how he wants to represent Partition; concomitantly, *Mammo* also tells us a great deal about how he wants to engage with concerns that became central to post-1984 (anti-Sikh pogrom) scholarship on Partition narratives. "Why is it that [survivors' testimonies] and other such accounts have found such little space in history?" Butalia queries as she maps her own project to provide precisely such accounts:

> Is it that this is not the stuff history is made of? Pain, trauma, loss, grief, the minutiae of daily living and the violence of upheaval, is there any way in which these experiences can find space in the way history is written?
> (2002: 140)

Arguably, Mammo's story constitutes a "survivor's testimony" – albeit she is not the kind of survivor Butalia interviewed – and it contains its share of "pain, trauma, loss, grief," although registered in a tone and (lack of) intensity at great variance with the one Butalia's "oral histories" make apparent: "I began work alone," Butalia notes, "After some time, however, it became very difficult to continue thus. The kinds of stories I was hearing were so harrowing, so full of grief and anguish, that often *I could not bear to listen to them*" (2000: 19; emphasis added).[24] Post-1984 scholarship on Partition has consistently referenced and/or centered these harrowing and deeply traumatic aspects of Partition, the evasion of which this scholarship sees as a hallmark of statist accounts in India and Pakistan. What does it mean for Benegal to bypass the extreme emotional affect that attaches to these aspects of Partition and select, instead, a narrative that addresses them through a resilient, humorous protagonist for whom survival translates to an enjoyment – both the taking of it for oneself and bringing it to others – of life and fighting for one's own (and one's family's) corner? Violence and trauma of the kind Butalia, Menon and Bhasin, Pandey, and Sarkar allude to and, in some instances, document is so overwhelming that it can stun its recipients into silence and paralysis: "Cataclysmic events," says Feuchtwang, "are a limit condition: the annihilation of history and the destruction of personality" (59).[25] Invested always in women protagonists who learn to become or are autonomous, self-determining subjects, Benegal's interest in Mammo's story seems entirely understandable. *Mammo* not only challenges the statist narrative of Partition – its very choice of a female Muslim subject, who embraces extra-legal means to [re]claim her "home," puts her at odds with what any (nation)state is likely to tolerate, far less accept – but also provides a different accounting of the Partition(ed) subject than the one provided in the revisionary, post-1984 scholarship, with whose concerns, as shown, the film is nonetheless clearly in sympathy.

Trikaal

> The narrative [of Trikaal] is built around the house, which was built in the seventeenth century. You can tell the history of its time – the whole story of Goa and as its transitioning into Indian time. The past comes through in nostalgic remembrances or nightmares.
>
> (Benegal, in an interview with me, February 21, 2011)

> Michael Lambek argues that if persons are understood … as in some sense bearers of their predecessors and their social role rather than being seen exclusively as individuals then the memory/history distinction becomes untenable.
>
> (Radstone and Hodgkin 2006b: 10–11)

In dominant and alternative narratives of the Indian nation, the historical context evoked by *Trikaal* – the demise of Portuguese colonialism in India and the incorporation of Goa into the Indian Union in 1961 – is not assigned anything even close to the status that 1857 or Partition are assigned. In fact, it is assigned no place at all: It has not been the subject of commemorative activities; its anniversaries having gone unremarked; certainly, it has not elicited the kind of scholarship – revisionary or otherwise – that 1857 and Partition have. Nor, on the basis of what both hegemonic and alternative narratives address, does it seem to have a bearing on India's forging of a post-independence, postcolonial identity. As Županov notes, "the history of the Portuguese colonial enterprise in India still appears marginal in terms of the long-term dynamics of change and development and compared, for example, with the importance of the Mughal and British empires" (2005: 21), both of which empires were implicated in the events of 1857, while British imperial policies of divide and rule are considered central to

Partition. Nevertheless, in a gesture that seems to refuse such marginality for the history of Goa and/or Portuguese colonialism, both the film's opening and Benegal's comments about *Trikaal* situate it within the narrative of the Indian nation as having a significant bearing on the secular definition of its identity that dominant nationalism observes, for the most part, in the breach. Thus the film's narrator, Ruiz Pereira, on returning twenty-four years later to Goa, remarks on the travels that have intervened – Bombay to Kampala to Bombay – only to assert the pull exerted by Goa, which he calls "my country," "my village" ("*apna vatan*," "*mera gaon*"), deploying a vocabulary associated with national belonging. On a different register, while noting his interest in recreating the lives and cultures of what Malcolm in his write-up on *Trikaal* calls "a little known society" (Malcolm 1988: n.p.), Benegal references the misapprehensions and stereotypes about Goans that abound in dominant Indian society (for example, Goans are "just people drinking *pheni* and dancing") only to insist:

> Goans have to be accepted by the majority. It is not for the minorities to accept the majority.... This is far more profound for me than anything else. Particularly in India today, there are so many people trying to create their own empires and not looking at the totality of it.
>
> (Interview with John 1986: n.p.)

With this foregrounding of minority claims on the nation, Benegal, in effect, returns, or looks forward, to one of the salient ways in which *Junoon* and *Mammo* respectively seek to negotiate their critical engagement with the dominant national narrative.[26]

At the same time, *Trikaal* addresses another, what most would consider peripheral, colonial presence and, through it, another layer that has gone into making Indian identities. Unlike *Junoon* and *Mammo*, furthermore, *Trikaal* self-consciously foregrounds the mechanisms – of memory, in particular, but also of séances that call forth ghosts from the past – through which resistant, suppressed, or marginalized pasts are recalled and thereby brought within the purview of the present as history.[27] The film's choice of memory and séances calling up spirits from the past as the modalities through which to represent the history of the Souza-Soares mansion and Goa/Portuguese colonialism and its demise reflects a quite specific relationship to the task of reconstructing the past the film seeks to represent. For memory, in recent scholarship, has often been construed as the modality through which history – especially, official, hegemonic history – can be challenged, resisted, re-envisioned (see epigraph; Radstone and Hodgkin 2006b: 10–11; see also, Hodgkin and Radstone 2006b).

The film begins with a visual enactment of memory and its workings, in which the past and present quite literally encounter each other in two intercut images: a figure, whom the viewer soon discovers belongs to the past, running across a green field carrying a coffin, and Ruiz, in the film's diegetic present, returning in a taxi to his "country," his "village." This palpable presence of the past *within* the present (or as van der Heide puts it, as if they inhabit spaces that are "co-temporal" with each other's [2006: 129]) is repeated in the very next scene when Ruiz, arriving at the Souza-Soares mansion again quite literally "walks into the past" (van der Heide 2006: 129) – into, that is, his ("recover[y]" of the) memory of Ernesto's funeral, engulfed by the music of a Portuguese *fado* that Dona Maria, the matriarch of the mansion, plays repetitively and insistently.[28] And although Ruiz's recollection of his past is framed by his hesitation proceeding from the fallibility of his memory ("What was the name of the *chowkidar* [caretaker]?" he asks himself; "I don't remember," he acknowledges, only to find out that the *chowkidar* does not remember him either), his memory (seemingly) delivers his past to him in glorious fullness with images of a mansion filled with family members and guests gathered together for Ernesto Souza-Soares's funeral – guests he then proceeds to introduce to the film's spectator, acting as an emcee, as it were. Datta remarks on how:

> the evocative mood of a past world and a mansion with period décor are largely the effect of art direction and camera … the light and camera creat[ing] a certain kind of top light typical of these mansions in which most of the available light [is] filtered through skylights," whereas "the night interiors were shot in candlelight.
>
> (2003:146)

All this infuses Ruiz's recollections with nostalgia and charm, which are belied somewhat by Ruiz's tone – urbane and affectionate, but also gently ironic and knowing – and are, furthermore, at odds with Benegal's desire to "film the … dramatic life of a feudal Catholic family in Goa, then a Portuguese colony" at a time of "upheaval [and] change" as Goa made its transition from being a colony to becoming an Indian Union Territory (R. Krishnamoorthy and Mohan Bawa quoted in Datta 2003: 142, 143). Indeed, Ruiz's (and the matriarch Dona Maria's) memories deliver both "nostalgic remembrances and nightmares." (See epigraph; Benegal's interview with me, February 21, 2011.)[29]

The past Ruiz "walks into" has at its center the matriarch, Dona Maria, who, surrounded by her extended family and friends (like the family doctor and his nephew, the narrator Ruiz) on the occasion of her husband's (the patriarch Ernesto Souza-Soares) funeral, is refusing to accept his death ("How to understand her refusal to accept Ernesto's passing away?" Ruiz ruminates). Ernesto has died just a few months prior to Goa's "liberation" by the Indian army.[30] *Trikaal*'s historical moment, thus, is a moment of transition, and the family doctor explicitly identifies it as such in the toast he raises to Ernesto – "not with Scotch, but with our native *pheni*" – after the latter's funeral ceremony. He equates Ernesto's passing away with the passing away of "our familiar [*jana pehchana*] Goa," and predicts the coming of a "new era [*naya daur*]" in which the "Indiawallahs will rule." The Souza-Soares mansion, by this logic, is co-extensive with, or a figure for, Portuguese-controlled Goa, a symbol especially of its passing away – its slow disintegration and abandonment by most of its residents, with the exception of Dona Maria and her maid and Ernesto's illegitimate daughter, Milagrenia, during the period covered by Ruiz's act of remembrance. Arguably, then, Dona Maria's refusal to acknowledge Ernesto's death is a refusal to relinquish this Goa within which her family has flourished, not least through its collaboration with the colonial regime: "Who apart from you wants the Portuguese out?" she challenges her dissident nephew, Leon, who has returned to the Souza-Soares mansion having escaped from a prison in Lisbon, where he was sent for rebelling against the Portuguese rule in Goa.

At the dinner following Ernesto's funeral, the fate of Goa on the verge of its takeover by the Indian army is one of the primary topics of discussion. Three alternatives, which were most likely part of the "historical real," are outlined: the expectation (and hope?) that Portugal will send troops and other personnel to Goa to defend its colonial territory (this possibility is dismissed as unfeasible because the Portuguese are judged to be too busy with their African colonial territories); the expectation (and hope?) that Goa will become a free, self-determining state – "*swatantra* Goa" whereby "Goa belongs to Goans" (this possibility is discredited almost as soon as it is articulated not least because its most vociferous supporter is Francis, an indulged and alcoholic mummy's boy); and, finally, the expectation that Goa will be incorporated into the Indian Union (this possibility did, in fact, come to pass, when the Governor-General of Goa disregarded his orders from Lisbon and surrendered Goa without a fight to the Indian army on December 17, 1961[31]). Identified by Francis and others as an "Indiawallah," the family doctor (and Ruiz's paternal uncle), articulates this last possibility for the dinner guests when he contests Francis's argument for a "*swatantra* Goa" first, by questioning him ("What freedom? The freedom to continue to live in luxury [*shaan shaukat rakhne ki azadi*]?"[32]); then, by affirming that "where ever a man is born, grows up, where he settles, that is his culture, his country"; and, finally, by locating Goa within the Indian Union: "Our nation is a quilt made up of many lovely patches, of which Goa is the most beautiful patch." Significantly, although the family doctor's view of where Goa belongs is based on what is best characterized as the hegemonic self-image of India – as a multicultural and multi-religious polity – among members of the Souza-Soares family and their other friends (some of whom are Portuguese citizens, and others who are getting ready to leave for Lisbon as they await the takeover), it represents a minority view, contested explicitly by Francis and more subtly by Dona Maria when she lets the doctor know that he is an outsider who does not belong to their community.[33]

For Dona Maria, acknowledging Ernesto's death is equivalent to acknowledging the death of her own identity ("I feel that if I forget Ernesto's face, I will forget mine. If he is gone what will be left for me?"), which is co-extensive, as is Ernesto's identity, with a Portuguese-ruled Goa. But while Dona Maria is deeply invested in preserving this identity, it does not exclude the Portuguese empire's long entanglement with, incorporation of, and assimilation to, the "native" Indian habitat and its socio-cultural and religious customs. Thus, although Dona Maria "is very Catholic … at the same time she sends her annual tribute of coconuts and rice to the temple" (Benegal to van der Heide 2006: 130). (Here we might also bear in mind that her holding the séance to bring Ernesto back from the dead transgresses her Catholic belief as well; in fact, the priest who performs the last rites at Ernesto's funeral characterizes such practices as a sin.) This aspect of Goa – as distinct from the tourists' Goa – is one that Benegal finds deeply attractive:

> There is a cultural formation in Goa, which is very fascinating and interesting; at the same time it is not very exposed. Goa has a certain distinct quality of life with a culture that is 500 years old. While the rest of India was ruled first by the Mughals, then the British, Goa, on the other hand was developing a different cultural configuration under the Portuguese. The place has a different atmosphere, yet it is very much part of India.
>
> (Quoted in Datta 2003: 141)

Furthermore, as Benegal suggests in his comment above, this character should be distinguished from how British colonialism operated, keeping the ruling class, particularly after 1857, separate from those they ruled. Županov characterizes Portuguese interactions with its colonies in India and elsewhere as a form of "tropicality" that entailed forms of adaptation sitting cheek by jowl with mechanisms through which the Portuguese "fenc[ed] themselves off" (2005: 20). Contrary, however, to Brazilian sociologist Giberto Freyre's argument about the intrinsic ability of "Portuguese culture (and blood)," by virtue of its "strong and plastic attributes," to "successfully" integrate "foreign and local elements," Županov, invoking Garcia da Orta, argues that "it was out of weakness that the Portuguese were forced to adopt local drugs, food, and certain customs in order to survive." Thus, "it was the Portuguese who were being incorporated and integrated into the larger networks of local Asian medical, economic, social, maritime, and religious markets and not the other way around" (2005: 12). After the 1560s, however, such "indigenization of the Portuguese in India" was denounced, setting the stage for the brutal operations of the Inquisition (2005: 11–12). Interestingly, most of the "cases tried by the Holy Office," Županov points out, "were due to the lapses into Hindu religious practices" (2005: 12). Dona Maria's "send[ing]" of "coconuts and rice" would surely exemplify the "tropicality" Županov talks about, as, possibly, would the priest delivering his sermon in Hindustani on the occasion of the first month of Ernesto's death.

Recalcitrant about acknowledging Ernesto's death, Dona Maria holds séances, with Milagrenia as the medium, to call up Ernesto's spirit. Instead of summoning Ernesto, however, she summons Vijay Singh Rane, which calls forth as well the subterranean history of insurrection that his ghost suggests is now built into the foundations of the Souza-Suarez mansion.[34] (With respect to this calling up of an underground, insurrectionary history, I find it significant that Milagrenia, who is Ernesto's illegitimate daughter, is the medium through which this is accomplished.) In his interview with van der Heide, Benegal remarks on how "the film," which is "a blending of fiction with reality," was shot in a house that "was built in 1680" and belongs to his friend, the well-known cartoonist Mario

Miranda. "Mario's great-great-grandfather", Benegal goes on to add, like Dona Maria's grandfather in *Trikaal*, "was one of the people who captured the rebel Rane and handed him over to the Portuguese governor. ... It turned out he was the wrong Rane" (van der Heide 2006: 128). *Trikaal* reprises this set of historical events in the séances that Dona Maria holds and, through the reprise, pursues several interrelated issues regarding the status of memory and history. The appearance of Rane's ghost (when Ernesto's has been called) demonstrates several things: that Dona Maria has little or no control over the past, which will "bubble up to the surface" (van der Heide 2006: 131); and/or that a past is never simply individual but always and already collective and social; and/or, finally, that a history of rebellion, arguably, not only cannot be suppressed, but is always and already an intrinsic or necessary accompaniment to power and domination (Rane says, for example, "I have now become a part of this [Souza-Soares] family"). But what are we to make of the fact that "he was the wrong Rane," a fact that the film retains? Are we to understand from this that both history and memory are fallible, that they make mistakes? By summoning the "wrong" subject – Rane instead of Ernesto – the film at a representational level underscores the "error" made by the Souza-Soares' (and Miranda's) grandfather, when he captured and imprisoned the "wrong" Rane. Benegal's representational strategy is also instructive in another respect, highlighting some of memory and history's performative character: Rane speaks in a highly stylized and theatrical fashion, as if he were playing a role rather than giving voice to real grievances.[35] And while Dona Maria continues to present a naturalistic demeanor and inhabit the "real" world, Milagrenia, as she thrashes about possessed by spirits, and Rane, with his stylized delivery, occupy a space marked off as performative, even anti-realist.

The ghost of Rane recalls for Dona Maria and *Trikaal*'s viewers a history of Portuguese colonialism in Goa associated particularly with the brutalities perpetrated by the Inquisition. In response to the perception that "Portuguese tropical colonies in India ... [had] 'gone native' in a religious and sociocultural sense," the Inquisition, Županov tells us, sought to "restore the purity of faith and blood" (2005:12). Rane also articulates colonialism's – all colonialism's – endemic modality, which the colonized find so problematic and, therefore, resist: When Dona Maria asks him, "Why do you keep coming back?" Rane responds, "You betrayed me. I belonged to this land, this earth ... but you people stole our names [*hamare naam chiin liye*], stole our identity [*astitva chiin liya*]." Dona Maria resists this "lesson" initially ("Why are all these people troubling me? How is all this my fault?"[("*yeh sab log mujhe kyon sata rahen hain, mera kya dosh hai*?], she complains to Milagrenia), but eventually learns from it. When she gives up on holding the séances through which she sought to "re-call" Ernesto ("I can no longer call Ernesto" ["*ab main Ernesto ko nahin bula sakti*"]), she draws attention to what she has learned from having undertaken the effort: "the treasure was in the search undertaken for it" ["*khazana usi khoj mein tha*"]), she tells Milagrenia; presumably the "treasure" she references here is the history of her family's collusion with the Portuguese that Rane has made her aware of. Benegal affirms that Dona Maria has indeed learned when, in response to van der Heide's question ("Do you think that Dona Maria faces [this unwelcome past] in the film?"), he replies: "She eventually does because she finally says she is not willing to call up the past [that Ernesto represented?]" (van der Heide 2006: 130). The narrative strand relating to Dona Maria concludes with the figure of the priest "cleansing" the Souza-Soares mansion of "sin." Arguably, however, the mansion is also being cleansed of a past history of Portuguese control over Goa that Ernesto's death has initiated but whose demise Dona Maria has to be "educated" into accepting.

It is instructive that of all the characters/subjects in *Trikaal* that Benegal could have asked his viewers to invest in, it is Dona Maria he selects for the viewer's attention – a selection he makes obvious from the outset by centering her visually and narrationally. Ruiz introduces each player in the story the film tells simply by name and relationship; however, even as he invests some (like Anna and Milagrenia) with more interest, his tone makes apparent that he is building up to something of significance – the introduction of the matriarch, Dona Maria – a build-up in which both the camera work and music participate: The camera first pans the back of her chair, isolating Dona Maria's figure from the rest of the space and from the individuals in the other room that Ruiz has thus far been working his way through. The camera comes to a rest, then jump cuts to her face, while the music, which has been playing continuously in the background also comes to a stop, the brief absence of sound investing the figure of the matriarch, Dona Maria, with significant power and distinction. Her presence, in other words, is dramatized and heightened even before she speaks. (Figure 3.2) Benegal also centers Dona Maria by making her the most complex, interesting, and three-dimensional figure, whereas those surrounding her, including her immediate family – her daughter, Sylvia, who as "borderline hysteric" (Benegal's characterization) is always shown screaming or crying; Sylvia's husband, Lucio, a bitter, comical house-husband (*ghar jamayi*), who does no work; Sylvia's children (Anna, the object of lust and desire of Ruiz, Erasmo, and Leon; Aurora, desperately in love with the alcoholic Francis; and two grandsons who dash in and out of Dona Maria's room) – are all one-dimensional or barely realized figures, associated with certain ideas and political positions or instrumental mostly in helping build a portrait of this little-known culture and society caught at a moment of transition.

Dona Maria's ability to make the transition from a Portuguese-ruled Goa to one on the verge of entering the Indian Union, thereby adding something valuable to the ongoing constitution of Indian identity, makes her significant for articulating the position that interests Benegal. This transition brings to the fore, as van der Heide points out, "the whole question about cultural identity" i.e., whether Goans are Indian or Portuguese or both? (2006: 131). As someone whose identity includes, but is not restricted to, being Portuguese – in fact is almost not Portuguese by virtue of an almost unconscious embrace of a hybrid Goan culture – Dona Maria is distinguished from her own daughter and son-in-law, for instance, whose primary allegiance is to Portugal (to which they

Figure 3.2 Dona Maria in the Souza-Soares mansion in *Trikaal.*

depart by the film's conclusion) and who are, therefore, unable to see themselves as anything other than Portuguese. Her position is also to be distinguished from Leon's; he is fighting for the liberation of Goa from the Portuguese, but is unable to see himself staying there at least at the historical moment when the transition is taking place (Benegal describes him as "confus[ed]" [van der Heide 2006: 131]); instead, he incites Anna to elope and return with him to Lisbon. Even the family doctor's position that Goa should become a part of what he views as the multicultural, multi-religious Indian Union does not seem to be the one the film endorses, at least not from the location the doctor occupies: there is a whiff of opportunism on his part that his interlocutors at the dinner recognize and draw attention to; moreover, as a comparison with Dona Maria's evolution seems to suggest, his position has not been arrived at deliberatively and seems to too easily accede to the hegemonic (Indian) conception of its national identity, without attending to the value of (Portuguese) Goan and/or minority difference. The comment from Benegal quoted earlier, about the majority having to accept the minority, suggests precisely this: That minority difference, rather than becoming an indistinguishable part of some conglomerate national identity, is something to be retained, valued, and engaged with by the majority, both continuously and actively. Benegal's desire to visualize, and have viewers visualize, the "different cultural configuration" Goa developed, while "the rest of India was ruled by Moghuls, then the British" (quoted in Datta 2003: 141) proceeds from a similar impulse. The attention his cameraman and art director lavish on the interiors of Mario Miranda's house and the aesthetic pleasure they expect the film's spectators to derive from their camera and art work are designed to convey not only, as indicated earlier, the nostalgia that infuses Ruiz's memory of this mansion, but also Goa and Goan culture's distinctive character. Concomitantly, when she actively calls forth her past by wanting to restore the deceased Ernesto, Dona Maria, who carries her (Portuguese) Catholic identity with(in) her, even as she daily negotiates the indigenous, mostly Hindu world around her, is surprised into an encounter with, and thereby made aware of, what the colonial Portuguese Catholic world has done to the places and people it has ruled over. This awareness, I think, transforms her into a self-conscious, informed historical subject able to negotiate her identification with, but also minority difference from, the dominant Indian identity in order to claim her (and Goa's) place in the Indian Union.

Both *Junoon* and *Trikaal*, unlike *Mammo*, which engages with a different form of liminality, focus on protagonists located between the indigenous and the colonizers' English or Portuguese worlds. However, the minority difference exemplified by Dona Maria is to be distinguished from the difference, better characterized as a form of deliberate separateness, displayed, even cultivated by Mariam in *Junoon*. For the latter's is a species of difference proceeding from a sense of entitlement based on British power and a sense of superiority, which translates to a refusal of Indian-ness: "Anglo-India [to which Mariam and her family proudly belong]," says G. Chakravarty, "remained more decidedly un-Indian that it was ever un-British," while "Anglo-Indian identity" was premised on a form of "self-exile from the immediacy of India" (2005: 103). Goa's, and, by extension Dona Maria's, difference, on the other hand, no less because of Portuguese colonialism's difference for reasons specified by Županov, translates to a difference in which India and Indian-ness does not disappear: "The place [Goa] has a different atmosphere," said Benegal to Datta, "yet it is very much a part of India" (2003: 141). For India (what its national cultures and identities are or should be) – and belonging to India – remain the significant frames of reference in the different permutations and interpretations aired in each of the three films this chapter has analyzed.[36] Nevertheless, certain preferences regarding national cultures and identities do emerge, often having to do with protagonists whose ways of looking at the world are privileged.

The introductory remarks that frame this chapter invoke Slotkin's claim that fictional/imaginative recuperations of an historical past enables "writer and reader [or filmmaker and cinematic spectator] to explore possibilities for belief, action, and political change unrealized in [or by] history." By doing so, "the novelist [or filmmaker] may restore, as imaginable possibilities, the ideas, movements, and values defeated or discarded in the struggles that produced the modern state" (Slotkin 2005: 221). Such fictional and imaginative recuperation does not so much reveal hegemonic or official history to be untrue or misleading as inadequate – unable or unwilling to represent positions and perspectives that are not a part of its value system and ideological predilections. Attention to these ignored, repressed, or marginalized positions and perspectives can not only fill out the "official" record, but also point to its limits and inadequacies, at the same time making a claim on behalf of the positions and perspectives that have been ignored, repressed, or marginalized. Benegal's fictional engagements with (national) history are of a piece with this latter effort.

4 A pantheon of national heroes

Nehru, The Making of the Mahatma, and *Bose: The Forgotten Hero*

> An intriguing aspect regarding the construction of public figures in India is its resistance to issues of private life.... Most autobiographies tend to lack a backstage, and, in a way, this is oddly true of even Gandhi's *Experiments with Truth.* Although it is a confessional to rank with the best, its stories are told as if each was a pedagogic act or moral message.... Consequently, our public figures are turned into icons or idols ... what is sorely missed is the warp and weave of a full life, where defects and idiosyncrasies of characters and dreams are woven creatively.... Is it any wonder that our icons are portrayed as one-dimensional bores, denied the freedom and license of myths, and with their biographies reduced to mere *curriculum vitae*?
>
> (Visvanathan 2007: 20)

> I continue to enjoy making documentaries. Although I must say that I'm not fully satisfied with documentaries, because you only deal with observable phenomena. With fiction you can explore things much more deeply – you are interpreting, you are exploring, you are re-shaping material. With a documentary you can't really re-shape material unless you want to be nonfactual.... But with fiction you can pursue what I call truth – which is very subjective in any case.
>
> (Benegal to van der Heide 2006: 31)

Some of the oppositions seen to exist in the preceding chapter, between fictional engagements with history and the disciplinary and disciplining practices of history proper, what Pandey calls "historian's history," also resonate within this chapter, except that the characteristics ascribed to the latter are mapped onto the assumptions that usually inform non-fiction films' representational practices. Thus, according to Beattie, "a claim or assertion at the center of all non-fictional representation" is that "a documentary depiction of the socio-historical world is factual and truthful," with such depiction's "relation to the real" conceived thereby, says Nichols, as "direct, immediate, transparent" (Beattie 2004: 10; Nichols 1991: 4). However, much like the recognition, particularly by contemporary historians of a poststructuralist bent, of the many mediations – including narrative and figurative tropes – through which reconstructions of the past called history are constituted, analysts of non-fictional films often concede that "representational styles and conventions and forms of narrative and argument together work to *produce* a realistic and authentic representation of the socio-historical world" (Beattie 2004: 14; emphasis added). Nevertheless, as Nichols notes, "as a general style, documentary realism negotiates the compact we strike between text and historical referent, minimizing resistance or hesitation to the claims of transparency and authenticity" (1991: 165). This is why conventional understandings of history and, indeed, of non-fictional films assume their ability (and based on this ability, their authority) to *factually* present the past or the world they reference as they *really* are. Such understandings have been enormously useful and have, therefore, been harnessed by various nationalisms to claim facticity for their version of their history of the nation. Official narratives of Indian nationalism are no exception to this rule.

Alternatively, as the previous chapter demonstrates, fictional engagements with national-historical events like the 1857 uprising, or the Partition of South Asia, or the demise of Portuguese colonialism in India in *Junoon*, *Mammo*, and *Trikaal*, while based on "true" occurrences about the lives and times of "actual" protagonists, in their commitment to an imagined and imaginative recuperation of the past open themselves to, or offer alternative, possibilities – "ideas, movements, and values defeated or discarded in struggles that produced" a given national or social formation (Slotkin 2005: 221) – through which quite different, even dissident, minority, or subaltern histories can be constructed. Self-authorized biographies of the nation can then be disrupted or, at the very least, put into question.

To move, then, from fictional engagements with history to the non-fictional ones that are the subject of this chapter – Benegal's documentaries and biopics about Jawaharlal Nehru, Mohandas Karamchand Gandhi, and Subhas Chandra Bose – entails a change of register and perspective in terms of both cinematic representation of and traffic with the dominant content and forms of Indian national history. Benegal's cinematic renditions of the three national heroes cannot, of course, be collapsed into one homogeneous or monolithic mode of representation, not least because they were sponsored by different agencies and thus negotiated the different imperatives of these diverse sources of funding and the audiences each presumed. *Nehru* and *Bharat Ek Khoj* (based on Nehru's *Discovery of India*; hereafter *Bharat*) were state-sponsored and funded enterprises, the first an Indo-Soviet production co-produced by, and made for, Films Division of India (hereafter FDI) and the latter a Doordarshan-sponsored fifty-three-part serial that Rajagopal situates under a category he labels "national programming" (1993: 92; Doordarshan is India's state-funded TV). Where the former is categorized as a documentary and relies on mostly archival footage of Nehru and his times and on Nehru's own words, the latter "sometimes use[s] the technique of a documentary, at other times drama in [its] narratives" ("Introduction," to booklet accompanying the DVDs); in the latter, furthermore, Nehru, played by an actor – Roshan Seth – who has appeared as Nehru in other films, guides viewers through what he considers to be exemplary episodes, rulers, and social, political, and cultural forms of India's centuries-old history. *The Making of the Mahatma* (hereafter *Making*), a feature film, was also funded by state agencies – the South African Broadcasting Corporation and the National Film Development Corporation (India) – but ones reflecting somewhat different interests than those of FDI and Doordarshan. And *Bose: A Forgotten Hero* (hereafter *Bose*), also a feature film, was privately financed, and co-produced by Sahara India Media Communications and Benegal's own production company, Sahyadri Films. Furthermore, whereas Benegal's documentary on Nehru and his adaptation of *Discovery* cover the entire arc of Nehru's (and India's) political life up to and a little beyond independence, his *Making* and *Bose* are more selective in their focus, concentrating exclusively on Gandhi's South African period – the period Fatima Meer characterizes as his "apprenticeship" – and the last five years of Bose's life respectively. Unlike *Nehru*, although like *Bharat*, finally, they are dramatic reconstructions with Gandhi and Bose performed by actors.

Despite their differences, however, Benegal (in an interview with me), drew attention to a crucial attribute shared by all three figures from the national pantheon: each possessed "a very coherently articulated vision of free India which no one else in the freedom movement had," and for each, "India had to be inclusive, and India had to be secular" (February 13, 2011).[1] In their generic affiliation as films about those whom Ramaswamy calls the "'big men' of the national movement" or "figures from the dominant nationalist pantheon" (2011: 181, 182), Benegal's films about them have more in common with each other than with those analyzed in the previous chapter. This commonality has less to do with hagiographic or uncritical renderings of the lives and works of national heroes (although the films about Nehru and Bose sometimes come close to seeming this way) than with the visual and narrative strategies that constitute them as exemplars of a species of heroism defined as national in character and scope from which the ordinary Indian is supposed to learn – become educated, that is, by the qualities embodied by these figures – but from which s/he is also, inevitably, excluded.[2] Concentrating almost entirely on their political lives, the visual and narrative strategies these biopics[3] deploy entail a striking elision with significant implications for what has been a central preoccupation in the Benegal films examined thus far: Benegal's films not only feature strong, compelling female characters, but have often relied on their perspectives to elicit a different account of the world Indians inhabit. In the documentaries and biopics examined in this chapter, however, women virtually disappear into the background; and this has to do with these films' conformity with dominant agendas of nationalist history that, I think, are not only part and parcel of their venues of production and the view of national history these venues assume, but also something endemic, not surprisingly, to a project that subscribes to a "great men" view of national history. Ramaswamy, studying the life and career of Bharat Mata (or Mother India) as an embodiment of, and figure for, the Indian nation in "popular and public art," notes that, while "women are hypervisible" in this art, "it is men who are accorded prominence in patriotic pictures, thus visually endorsing a prevailing truth about nationalism as a masculinist project, fantasy, and hope" (2011: 178).[4]

This chapter examines Benegal's portrayal of Nehru in his three-part Indo-Soviet documentary *Nehru* (1984), with extensive reference to Doordarshan's fifty-three-part serial, *Bharat* (1988), and passing reference to the documentary *Satyajit Ray* (1984) that Benegal made for Films Division contemporaneously with *Nehru*.[5] Drawing on some of the extensive scholarship on Nehru's (political) life and on his *Discovery* as the vision par excellence of what he wanted an independent India to become, I contextualize my analysis of the documentaries and *Bharat* (also) through a brief history of their sponsors – FDI and Doordarshan – and the kinds of historical reconstructions they privilege. For Benegal's portrayals of Gandhi and Bose, I focus on the two feature films about them, *Making* (1996) and *Bose* (2005) respectively. I situate *Making* via its relationship to its primary source, Fatima Meer's *The Apprenticeship of the Mahatma*, and contextualize both, through scholarship, on the integral place of his years in South Africa in *making* Gandhi into the leader who helped secure India's independence from the British. For *Bose*, which restricts itself to Bose's last five years, from his "great escape" from house arrest to his years in Germany and then south-east Asia and, finally, his much-contended death in 1945, I draw primarily on accounts of these final years in the scholarship on Bose. However, I sometimes have recourse to accounts of earlier events and activities that had an impact on his evolution as a particular kind of leader to contextualize both Bose's actions and predilections and Benegal's cinematic rendition of these.

In stating his preference for "fiction" (or "feature") films over documentaries (see epigraph; van der Heide 2006: 31), Benegal specifies how fiction enables one to "explore things much more deeply" because it allows for interpretative "reshaping" that, in turn, enables "truth – which is very subjective in any case" – to emerge. In his non-fiction documentaries/biopics, however, Benegal tacitly eschews "fiction" because of an "obligation to factuality" that documentaries, in his view, are supposed to reflect. This is accompanied by what Visvanathan defines as an "intriguing aspect" of "the construction of public figures in India" – its "resistance to issues of private life" such that "the warp and weave of a full life, where defects and idiosyncrasies are woven creatively" are excised (see epigraph; 2007: 20).[6] Fact vs. Fiction, Public vs. Private, Documentary vs. Feature Film become implicit and explicit oppositions through which the representational practices of these films are organized, arguably with the emphasis in the documentaries/biopics falling on the former and in the films examined in the previous chapter falling on the latter, and this despite the fact that *Making* and *Bose* are labeled "feature films." This chapter, read comparatively with and alongside the previous one, enables us to see the intersections between "historian's history" and national self definition, but also the blurred and ambiguous boundaries between historical fiction and historical fact, which, in turn, raise questions regarding history's referential ambitions. Furthermore, when read together with and against each other, the two chapters that comprise this section on "Alternate and Self-Authorized Biographies of the Nation," also hope to render visible the processes of selection that go into fictional versus non-fictional reconstructions of India's (national) past, much as they hope to demonstrate Benegal's cinematic *oeuvre* as internally differentiated and heterogeneous.

The idea(s) of *Nehru*

> Nehru's task … [lay] in securing and consolidating the hard-fought independence.… The figure of the man is that of the nation-building moment.
>
> (Ramaswamy 2011: 203–204)

The subtitle of this section departs from the way discrete segments of chapters have been subtitled thus far. Instead of alluding to a particular film, the subtitle here references a theme or preoccupation that ties *Nehru* and *Satyajit Ray*, both undertaken simultaneously in 1981 and exhibited in 1984, and *Bharat* (1988) together: At the center of all three (and other Benegal films) lies an ideological alignment that Benegal characterizes as "Nehruvian," adding, in his interview with van der Heide, that he "admire[s]" Nehru "greatly [for] provid[ing] us with a worldview and [for] creat[ing] in some ways a consensus on the kind of worldview that India could possibly have" (2006: 19). Arguably, it was in recognition of this alignment that he was commissioned to direct the Indo-Soviet documentary *Nehru* followed by the Doordarshan-sponsored *Bharat.* As Benegal's comment suggests, being "Nehruvian" entails embracing ideas and a worldview associated with the figure of Nehru, recognizing, of course, that many of these originated with, or were propagated by, Nehru himself. My subtitle seeks to capture this double – i.e., metaphorical and literal – valence: Nehru as an idea, or stand in for, and Nehru as source or initiator of, ideas that characterized India in its first decades of independence from the British. These ideas included: a commitment to modernity and to development projects considered integral to its functioning; secularism as the crucial instrument of tolerance between peoples from culturally and religiously diverse social formations; and the dismantling of gender, class, and caste discrimination. Being "Nehruvian" also entailed, most significantly perhaps, belief in the state as a central agent of social mobility and transformation: The "enduring legacy of the Nehru period," says Khilnani, was "the establishment of the state at the core of India's society," such that "a distant alien object," inherited from India's colonial masters, was transformed into an entity that "proclaim[ed] itself responsible for everything [Indians] could desire: jobs, ration cards, educational places, security, cultural recognition" (1999: 41).

This association of Nehru with a particular set of ideas, and a worldview, indeed of Nehru as *the* "idea of India" (Nehru's phrase [quoted in Som 2004: 69]), which is a staple of standard Nehru biographies, is a product of specific historical circumstances: With Gandhi dead, Nehru, as his chosen heir and the first Prime Minister of a newly independent India, was given the opportunity to have an indelible impact on a polity and society that could and did take shape under his direction. It was an opportunity Nehru embraced; and it was an impact that, as Brown's account suggests, Nehru actively sought to exercise both via his position as Prime Minister ("with immense powers of advise to the President" and as "head and lynchpin of government on a daily basis" [2003: 205]), and "by dominating the cabinet and Lok Sabha" and assigning himself important portfolios like that of External Affairs Minister and the role of Chair of Planning Commission (2003: 206) that enabled him to forward his vision of international relations and the developmental agendas so central to his conception of a modern India. In these roles, by assigning centrality to the state for enacting his "idea of India," Nehru was able to put himself, Brown adds, "in a unusually prominent position" (2003: 222).

It is interesting to observe how often these historical circumstances and Nehru's active role in determining his own centrality to India's biography is effortlessly transmuted into an understanding of him as an iconic figure whose life (reduced – or amplified – persistently to mean only his "political life") is rendered seamlessly co-extensive with the life of the Indian nation and its peoples.[7] To know the one, this understanding suggests, means also to know the other. Thus, in her November 1980 "Foreword" to Nehru's *Discovery*, Indira Gandhi characterizes her father, Nehru's *Autobiography* "as not merely the quest of one individual for freedom, but as an insight into the making of the mind of new India."[8] An analogous tendency is at work in Khilnani's *The Idea of India* whose definition of India derives from the idea(s) – and, indeed, iconic figure – of Nehru. Pithy invocations such as, "In India, the 1940s and 1950s were the Age of Nehru, just as the 1920s and 1930s had been the Age of Gandhi" (Guha 2011: 299) and "In the years between independence in 1947 and his death in 1964, India in many ways was Nehru" (Som 2004: 1), are commonplace in the scholarship on Nehru and India. Indeed, Brown "design[s]" her 2003 biography, *Jawaharlal Nehru: A Political Life*, "to enable the reader to see through his life many of the issues facing his generation, and many of the influences at work in a historical period of rapid and momentous change." Her biography "also uses," she adds, "his life as a window into Indian politics and shows how his life and concerns, his ambitions and failures can help the analysis of some of the deeper forces operating in the Indian polity." She concludes her study by reiterating the centrality of Nehru's life to the "creation of modern India" (2003: 3–4, 338).

Although Brown is explicit about how her framing of Nehru's "political life" is designed to achieve specific ends, most other studies of Nehru assume the correspondence between Nehru and India (and/or a decolonizing Asia and Africa) as a given, and as in fact proof of Nehru's self-evident significance, thereby displacing or eliding the willed or constructed aspects of his biography on their, and his, part or as a powerful trope deployed by narratives of nation to affirm the "greatness" of "big men." By not acknowledging any mediation, such assumptions are ideologically congruent not just with documentary films' assumption of their unmediated access to the real, but also traditional or disciplinary history's assumption of its unmediated access to facts. Both these factors constitute an important context for Benegal's films on Nehru and Ray, much as they provide a significant context through which to understand their sponsor, FDI's agenda with regard to its programming. *Bharat*, on the other hand, conforms more with Doordarshan's brief to "merge entertainment with 'socially oriented' programming" (Mankekar 1999: 73), reconstructing Nehru's reconstruction of India's past through recourse not just to the narrating presence of an actor playing Nehru, but also to a treasure trove of stories, legends, and myths, as well as cultural forms such as the novel, classical, and regional dance forms and classical and vernacular theatre traditions.

To turn, first, to FDI: there is, in some respects, a homology between the role exemplified by Nehru and that which FDI took on as its *raison d'être* – to be bearer of the nation's identity and also its architect: For K.L. Khandarpur, "[t]he history of Films Division and the history of free India are closely linked" (quoted in Jag Mohan 1990: 45). Nor is this close link accidental, for, as Jehangir Bhownagary, who was deputy chief producer of FDI from 1954 to 1957, and was subsequently asked by Indira Gandhi, then Minister of Information and Broadcasting (I & B) to return as chief advisor for Films in her Ministry from 1965 to 1967, notes: FDI from the outset undertook to make "*films that would help build the nation, build a sense of citizenship and community*"; this involved bringing "*[t]he common heritage ... to light for the truth of unity to be proclaimed, to be illuminated by the gift of the diversity so that we, as a subcontinent, may in our unity be enriched by our differences.*" "After the 'know your country phase,'" he adds, "the people had to be informed of *the mobile social and economic structure of the country and its progress*" (quoted in Jag Mohan 1990: 75, original emphasis). Similarly, Jagat Murari, reminiscing about his own tenure at FDI, observes: "The [FDI] Documentary became a means of constructive interference in the lives of the people for a better tomorrow. It meant shaping and reshaping the minds of the people in all fields" (quoted in Jag Mohan 1990: 53).[9] Nehru himself envisaged FDI documentaries as informing "our people [about] the magnitude of the task that is being done in India at present." He made clear that this information was to be geared to presenting the (nation-)state's efforts in a favorable light as well as to create a consensus – indeed, "understanding and enthusiasm" – for "a certain unity of outlook in our national planning" among a diversely located, significantly heterogeneous peoples. Thus "it is not enough to just give a glimpse of something being done. It should be a longer and more educative picture and it should be taken in mobile vans to remote villages" (quoted in Jag Mohan 1969: 4).[10]

Although it is hard to fault an effort to bring about comity among the multiethnic, multi-religious, multicultural, and multilingual peoples such as India contained, the desire for unity in this case was also tied to, and in support of, the (nation-)state's agendas for its peoples. Examining the "visual representations of the nation produced by state and non-state actors in postcolonial India," Roy focuses on FDI as an instance of the former to argue that, with "citizenship and representation" as "moving targets during these transitional years" – conceived, that is, "as an ongoing process" – "guidance [from] the state" – via state organs like FDI – was considered crucial to the project of "'becoming Indian' rather than 'being Indian'" (2002: 233, 236). Following from this conception, Roy characterizes the visual rhetoric of FDI documentaries as a species of "seeing like the state" (a term she borrows from James C. Scott), which sets up a "vertical or hierarchical relation of authority between film-maker and film-viewer and by implication between state and society," a relation, that is, that assumes an "ethically incomplete audience – an audience that needs to be made aware of something" (2002: 241). Both Waugh and Roy draw attention to the fairly commonplace use of "authoritative voice-overs" (part of "the same dread Griersonian legacy"), or "disembodied 'voice-of-God' interpretive narrations," as the classic technique through which such documentary filmmaking signals the state's hierarchical relationship with its peoples, although Waugh does recognize it as a function as well of FDI's effort to negotiate the imperatives of a multilingual nation: "Easily dubbed in the seventeen or so official languages, this device had the welcome additional political advantage for Bombay–Delhi bureaucrats of the full discursive control inherent in one-way top-down communication" (Waugh 1988: 29, 35; Roy 2002: 240).

Despite their implication, in hegemonic nationalist efforts, to present a particular image of rulers/leaders and a specific, delimited understanding of the nation, however, FDI documentaries were made by diverse filmmakers, some who agreed with, and others who dissented from this image and understanding: As Roy points out, "with the state as the biggest patron of the short film in the 1950s and 1960s, filmmakers were eager to sign contracts with the Films Division of India," whose work they "viewed ... in very favourable terms";[11] she adds that "filmmakers interested in establishing themselves as creators of serious or intellectual cinema frequently turned to Films Division of India for sponsorship and financial support"; a list of such filmmakers would include Satyajit Ray, Mrinal Sen, Shyam Benegal and others (2002: 237). Apart from the documentaries on Nehru and Satyajit Ray, for example, Benegal made *Close to Nature* (on the tribal communities of Bastar; 1967); *Indian Youth* (on the 20th anniversary of India's independence; 1967); and three ten-minute films on Indian classical music – *Tala and Rhythm, Raga and Melody*, and *Shruti and the Graces in Indian Music* (1971) – for FDI.

Following the decline in the 1980s of state financing for "alternative" or New Indian Cinema, state-owned television, Doordarshan, stepped into the breach, becoming the sponsor that filmmakers like Benegal, Govind Nihalani, and Saeed Mirza looked to for some of their own cinematic efforts. In the 1980s, furthermore, Doordarshan "became the Government's favoured child," says the header framing Garga's "The Indian Documentary," "while Films Division, most always inclined to do a balancing act ... seemed to have lost the will to live altogether" (1988: 26). For Doordarshan, too, Benegal has made several serials: the fifteen-part *Yatra* (Journey; 1986); adaptations of ten international short stories, *Katha Sagar* (Sea of Stories; 1986–1990); the thirteen-part short stories, *Amravati Ki Kathayen* (Amravati's Tales; 1994); the ten-part series on the first fifty years of independent India, *Sankranti* (1997); and the fifty-three-part *Bharat*.

The titles of the films Benegal has made for Doordarshan signal a shift in subject matter from those he made for FDI, with the emphasis falling, albeit not exclusively, on stories and story-telling. *Bharat*'s many episodes are replete with stories – deriving from India's two major epics, *Ramayana* and *Mahabharat*, and other sources, including regional and folkloric ones – that mediate Benegal's cinematic rendering of Nehru's reconstruction of India's glorious and sometimes not-so-glorious, past. This shift is a product, in significant part, of a shift in the historical circumstances when Doordarshan, like FDI before it, became the disseminator of national identity and culture. For, as Mankekar notes, although state-run television had been introduced as early as 1959 "as part of the larger nationalist project of building a modern nation," "it was not until early 1980s that it acquired much political and cultural significance" (1999: 5). Rajagopal, in turn, locates the years of the National Emergency (1975–1977) as the period during which "experiments were carried out in satellite broadcasting (SITE, or Satellite Instructional Television Experiment) for national telecasts, and the first moves were made towards systematic testing of the programming aimed at the majority population"; and he points out how state-sponsored television's further development took place "in tandem with Rajiv Gandhi's New Economic Policy" liberalizing India's economy, "with the introduction of commercially sponsored programming for a few hours everyday." In this context, historical and mythological serials provided examples of "pre-existing culture" through which the television audience could be enlarged (2001: 73).

Doordarshan's "new clothes" should not, however, mask a continuity of purpose and perceived national need with FDI, even as this purpose is itself marked by, and in response to, changed historical circumstances. For, as both Mankekar and Rajagopal demonstrate, a preoccupation with national integration and the effort to forge a modern Indian culture remains as central to Doordarshan as it was to FDI, albeit in altered historical circumstances, much as these circumstances are central to the "official" narrative of the nation: "As secessionist movements in the Northeast, Punjab, and Kashmir gathered momentum," observes Mankekar, "the constitution of *a* national culture acquired greater urgency" (1999: 10, original emphasis). Analogously, characterizing "Indian television as state apparatus," Rajagopal sees the historical and mythological serials that constitute Doordarshan's "imprimatur" as the instruments through which "a shared past, behind and above all divisions, [can be] projected as the crucible in which a distinctive identity was shaped" (1993: 92).

There is one other context relating to Benegal's non-fictional films on Nehru, Nehru's *Discovery*, and Satyajit Ray worth noting: The attributes associated with the term "Nehruvian" denote something that has passed (and/or is of the past – at some distance, that is, from the historical present in which it is being mobilized). For, as Rajagopal, who, like Benegal, uses the term "Nehruvianism" to characterize "the consensus undergirding the Indian development state, referring to a particular distribution of political power and its legitimating vision of secular, autarkic growth," points out: "Nehruvianism" is "a term *retrospectively* applied to the first decades of the post-independence period" to characterize this consensus, which came to an end with Indira Gandhi's declaration of Emergency in 1975 (2001: 32; emphasis added). Furthermore, not only are "Nehruvian" or "Nehruvianism" terms coined to signal an era *before* the Emergency years of 1975–1977, they are also terms associated with state-driven projects whose value was being radically questioned during and post Emergency. Thus, Benegal, while concurring with van der Heide that Nehru and Ray "represent … the potential of Indian society and Indian culture," goes on to add: "This is an approach which of course today a lot of people are questioning … both the world view that was created by Nehru, just as much as the view on the cinema advanced by Satyajit Ray" (2006: 20). Elsewhere, in another interview with van der Heide, Benegal repeats the same assessment regarding the consensus forged by Nehru as the basis for taking on the project that became *Bharat*:

> We had a national consensus about our nation, our people, our country, our democracy, and our constitution. But this consensus is now being questioned in different ways. This concept of national consensus has come back into public discourse in a way it hasn't for many years. Perhaps the time has come to again examine our definitions.
>
> (2006: 142)

Nehru, as idea and person, and the assumptions that undergird his narrative of India's multifaceted, multi-layered identity in *Discovery* are, in other words, being recuperated by Benegal at the historical moment of their erosion.

A government of India and Soviet co-production, *Nehru*, a three-hour long "feature documentary" (Benegal's characterization), is the product of what Benegal described in his interview with me as "a long, tough negotiation over defining Nehru" – a negotiation he seems to have won given that "the script was written by [Benegal's] team, not by the Soviets" (February 11, 2011). Divided into three parts – "The Awakening," "The Struggle," and "Freedom" – in what is a familiar, even conventional organization, it's a linear reconstruction of Nehru's political life, which is also the teleology (for the standard scholarship on Nehru and India) of the Indian nation as it made its transition from colonial to postcolonial status. This feature documentary is composed almost entirely of newsreel footage of Nehru himself and of events in which he was a participant and/or events constituting the political contexts from which he emerged, as well as photographs, letters, and colonial documents. The crucial agent of historical reconstruction and, therefore, representation in this feature documentary are Nehru's own words, gleaned from his writings – his *Autobiography, Selected Works, Glimpses of World History* and his speeches – albeit not his own voice: With Nehru already dead, his voice is substituted with that of Saeed Jaffrey's, which provides the voiceover for the entire documentary.[12]

Significantly, in what constitutes an intriguing disruption whether conceived this way or not by Benegal, Jaffrey speaks in Hindustani, whereas Nehru's writings are all in English that, according to Rajagopal, "by virtue of being subsumed as the Nehruvian language of command, continued a colonial practice of aloofness and unfamiliarity with local traditions" (2001: 14).[13] Two interrelated implications result from this disruption: First, whereas voiceovers are often perceived, as already noted, as "disembodied 'voice-of-God' interpretive narrations" (Roy 2002: 240) through which a hierarchical relationship between narrator and audience (or, in the case of FDI documentaries, the state and its peoples) is established, Jaffrey's supple voice (speaking in Hindustani as it moves among and between different affective registers) establishes, if not intimacy with its audience, then at least parity with them. Second, in so doing, the voiceover paradoxically invokes a Nehru who seems audibly palpable, even as his screen presence, highlighting his participation as leader in entirely political happenings and events, distances him visually from his audience.

Voiceovers, which Bruzzi characterizes as "the *sine qua non* of the Expository mode" in documentary film, are "a means of making sense of a montage of images" and often complement "archive material," which is "rarely used unadulterated and unexplained within the context of documentary film" (2000: 14, 45, 21). While archive material accompanied by voiceover can be (and is) used "critically as part of a more politicized historical argument or debate," according to Bruzzi, it can also be (and is) used "illustratively, as part of historical exposition" (2000: 21). When used "illustratively," the deployment of archival material is, Bruzzi notes, "straightforward in that it is not asking the spectator to question the archival documents but simply to absorb them as a component of a larger narrative" (2000: 21). Benegal's *Nehru* deploys archival material – newsreels, photographs, letters and so forth – illustratively; hence, the voiceover accompanying these materials, despite the initial estrangement it provokes, settles into its more conventional uses.[14]

For the history of Nehru and of India and their symbiosis that this voiceover relates is the dominant anti-colonial, nationalist rendering we have encountered before. Nehru's birth and development is presented in tandem with events on the national stage. Thus, part one, "The Awakening," which begins with mention of Nehru's birth, childhood in Allahabad, and then his student days at Harrow and Cambridge, also "chart[s]," as Habibullah observes, "through [Nehru's] eyes and responses … his commitments, on his return to India, to the nationalist movement" (1985: 136). Part two, "The Struggle," documents Nehru and his family's increasing involvement in the anti-colonial nationalist struggle. Several well-known events in this struggle (Rowlatt Bill, Jallianwala Bagh, Dandi March, Round Table Conference and so on) and well-known nationalist leaders (like Gandhi, Bose, Jinnah, and others) get extended or brief mention and are visualized through newsreel footage or photographic stills, while mention of personal events in Nehru's life are kept to the minimum. Clearly, it is Nehru the leader, Nehru the public figure whose biography is being rehearsed here for the audience's edification. Part three, "Freedom," focuses on a post-independence India, and though focused on Nehru, it brings India much more into the foreground. Thus, while it references the Partition and Gandhi's assassination and Nehru's anguished response to both, in its initial moments we are also situated within familiar Benegal territory when presented with ethnographic details of the daily lives of rural women fetching water, bathing children, planting paddy, that also not-so-subtly insinuate regional or confessional community identifications, like the image of the Sikh male child studying from a book. Arguably, no account of Nehru can ignore his statist vision that included both investment in development projects – huge dams/hydroelectric projects – and support for the arts – the Akademies his government funded. Nor can an account of Nehru ignore his presence on the world stage. "Freedom" references all these through images of Bhakra Nangal, insets of Indian dancers and classical music as background, and, of course, Nehru's visits abroad and his meetings with world leaders.

In his interview with van der Heide, Benegal points out that his documentary about Nehru (and Satyajit Ray) uses an approach he characterizes as "a first-person biography … because [Benegal] used only his words"(2006: 19). To me, Benegal said that, confronted with the "problem of creating a composite character on the basis of many divergent opinions" – a charge that did not particularly appeal to him – he decided: "Why not let Nehru speak for himself?" (February 11, 2011). Benegal's remark suggests it is Nehru's idea of himself and of India that is on display here. But, as already noted, it is an idea of Nehru/India being recuperated at the historical moment when it was on its way out, an object of interrogation and critique, not only because the national consensus it helped forge had become a casualty of the Declaration of National Emergency in 1975, but also because an influential intellectual strand of anti-modernist critique insisted that Nehru's state-sponsored secularism and modernization were deeply flawed national projects. Arguably, then, the conception of India that I have been calling dominant, fuelled by hegemonic nationalist myth-making, in being viewed as problematic and/or inadequate to its tasks was being shorn of its authority and significance. Indeed, as Benegal put it in his interview with me, his decision to let "Nehru speak for himself" was crucially tied to what he described as "the anti-Nehru stance of the Janata government": to "let Nehru speak for himself" was to enable "the spectator" to "make up his mind about him" (February 11, 2011). Benegal's hope was that Nehru's portrait of himself and of India would elicit the same admiration Benegal feels for Nehru for "provid[ing] us with a worldview and [for] creat[ing] in some ways a consensus on the kind of worldview that India could possibly have" (Benegal to van der Heide 2006: 19).

Benegal's documentary on Satyajit Ray – made contemporaneously with that on Nehru for FDI as a "first-person biography" – is informed by a similar intention, although, unlike Nehru, Ray does get to speak in his own voice, not just in his own words. The documentary is structured as an interview in which Benegal, as interviewer and filmmaker, is intermittently audible and visible. This produces a somewhat different effect than that produced by *Nehru*. In the opening scenes, Ray is shown at work filming a scene from his *Ghare Baire* (Home and the World); the emphasis here falls not so much on this well-known director's film-making as it does on the ease, humor, and warmth with which Ray interacts with his crew and actors, although scenes from Ray films are interspersed with Benegal interviewing Ray, recalling and reconfirming for the viewer Ray's status as a filmmaker. From this combination of interview, scenes from Ray films, and an extended repertoire of Ray's drawings that Benegal also includes, a very generous portrait of Ray emerges as someone cultured, intellectually sharp, and well-informed about the arts, films, and the world. Waugh invokes Nichols to remark on how "the interview film" enables a "structure in which the authorial voice [is] disguised, or abdicated, or both, in which the filmmaker bec[omes] a ventriloquist hiding behind carefully selected charismatic subjects" (1988: 34). Something similar is at stake in Benegal's "interview film," and to an extent can be applied to *Nehru* as well, even though the latter is not structured as an "interview film." The two documentaries, I suggest, offer us what is also a self-portrait of the man making them, for whom Ray and Nehru are not just figures to be admired, but also figures to be emulated, models through whom to shape his views about the world, the nation, and his profession. In this context, it bears repeating that not only is Benegal seen as the filmmaker who comes closest to being Ray's heir, but that he is also frequently described, by himself and others, as Nehruvian.

To "let Nehru [or Ray] speak for himself," however, can entail, potentially at least, a lack of any critical analysis and evaluation about either of them and their idea of India, or of films.[15] I say "potentially," because it need not entail this: Udaya Kumar, while analyzing Nehru's autobiographical writings and their vernacular successors, makes much of the instabilities and uncertainties in Nehru's conception of himself – "the peculiar relationship between self-questioning and egotism" in his autobiographical writings, so that any idea of Nehru, any affect structure connected with Nehru can (and should) call forth a complex visuality, not amenable to singular or linear forms of representation (2011: n.p.). Nor is the narrative of India as it moves toward independence and of its early decades of independence, viewed as co-extensive with Nehru's own development, amenable to, or amenable *only* to, a linear historical reconstruction shorn of all contingency and contradiction: Hasan, for instance, in his "Introduction" to *Select Speeches* of Nehru notes that "the character of the future independent India was a keenly contested one for most of Nehru's early career too, with various ideological trends, even within the Congress, jostling for hegemony"; thus, the speeches Hasan selects are geared toward "captur[ing] some of the rough and tumble of the early days of that tentative planning…, the heat and the dust – or the 'prose' as Nehru called it – of attempting to translate that blueprint into reality" (2004: 3–4). Analogously, Khilnani speaks to the "contingencies that put Nehru in control of his party and then over the state of independent India" (1999: 29) as does Khan, who examines "Gandhi's assassination as a critical element in the consolidation of the Nehruvian state" (2011: 57).

But this is not how Benegal proceeds. His feature documentary evacuates the ambiguities and contradictions that prevail in self-formation and narrates, instead, a portrait of Nehru that is seamlessly teleological – one that detractors as well as admirers deploy, albeit keyed into quite different ideological assessments – shorn of contingencies, contradictions, and self-reflexivity, and focused on a political, public self, which is allegorized as India's self too in the early decades of independence. In this it also hews closely to traditional documentary practice that FDI documentaries embraced, which, in their assumption of objectivity, eschewed all overt markers of the perspective from which its representations proceeded. Thus, Nehru's words (albeit translated into Hindustani), but not voice, constitute an unmarked element of the feature documentary's narrative, even though Benegal brings attention to them in his own comments to his interviewers – outside the documentary itself.

Viewing Benegal's other film that deals with the idea(s) of Nehru – the fifty-three-part serial, *Bharat*, which is separated from *Nehru* and *Satyajit Ray* by just four years – however, is a quite different experience from viewing the latter two: Deploying a host of voices and genres, Benegal's *Bharat*, in the sheer range of perspectives and stories it harnesses to reconstruct what is, for the most part, Nehru's history of India from the Indus Valley civilization to independence, is more like the experience of watching several discrete, but also interrelated, feature films. Indeed, Benegal said as much in his interview with me when he noted that it "was like shooting 25 feature films" (February 11, 2011). Benegal has also distinguished it explicitly from his documentaries: In his interview with van der Heide, for example, he compares it with making "the fiction film, the feature film" (2006: 31).

Approaching it as a "feature" as opposed to "documentary" film seems to have freed Benegal from the constraints he views as characterizing " 'the obligation to factuality' documentary films impose" (see epigraph; van der Heide 2006: 31). In his conversation with me, for example, while noting "the gap" between "Nehru writing in jail," pre-independence – from the top of his head since he had little or no access to books – and Benegal himself making the film post-independence in the 1980s, with Nehru being played by an actor, Benegal seemed acutely conscious of the constructed, mediated, even fictive status of history (February 13, 2011). For, although the history Benegal reconstructs is dotted with familiar events, personalities, and movements that Nehru's (and India's dominant nationalist) history invokes, his reconstruction engages explicitly and implicitly with this history's intersection with the fictive – myths, legends, epics – as it appears and/or is embodied in a variety of literary genres – novels, plays, short stories – and performative traditions – classical, regional, and popular dance forms and theatre, and different traditions of oral story-telling. Each of these modes and genres, furthermore, are cast in and/or demand different representational registers from overtly theatrical melodrama (as in the reconstructions of episodes from *Ramayana* or *Mahabharat*) to understated *Ankur*-like realism (as in the two episodes dedicated to a highly mediated account of Gandhi's rise to national prominence through a dramatization of Raja Rao's novel *Kanthapura*). Thus, while the figure of Nehru who, by opening and closing each episode with his commentary, serves as the voice and presence that makes the whole series cohere, each episode (dedicated to a particular social, cultural, or political form, historical figure, kingdom, civilizational ethos, or mode of governance) contains within itself other narratives and narrative/performative forms that dramatize these facets of India's history. The single and singular narrative presented by Nehru constitutes the outermost frame of many other narratives that nest within it, interacting with, but also working independently of, the frame narrative, giving the viewer access to the enormous diversity that makes up the social, cultural, and political identity of India.

The following are but a handful of examples of the representational practices mobilized by Benegal in *Bharat*. Episode four on "Caste Formation," shows the evolution of caste by dramatizing the Eklavya story from *Mahabharat*, while episodes five and six, devoted to select events from *Mahabharat*, dramatize these events via recourse to a folk art form from Chattisgarh – Pandavini – performed by one of its leading exponents, Teejan Bai; Kathakali, a high classical dance form; and select scenes from contemporary Hindi playwright Dharamvir Bharati's *Andha Yug*. Episodes seven and eight, devoted to India's other famous epic, *Ramayana*, represent exemplary events from the epic through kathakars (oral story-tellers); Chhau – a form of Indian tribal dance from Orissa, Jharkhand and West Bengal that uses masks – and Kathakali dancers; and excerpts from Bhasa's play *Pratima Natak* and Valmiki's *Ramayana*. Episodes eighteen and nineteen on Kalidasa and his work, *Shankuntala*, open with Nehru quoting from a French critic, Sylvan Levi, to speak to theatre's value as "an expression of civilization," and move on to an example (scenes from the play *Ashadh Ka Ek Din*, by a twentieth-century playwright, Mohan Rakesh) to invoke Kalidas's personality, while also including a scene from Kalidasa's *Abhijnana Shakuntalam*; such a juxtaposition of the contemporary with the ancient allows each to act as commentary upon the other, while keeping the viewer engaged with the value of the past captured via a contemporary exposition. Architectural forms, music, and sweeping views of the natural landscape of India all constitute the viewer's sensorium. Arguably, *Bharat* mobilizes such a diversity of narratives, cultural forms, and traditions in response to, as already noted, its sponsor Doordarshan's brief to "merge entertainment with 'socially oriented' programming" (Mankekar 1999: 73). I believe, however, that there are more compelling reasons for the kinds and range of representations Benegal mobilizes to reconstruct the history that Nehru tells.

Scholarship on Nehru's *Discovery* argues that, besides being a work of self-making on Nehru's part, it is also an attempt by one of official Indian nationalism's spokespersons to *shape* India into a nation, emerging out of two centuries of British rule. This shaping has been described as a positivist attempt at forging unity, asserted, paradoxically, as both a pre-given essence and as something to be achieved. The possibilities for the likelihood of this achievement are illustrated through references to a long history of synthesis and incorporation as diverse rulers, peoples, and their cultures arrived and were absorbed within the already existing communities and cultures, but without entirely losing their difference or distinctiveness.[16] Nehru's most powerful concept allegorizing this process of differential incorporation is the palimpsest, which can represent layer upon layer of new forms of cultural practices, religious belief, and social and political formations that cover, but do not entirely obscure, what has existed before. Benegal's mobilization of the sheer diversity of narratives, performative traditions, architectural forms, music and so on, with multiple narratives and/or cultural forms nesting within one other, constitutes the visual and palpable equivalent of the process that Nehru's narrative can only describe and/or reference by invoking the concept of the palimpsest. Benegal thus remains loyal to the central idea animating Nehru's text. Benegal also remains loyal to the culturalist bias of Nehru's *Discovery*, to what Brown has characterized as an emphasis on the "role of culture in historical change rather than socio-economic forces" (2003: 152).

Thus, even as Benegal marks his own distance from certain aspects of Nehru's reconstruction of India's history, he also simultaneously embraces the worldview that this reconstruction purports to illustrate. For instance, almost as if he were authorizing his own *Bharat* over Nehru's *Discovery*, Benegal has remarked on the twenty-two historians he and his team chose to work with on the serial – as "consultants for different periods of history" – all of whom he describes as "eminent, with impeccable credentials" (interview with me, February 11, 2011). In his interview with Shoma Chatterjee he says, *Bharat*:

> is a free interpretation of [*Discovery*]. I am absolutely faithful to the original work till the point it remains true to history. But a lot of things in the book are dated today … many more facts have been unfolded in regard to the Harappan civilization since Nehru's time. We have added this knowledge.
>
> (1988: 19)

To this end he uses a second narrator – a counter-voice – in tandem with Nehru, who takes over at various points. At the same time, he prefaces his remarks to Chatterjee with the comment that he and his team "chose historians who were sympathetic to Nehru's work … especially his views in *Discovery of India* because we could not afford to take on a historian who did not agree with the views proposed by Nehru" (1988: 19). Despite the suggestion of an external constraint ("we could not afford to…"), the constraint that operates in *Bharat* is almost entirely internal and voluntary, for not only did Nehru's *Discovery*, in Benegal's estimation, provide a picture to live and grow with, but in its focus on "the adhesive factors that went into fashioning India," it was as needed in its own historical moment as it was during the one in which it was transmuted into a different (i.e., cinematic) medium (interview with me February 11, 2011). Futhermore, despite all the differences signaled by the deployment of multiply inflected representational practices, and the dispersal and disaggregation they entail, the use of Nehru as framing narrator for each episode of *Bharat Ek Khoj* seems like a return to the assumptions undergirding the technique of "first-person biography" and thus constitutes a continuity with, rather than a departure from, *Nehru* and *Ray*: "Shama Zaidi and I decided," says Benegal in his comments to Shanbag and Pruthi:

> that the only way to deal with the book [*Discovery*] was to make Nehru the person through whom we view Indian history, that is, take some of his sensibility towards Indian history. Because Nehru's concern was also the concern of the nation coming into being.
>
> (1988: 7)

The Making of the Mahatma

> India was most decisively imagined in Johannesburg.
>
> (Hyslop 2008: 128)

In *Bharat*, the two episodes –forty-nine and fifty: *And Gandhi Came*, Parts I and II – dealing with Gandhi's arrival on the Indian national scene, represent Gandhi through several layers of mediation. Framed by Nehru's commentary, which constitutes the outermost layer, the two episodes focus almost entirely on dramatized selections from Raja Rao's *Kanthapura* invoking Gandhi's efforts at mobilizing the Indian (particularly rural) masses in the praxis of *satyagraha* and non-violent struggle against colonial and feudal oppression via a Gandhi-like figure, Moorthy, who successfully converts a skeptical, caste conscious Rangamma to the Gandhian cause; Rangamma, in turn, proceeds to mobilize fellow female peasants in the Gandhian cause. Not only does Gandhi not appear in his own person in these two episodes dealing with him, but Moorthy and Rangamma's narratives of peasant mobilization themselves nest within the story narrated by Gangamma, a female denizen of the village, who retrospectively recalls the destruction of Kanthapura, the village, and while mourning its loss concludes, "I am still Gandhi's follower." Central to Benegal's representation of Gandhi in *Bharat*, then, is not Gandhi himself so much as the force of his ideas, the impact, on the masses, of what he was asking his followers to undertake. And while what *Kanthapura* portrays is part of the dominant mythology surrounding Gandhi and the influence he exerted whilst leading India toward freedom, the choice to let an involved, but not central, character in Rao's novel speak to this rather than documentary images and the person of Gandhi himself points, I think, to Benegal's belief in the power of fiction to achieve what documentary footage may not accomplish as effectively. I also think it is somewhat unusual on Benegal's part to represent one of India's "big men" in so mediated and oblique a fashion, constructed through Gangamma's recollection (and perspective) of what passed in the village of Kanthapura when "Gandhi Came" in the person of Moorthy.

Even when Benegal, in *Making*, represents Gandhi in person, as it were, engaging directly with the events of his biography, he does so through the unusual choice of focusing entirely on his South African years (1893–1916). This is a Gandhi his grandson, Rajmohan Gandhi, describes as the "Gandhi you may not know" – a characterization confirmed by scholars who, intent on recovering the South African Gandhi, remark on the marginalization of this Gandhi in the substantial body of mainstream and specialist scholarship on him, despite South Africa's integral place in his political and personal formation. In part, Benegal's choice is a product of happenstance: In 1990, the year Nelson Mandela was released, Meer, a political activist and member of the African National Congress (ANC) and a biographer of both Mandela and the young Gandhi, met Benegal at the Indira Gandhi seminar in which they were both participants. She asked Benegal if he would make a film on Mandela based on her biography about him. Benegal balked because he did not know much about

Mandela at that time. Meer then sent Benegal her *Apprenticeship of a Mahatma* to consider making into a film. Benegal agreed, not least because, as he told me, "South Africa was the crucible in which [Gandhi's] philosophical and political ideas were tested"; Gandhi's tenure in South Africa, moreover, provided an answer to the "provocative question" regarding "how this ordinary man, from an ordinary family, became this extraordinary figure"; finally, a focus on Gandhi's South African years allowed Benegal to represent "a Gandhi no one knew" (interview with me, February 16, 2011). All three reasons Benegal offers are also articulated, with varying degrees of emphasis, in the small, but rich and often theoretically sophisticated scholarship on the crucial place of South Africa in the "making of the Mahatma," with "making" understood in all its fullness as a creative act in which personal circumstances and predilections interacted dynamically with the social, political, and cultural milieu within which Gandhi found himself in South Africa.

Gandhi first went to the colony of Natal on a one-year contract as a legal representative for Muslim Indian traders based in Pretoria. Brown suggests that this was to escape from the "failure and frustration" that were his lot as a lawyer with few or no powerful patrons in Rajkot (1996b: 114). He stayed for twenty-one more years because from the outset he "quite unwittingly stepped into the politics of racial discrimination and released a voice of protest which, in a few years would challenge the whole country" (Meer 1994: 26). Gandhi's own writings refer to incidents of racial discrimination, which produced in him a febrile sense of fear and anxiety, and a deep sense of humiliation, but also the resolve to combat them. Virtually iconic among these is an early incident when he was ejected from the train taking him to Pretoria for refusing (having bought himself a first class ticket) to leave the first class compartment voluntarily. The story, as recalled by Gandhi in his *Autobiography: The Story of My Experiments With Truth*, "belongs," according to Gopalkrishna Gandhi, "to the genre of epic transformations," with the reflections that ensued after his ejection encapsulating what "Gandhi himself later traced [as] the genesis of his resolve to oppose injustice" (2000: n.p.):

> I began to think of my duty. Should I fight for my rights or go back to India, or should I go to Pretoria without minding the insults, and return to India after finishing the case? It would be cowardice to run back to India without fulfilling my obligation. The hardship to which I was subjected was superficial – only a symptom of the deep disease of colour prejudice. I should try, if possible, to root out the disease and suffer hardships in the process.
>
> (M.K. Gandhi 2004:105)

During his twenty-one years in South Africa, a great deal of his energy – intellectual and philosophical, moral, political, social, and personal – was directed towards combating discrimination. Specifically, he addressed, opposed, and mobilized Indians (and also, in some instances, the Chinese) settled in South Africa against a series of discriminatory laws that sought to curtail their franchise; demanded compulsory registration of all Asians over the age of eight; imposed a poll tax on primarily indentured Indian labor over the age of thirteen; restricted their immigration; and declared marriages not performed by Christian rites null and void, so that "with one stroke," says Meer, "the wives of most Muslims, Hindus and Zoroastrians, became concubines, their children illegitimate" (1994: 96). In mobilizing against these discriminatory laws, the activism, strategies of resistance, and worldview – including his introduction to the philosophies of John Ruskin and Leo Tolstoy and, through them, the valorization of communal living and embrace of a rural, self-sustaining lifestyle on farms – indelibly associated with Gandhi were forged. Upon his return to the Indian subcontinent, this activism, strategies of resistance and worldview were then brought to bear on the freedom struggle of Indians against British rule.

Gandhi's definition and embrace of the interrelated terms and activities constituting instruments of resistance against discrimination and injustice – non-violence, passive resistance, or *satyagraha* – were elaborated and practiced via the series of actions undertaken to oppose the discriminatory legislation directed at compulsory registration: "Up to 1906" – the year in which the compulsory registration of all Asians over the age of eight was introduced in the Transvaal legislature – Gandhi recalls, "[he] simply relied on an appeal to reason"; he "found," however, that "reason failed to produce an impression when the critical moment arrived in South Africa." With his "people" talking about "wreaking vengeance," he had:

> to choose between allying [him]self to violence or finding out some other method of meeting the crisis and stopping the rot, and it came to [him] that we should refuse to obey legislation that was degrading and let them put us in jail if they liked. Thus came into being the moral equivalent of war.
>
> (quoted in Itzkin 2000: n.p.)[17]

Of the terms that came to signify this modality of refusal – passive resistance and civil disobedience – which have become synonymous with the name of Gandhi, Itzkin remarks on how Gandhi chose "*satyagraha*" to replace the former term, because it was "different from what people generally meant in English by the phrase 'passive resistance,'" signifying, rather, "'truth force'" and "a philosophy of non-violent non-cooperation, which call[ed] for self-sacrifice and willingness to undergo suffering without resorting to violence no matter what the provocation"; Gandhi also substituted "passive resistance" with *satyagraha* because it "'appeared shameful to permit this great struggle to be known only by an English name'" (2000: 3), see Figure 4.1.

Scholars writing about the significance of South Africa for Gandhi's evolution as a leader committed to the notion of an inclusive polity and culture, and to an idea of Indian-ness that was "eclectic, expansive, tolerant deriving from all the diverse groups who had made India their home," observe that Gandhi learned the "transcendence of narrow nationalism" in the crucible of South Africa, Johannesburg, in particular. Not only was his campaign against compulsory

Figure 4.1 Gandhi with members of the Hamidia Islamic Society in *Making of the Mahatma.*

registration initiated at the Hamidia Islamic Society, with its leaders, H.O. Ali and Haji Habib "reach[ing] out to Hindus, Parsis and Christians," it was also through this experience of collaboration that "Gandhi, the high-caste Hindu embraced Muslims, low-caste Hindus and others as fellow Indians in a way that social boundaries would have made it much harder to do at home" (Hyslop 2008: 123, 128; see also Brown 1996a: 26). Hyslop also invokes Markovits to emphasize the "oppressive context of South Africa," especially Johannesburg, which contributed significantly to Gandhi's experience of and opposition to discrimination, while noting as well that, insofar as the act requiring compulsory registration "did not differentiate between strata within the Indian community concentrated in the city, the Indians found themselves in a common situation, faced by draconian measures that cut across their various ethnic, religious and social divisions"; Gandhi was thus provided with a commonality he could draw on in articulating his vision of a capacious Indian identity not hobbled by such divisions (2008: 126–127). In this regard, both Hyslop and Brown make much of Gandhi as an "outsider," a critical outsider, who by virtue of his extended sojourn among Indians in South Africa, whose internal divisions had been erased or rendered moot, could craft an Indian-ness that "emerged in the context of another continent and which was profoundly influenced by the spiritual enrichment he experienced away from India." At the same time, "drawing on the alternative experiences and ideas" encountered in South Africa, Gandhi was able to see India and its people, on his return, "with particular insight and clarity"(Brown 1996a: 27, 22).[18] There is also, finally, the centrality of Gandhi's experiments in setting up and living in a " 'co-operative commonwealth' " that, first the Phoenix Settlement, and later Tolstoy Farm, came to signify in the development of his conception of village republics, through which his activities during the freedom struggle in India were waged.

Distinguishing his "image of Gandhi" from that in Richard Attenborough's much-feted film, *Gandhi*, (1982), which was also financed in part by the National Film Development Corporation (NFDC) of India, Benegal underscores his interest in "the evolution of Gandhi, which for Attenborough was a prelude that is dispensed with in the first fifteen minutes," whereas, says Benegal, by the time "Gandhi came back to India, his evolution had already taken place" (van der Heide 2006: 160). One would have thought that Benegal would, therefore, choose a cinematic method that would enable him to represent such an evolution – deploying continuity editing, for example, or dissolves – to establish smooth transitions and cause and effect relationships between scenes depicting different stages of Gandhi's development. Instead, *Making* is almost entirely organized as a series of vignettes that, rather than allowing for a smooth transition from one scene to another, seem to frame individual events, interactions, friendships, and acquaintances in Gandhi's life in South Africa as discrete, self sufficient units, thereby rendering each such unit iconic and loaded with considerable symbolic freight. These vignettes, furthermore, draw on a documentary register in representing Gandhi, largely eschewing affect and thus, for the most part, preventing identification with either the protagonist or the events. And these vignettes are more or less shorn of contextual detail (few dates are mentioned, for example) and depend for their intelligibility on the viewer's familiarity with the specificities they address – a curious presumption given Benegal's claim that Gandhi in South Africa was a "Gandhi no one knew." Possibly, the presumption of familiarity on the viewer's part, especially as pertaining to the qualities of Gandhi these events signal, accrues from the fact that these qualities are part of Gandhian lore crafted, for the most part, by him and then incorporated by his later biographers into their accounts.

This last attribute is in some measure a function of the "archives" that Benegal mines: *Making* is based on Meer's *Apprenticeship of the Mahatma*, which itself draws on Gandhi's *An Autobiography: The Story of My Experiments with Truth*, which Benegal also consulted in addition to Tendulkar's eight-volume biography of Gandhi.[19] In his *Ungandhian Gandhi*, Markovits decries the general lack of Gandhi biographies that escape "the hagiographical mode," which he finds inadequate for representing "the complex and contradictory individual" that Gandhi was (2004: 44). Excepting a couple of examples, this lack is also true, he says, of Gandhi's stay in South Africa because virtually all accounts of this period rely on, and accept as authoritative, Gandhi's own accounts of this period, which were written retrospectively "ten years after his departure from South Africa, entirely from memory, without the help of written notes"; hence, "serious doubts exist as to the reliability of such memories uncorroborated by other testimonies" (2004: 45). For Markovits, not only does "the process by which a small-time merchant became a Mahatma" remain a mystery, but this mystery is, in part, a result of Gandhi's own actions: "His *Autobiography* tries to cover his tracks so as to discourage all attempts at reading his trajectory in worldly terms. The Gandhian myth originates in Gandhi" (2004: 50). Analogously, earlier in this chapter in the section on Nehru, I argue that most Nehru biographers efface or elide Nehru's active role in determining his centrality to India's biography. "Big men," it seems, are *made* big (whether or not through their own active intervention) precisely by disregarding and/or erasing the signs of such making.

From the outset, *Making* reprises, via individual vignettes, the many incidents of discrimination Gandhi encountered and resisted that enjoy an iconic status in accounts of his South African period, presenting them as constituting the *raison d'être* of his evolution as a particular kind of leader: a man dedicated to non-violence; practicing *satyagraha*; open to negotiation but, at the same time, a man wedded to principle. Thus, a series of vignettes portray a recently arrived Gandhi balking at being ordered to take off his turban in front of the magistrate as a sign of his respect – more precisely, obeisance – toward the latter; a resistant Gandhi being thrown out of the first class railway compartment; Gandhi taking on the legal battle to prevent Indian merchants' disenfranchisement; the quarantine (and hardship) imposed on the ship bringing back Gandhi, his family and other Indians to South Africa to prevent, primarily, the political mobilization of Indians against "white" people's interests; the infamous "Black Act," which required all Asians to register; and the imposition of a poll tax and anti-immigration laws directed against (primarily indentured) Indian laborers. The film also documents Gandhi's meeting with the Europeans who became his life-long friends and supporters – West, Polak, Kallenbach – as, too, it documents the inception of the two experiments in collaborative living he devised – Phoenix and Tolstoy Farm – and it documents the birth and ongoing life of the newspaper, *The Indian Opinion*, created by Gandhi to disseminate information about his projects and bring attention to the discrimination directed against Indians. These, and more, are familiar, not least because they turn up in most accounts (including Meer's) of Gandhi's South African years. Relying uncritically on his own rendition of these events, the vignettes end up privileging Gandhi's retrospective take on them, which, inevitably perhaps, centers him as the primary agent of change – both material and spiritual – in the lives and events he encounters and intervenes in. I already have referred to Hyslop's "correction" regarding the person who urged the audience at the Hamidia Mosque (when the response to the legislation requiring Asians to register – the infamous "Black Act" – was being debated) to take an oath to go to jail rather than accede to oppressive legislation: it was Haji Habib, not Gandhi (see note 17). Markovits, following T.K. Mahadevan's "iconoclastic" account of Gandhi's South African years, provides another "correction." The film, following Gandhi, dramatizes his first decision to stay on in South Africa as a consequence of a newspaper item he read at the farewell reception held for him by his hosts, which focused on a bill disenfranchising Indians of the right to vote. He notes how, when bringing this to his hosts and other Indians' attention, they persuaded him to stay to help them challenge it. Markovits, contesting Gandhi's representation, remarks on the implausibility of this account citing, first, the virtual impossibility of the merchants' being unaware of legislation affecting them so crucially, and second, the slim likelihood of them hiring Gandhi "spontaneously" without first discussing the possibility among themselves. Yet, this account has become part of the Gandhian lore without anyone questioning its plausibility. Certainly, it is represented in *Making* the way it is in Meer's book, which itself derives from how Gandhi recalled it. What these "corrections" suggest is the importance of taking seriously the involvement of Gandhi's own self-interest in crafting his biographical self-presentation.

While a 145 minute film documenting a twenty-year stretch packed with significant political mobilization and personal evolution (such as Gandhi's years in South Africa represent) must inevitably compress these years and the activities associated with them, such compression, also perhaps inevitably, denudes Gandhi's career in South Africa of some of its contradictions and historically-specific dimensions, although it highlights other dimensions. Markovits points out that Gandhi's work on behalf of Indians was, in the initial years in South Africa, confined almost exclusively to "the tiny milieu of mostly Muslim Gujarati merchants who formed a bulk of the élite within the Indian community in South Africa." Only in 1913–1914 did his actions begin to address the "problems of indentured workers, who accounted for the vast majority of South African Indians" (2004: 46). Gandhi's actions, moreover, were in response to a growing lack of commitment on the part of the élite that he then dealt with "by enlarging the appeal of the struggle to include specific groups of indentured workers such as the coal miners of New Castle, among whom he found at last the determined hard-core he needed to pursue the struggle" (2004: 49). Yet, the film shows Gandhi engaging with the problems of the indentured workers from the outset through an early vignette portraying the oppression of an Indian female house servant whose baby dies because she is unable to address its needs while meeting the demands of her white employers. And despite Benegal's (but not Meer's) finely tuned awareness of the stratification, based on class and ethnic belonging, among Indians in South Africa (see interview with van der Heide 2006: 156–157), the film does not represent this stratification, although it does foreground subalternity as the more powerful site of resistance. Thus, in a departure from Meer's book and, likely, from the other canonical accounts, the film gives more prominence to the mobilizing of the miners, more even than what it gives to the virtually defining act with which Gandhi's tenure in South Africa is associated, the call for opposing the Asiatic Registration Act. The mobilization of and by the miners is accompanied by a rousing rendition of "Vande Mataram" as background music, thus constructing subjects marked by subaltern, not élite, status as truly revolutionary subjects.

Among a handful of ways (and instances) in which *Making* foregoes (or escapes) its predominantly documentary register is, first, linked with the actor playing the role of Gandhi; Rajit Kapur, sometimes *performs*, rather than simply *inhabits*, Gandhi, although in doing so, he also reprises Gandhi's own attempts at staging his persona. In her piece on "Khadi," Tarlo remarks on how:

> as a young man Gandhi was attracted to what he would later call "the tinsel splendours of Western civilization." Like most of the other élite educated Indian men of his generation, he made considerable efforts to adopt Western dress and manners in public life, associating these with the values of modernity, civilization, and progress.
>
> (Tarlo: n.d.)

But, she goes on to add, Gandhi "experienced the feelings of alienation and discomfort that the adoption of Western clothes entailed" (ibid.). In this piece, Tarlo also highlights the theatrical and deliberately crafted aspects of Gandhi's use of particular styles of clothing and particular kinds of cloth when she examines how *khadi*, a handspun, coarse indigenous cloth "became a key visual symbol of India's struggle from colonial rule" – in developing which symbolism Gandhi played a crucial role. For those of us brought up on iconic images of a dhoti-clad Gandhi, it comes as a surprise to see Gandhi clad throughout *Making* in Western clothes, with his public appearances always marked by him wearing suit and often the hat that came to replace his turban. Almost as if Kapur (and Benegal?) perceives Gandhi the same way Tarlo does, he, through infinitesimally small and subtle – mostly facial, but also bodily – gestures conveys both an element of display and discomfort with what he wears. Thus, visually, he appears as both a dandy and a man at odds with his western clothes and suited self.

By performing, rather than simply disappearing into his role as Gandhi, Kapur also manages to draw attention to the craft and rhetorical skill that has gone into Gandhi's self-fashioning as manifested in his *Autobiography* (which serves as the master text for Gandhi's later biographies) through his staging of a Gandhi persona that foregrounds the latter's allegorical dimensions. In an incident referred to earlier –the account of being thrown out of the train for refusing to move from the first to the third class compartment – Gandhi's *Autobiography* represents this incident as moment of spiritual transformation when he committed himself to a moral conception of "duty," "obligation," and "suffering." Its resonance with other narratives of spiritual transformation is overt to some commentators: Gopal Krishna Gandhi, quoted earlier, characterizes this incident as belonging to the "genre of epic transformations." In *Making*, as Kapur (in his aspect as a lone Gandhi) sits on a bench at the railway station, with his shoulders hunched forward, surrounded by the dark of the night, his face alone visible in the glow of a light, a bewildered, hurt look appears on this face before it is resolutely smoothed out and made to settle into determined lines. In this brief moment, Kapur makes the transformation both visible and overtly theatrical, staging it so as to draw attention to its carefully crafted aspect.

Another way that *Making* escapes its predominantly documentary register to present a more complicated portrait of Gandhi than a singular focus on his political activism in South Africa, allows for is through the all too-few-vignettes devoted to Gandhi's wife, Kasturba, and his oldest son, Harilal.[20] Gandhi's interactions with his wife and son, respectively, confined for the most part to the personal and domestic spheres, reveal an inflexible, authoritarian Gandhi unwilling and unable to entertain any (supposed) violations of his principles, although in his public, political aspect he is shown as someone open to negotiation with his opponents. Kasturba's intermittent narration in the film makes this inflexibility explicit ("Without any thought Bapu departed," she says at one point in a voiceover, while at another she speaks of him as "such a hard, uncaring man"). In their verbal skirmishes with Gandhi, both Kasturba and Harilal draw attention to the harshness of Gandhi's demands for self-sacrifice and suffering, articulating their resistance to them and suggesting that they merely feed Gandhi's ego.

In his interview with van der Heide, Benegal suggests that allowing Kasturba to narrate was a means of creating space for her in a film essentially about Gandhi: "His wife was a person of great strength herself. She eventually became his most devoted disciple but … she didn't allow him to walk all over her"; and again, "one of the interesting things was that she was totally unlettered and she resisted learning from him. That was her kind of defiance" (2006:157). But as van der Heide astutely points out, while Kasturba is "given a voice," she speaks about Gandhi, not herself (2006: 157). Gandhi, on the other hand, continues to occupy the center, and these vignettes devoted to his faults and failures seem like mere hobbles in a cinematic narrative about the *making* of the Mahatma. What's more, despite South Africa's place in this making, "India," although "invisible" is, observes van der Heide, "ever-present in the film"; Benegal concurs: "Gandhi himself said that his battle was to be fought there, and not in South Africa" (2006: 159). To me, he said, "Gandhi was in South Africa and got involved, but he never saw himself as South African. He was always an Indian" (interview, July 31, 2012).

Bose: The Forgotten Hero

> Netaji serves in a sense as "an alter-ego to the nation's power structure" (Gopal Krishna Gandhi). Whenever justice is threatened, wherever freedom is menaced, he continues to be evoked.
>
> (Sugata Bose 2011: 327)

In her chapter on visual renditions – "patriotic pictures" – of the " 'big men' of the national movement" in "popular and public art," Ramaswamy examines one entitled *Bharat Mata ka Bandhan Mochan* (Mother's liberation from enslavement) as a "revealing example of Bharat Mata's role as an instigator of male militancy," in which Subhas Chandra Bose is accorded centrality. In this picture, Mother India is represented as "a four-armed goddess" standing "on a globe almost entirely covered with a partial map of India. In one of her hands she holds a spinning wheel that she seems to be handing over to Gandhi," while Nehru "perch[ed] on the globe on her other side" holds his hands out for the "symbol of the new independent state" – "the Indian tricolor" – that, says Ramswamy, symbolizes Nehru's association with "conventional statist politics" and, one could add, his association with the formal governance of an independent India in its opening decades. Positioned at the center of "this pictorial tableau," Bose appears "dressed in a soldier's uniform, … kneel[ing] down in front of the mother … waiting to accept a sword that she holds out toward him." Invoking Christopher Pinney's "nuanced reading of this image," which for him "symbolizes 'the accession of non-violence to the power of violence,'" Ramaswamy remarks on the contrast between the "evolving consensus of 'real time' Indian political culture that by the mid-1940s increasingly favored the statist approach of Nehru over Gandhi's ascetic path and the militant ways of Bose" and "the patriotic pictures" that, by establishing "a commensurability between Gandhi's freedom through spinning, Nehru's through conventional statist politics, and Netaji's liberation through the sword," allow "all three models … to flourish and proliferate and no tidy resolutions are offered" (2011: 181–182, 178, 189–190). Arguably, Benegal's decision to represent more selectively the biographies of Gandhi and Bose, while representing Nehru's political career (which is also represented as the career of the (nation-)state in dominant accounts) in substantial detail and almost in its entirety, speaks more to "'real time' Indian political culture" than it does to the contrasting approach the "patriotic pictures" suggest. However, as noted earlier, each national leader's biography or partial biography is being recuperated by Benegal because, in the "real time" of the biopics' making, that contribution is being interrogated or undergoing erosion (Nehru); or some significant dimension of it is little known (Gandhi); or because it has been forgotten (Bose). The biopics, in other words, are dedicated to reviving and making relevant again these national figures and the ideas and visions of India associated with them, albeit in official nationalist terms.

Of course, Bose's status as a national figure, by virtue, not least, of his endorsement of violence as an important instrument of emancipation from colonial servitude, goes comprehensively against the grain of the hegemonic ideology of non-violence that official Indian nationalism embraced; the appellation "forgotten hero," then, carries the added freight of a deliberate forgetting or elision.[21] Benegal's film underscores Bose's militancy and hegemonic Indian nationalism's refusal of such militancy from the outset by opening, before the titles, with a conversation between Bose and Gandhi, the emblematic figure for the ideology of non-violence, that leads to their parting of ways. Alluding to his successful bid for Congress President a second time, Bose gently berates Gandhi for the latter's refusal to support him this time round, whereas, he acknowledges Gandhi had been responsible for making him Congress President the first time. Their conversation turns on Gandhi's opposition to Bose's refusal of the claims of non-violence ("Non-violence was fine weapon once," Bose tells Gandhi, "it no longer is") and his argument for more aggressive action against the British (with the British at war with the Axis powers, Bose feels that "this is not the time to keep quiet"). Averring that his "love is tender as a flower, but can be hard as flint," Gandhi responds by suggesting that the time may have come for the two to go their different ways ("*hamein alag alag raaste per jana padega*"). In the conversation, Gandhi characterizes Bose as his spoilt son ("*aur tum bhi mere bigdhe bete ho*"), evoking thereby his oldest son, Harilal, with whom he also had a very contentious relationship.[22] In as much as Bose's preparations for escape from his house arrest by the British follow soon thereafter (after the titles, that is), his departure can be viewed as a form of (self-)expulsion of (the figure of) violence from the body politic of hegemonic Indian nationalism.[23]

Benegal's decision to focus on Subhas Chandra Bose's last five years, like his decision to focus on Gandhi's South African years, is neither idiosyncratic nor without considerable symbolic meaning. Much like Gandhi's years in South Africa, for example, when and where he honed several of his primary modes of resistance against the depredations of the British empire, Bose's last five years were *defining* years for him as an implacable opponent of the British empire. During these years, he put together his vision of an independent India made material through the Provisional Government of Azad Hind (or Free India) that he proclaimed in October 1943 while in exile in Singapore, "drawing," says his great-nephew Sugata Bose, "on Indian history and on elements of the Irish and American declaration of independence" (2011: 5); it was a vision that sought to establish "communal and gender unity" and accomplished "the almost impossible feat … of knitting together men and women from different religious communities and socio-economic backgrounds into one force" (Som 2004: 167). Furthermore, as Brown notes, if Gandhi:

> came to [political] maturity outside India, outside its social and political patterns; someone who, looking from the outside was able to perceive India's problems and the issues at stake … with a particular insight and clarity because he was drawing on alternative experiences and ideas,
>
> (1996c: 26, 27, 22)

something analogous can be claimed on behalf of Bose's vision of an independent India, also materialized in exile, and drawing, moreover, on "alternative experiences and ideas."

Apart from their place in Bose's development as a particular kind of national leader, these years also encapsulate an inherently dramatic and exciting story, starting with Bose's late night "great escape" from house arrest by the British. Fleeing first to Afghanistan in hopes of securing Soviet help, then to Germany and finally south-east Asia, where he set up a government in exile, he ultimately commanded an Indian National Army (INA) that, accompanying the Japanese, moved briefly into Indian territory – Imphal and Kohima on the north-eastern frontier of India – before being beaten back and forced to retreat. Indeed, in his conversation with me, Benegal observed that the most "fascinating part of Bose was when he functioned most independently – during the last five years, that is, before he disappeared." "Cinematically also," said Benegal, when "he escaped from house arrest, [and] formed the INA," was "much more exciting" (interview with me, February 19, 2011).

Benegal's film is divided into three parts of roughly equal length. The first focuses on Bose's sojourn in Afghanistan, where he awaited papers and instructions to travel to the Soviet Union via Kabul (as it turned out, the Russians, from whom he sought support for his anti-colonial struggle against the British, disappointed him so he went to Germany instead – "If not to Russia, then to Germany," he says, "for India's freedom I am willing to deal with the devil"). The second focuses on his tenure in Germany, where he founded the Free India Center in Berlin, cobbled together the Indian Legion, composed of several thousand soldiers, formerly of the British army, who had been taken as prisoners of war in the North African war theatre by the Axis forces, and broadcasted on German-sponsored Azad Hind Radio. The third focuses on the site of Bose's most sustained development of an Indian polity in exile, particularly through his accession to the leadership of the Indian National Army (INA), which included a separate women's unit called the Rani of Jhansi Brigade, named after the queen who famously fought the British in the 1857 uprising; through his massive organizing of support and funds from the expatriate Indian population in southeast Asia; and through his proclamation of the provisional Azad Hind (Free India) government.

The narrative of Bose that the film disseminates, hews closely to details that are part of standard, *documented* biographies of Bose's last five years, much as the film incorporates several well-known slogans associated peculiarly with him: "*Dilli chalo*" ("On to Delhi")[24]; "*Tum Mujhe Khoon do; mein tumhe azadi doonga*" ("Give me your blood, and I will give you your freedom"); "*Jai Hind*" ("Victory to India") – with the last used by all the INA soldiers and Bose's other cohorts as a standard greeting, which then framed all interactions as directed toward and determined by the imperative to free India.[25] Given the film's conformity with documented biographical facts, given, furthermore, its commitment to historical verisimilitude, evident not least in featuring an actor who looks remarkably like him to play the role of Bose, it seems curious that of all the biopics examined in this chapter, this film alone opens with the disclaimer: "This film is a fictional representation based on historical facts." This invocation of "fictional representation" may be referencing a distinction Benegal made in an interview with me, when he noted that, "whereas *Nehru* and *Satyajit Ray* are feature documentaries, *Making of the Mahatma* and *Bose: the Forgotten Hero* are feature films" (February 16, 2011), except that a similar disclaimer does not appear in *Making*. Or it may reflect the difference that while both *Nehru* and *Ray* depend almost entirely on their (Nehru's and Ray's) "own words," the film on Bose does not, except, again, neither does *Making*, which derives primarily from Meer's *Apprenticeship of the Mahatma*, and which, while drawing on Gandhi's autobiography, is no less an historical reconstruction than *Bose* is.

What does distinguish *Bose* from *Making* is its mode of presentation, marked by continuity editing and smooth transitions linked to the project of seamlessly stitching together a dramatic narrative. It is a mode of presentation, furthermore, identified more with imaginative (even fictional) not documentary films. A large part of Bose's sojourn in Afghanistan, for example, where he meets up with the various people who are to put him in touch with the Soviets or who provide him with shelter and companionship in his exile, is rendered via a realism we have come to associate with Benegal's fictional films, deploying ethnographic details of landscape and cultural forms in combination with plausibly delineated social interactions, which foreground important aspects and thematic preoccupations of the narrative and move it along.

A more significant difference accrues from the film's cultivation of affect, through which it seeks to enlist a sense of identification and/or empathy for Bose. Although deployed sparingly (predominantly, the film conforms to the biopic genre in its focus on the public and political life of its protagonist), *Bose* has recourse to the familial and private space of its protagonist's interactions, primarily with his mother and, later, his Austrian lover and then wife, Emilie Schenkl as a source for such affect. These interactions revolve around leave-takings of one kind or another that, always involving the presentiment of danger, are designed to engage the film's audience emotionally. Additionally, a couple of flashbacks – infused with romantic longing and nostalgia – that address Bose's recollections of his wife are designed to give Bose more three-dimensional depth[26] than he would otherwise possess given the film's significant and extended focus on his heroic attributes,[27] which are signaled via his figure, clothed always in a soldier's brown uniform.

Bose deploys affect to signal another dimension of Bose's specific appeal as a national figure: To underscore the affective content of Bose's patriotism – its ability to both be a site for and to generate emotion. There is, in other words, something intrinsic to Bose's anti-colonial nationalism that calls forth an excess of emotional commitment that the cultivation of affect is meant to underscore.[28] As he is departing from Kabul, where he has been staying with an Indian business man (Uttamchandra Mehrotra), the businessman's wife while giving him three gold guineas for the cause of freeing India, movingly remarks on how "helping [Bose] has allowed [her husband and herself] to experience the possibility of freedom." Additionally, *Bose* mobilizes affect as a response to its protagonist's willingness to sacrifice himself in battle for the freedom of the Indian nation, on the basis of which willingness he had little or no hesitation in asking his expatriate Indian compatriots to their shed blood also ("*Tum Mujhe Khoon do; mein tumhe azadi doonga*"). The film registers this sentiment not only via its deployment of this slogan, but visualizes it – literalizing it in the process – as a moment within the cinematic narrative when an Indian expatriate woman, accompanied by her son, tries to hand over her jewelry to Bose at one of his rallies as her contribution to the freedom of India. Bose tells her "Ma, I don't want your jewelry; give me your son." When she demurs ("But he is an only son"), Bose responds ("Am I not also your son?"). In this scene, the invocation of "Ma" (Mother India?) and the call for the willingness to sacrifice one's life as an important modality of the struggle for freeing the Indian nation come together to identify Bose's nationalism as a heady and defining mix of both.

"No man," says Sugata Bose, "could have elicited such conflicting emotions as Bose did upon the approach of Indian independence" (2011: 6) – not just "upon the approach of independence," as a piece by Mike Thomson, "Hitler's Secret Army," (September 23, 2004) for BBC News makes clear. Sugata Bose presents this primarily as a conflict between British (and the West more generally) and South Asian assessments of Bose. Thus, "Britain's imperial hands could not forgive [Bose] for subverting the loyalty of the prized instrument of colonial control: Britain's Indian Army" and "the taint of Axis collaboration and negative wartime propaganda," he adds, "had definitely sullied his image in the West" (2011: 6). Against this highly critical assessment, Sugata Bose opposes the South Asian subcontinent's tremendous "adulation" of Bose as "a great popular hero" – an adulation that is "on par with [that lavished on] Mahatma Gandhi" (2011: 6–7). Benegal locates himself firmly (as does his film) within the South Asian camp, making short shrift of negative British assessments: "The British," he says to van der Heide, "have dealt with [Bose] very unflatteringly. He's the only nationalist leader from any of their colonies who is still regarded as a traitor. They've never forgiven him because he was an implacable foe" (2006: 200). Regarding the "taint of Axis collaboration," the film asserts Bose's highly critical response to German assumptions of racial superiority in a remark he makes to Adam von Trott who, in turn, cautions him not to put too much faith in the Nazis. The film also shows Bose's one and only encounter with Hitler as a contentious one, in which Bose challenges the Fuhrer's view of India as backward and uncivilized. As Bose gets ready to leave Germany for Japan, his colleague Nambiar suggests disbanding the Indian Legion he had put together from the Indian prisoners of war who had fought on the British side in North Africa, but Bose demurs, not wanting them to become prisoners of war again, not least because, he says, "they too have dreamed of freedom with us" ("*unhone bhi hamare saath azadi ka sapna dekha hai*"). This sensitivity on Bose's part directly contests the view reprised in Mike Thomas's piece, "Hitler's Secret Indian Army," that claims that Bose disappeared secretly without informing the soldiers he had recruited for the Indian League, and who, therefore, were left without a leader and became demoralized.

The spectator's final view of Bose is of him getting into the plane en route to Japan, which is preceded by a scene in which, having just learned of the US bombing of Nagasaki and Japan's preparations for surrender, he tells a member of his inner circle: "We are the only ones left in the world who have not knelt before the Allies. We will not surrender." He then instructs his cohorts to disband the INA so its members do not fall into the hands of the British, "make sure everyone gets paid, gets his share." Both his words and demeanor confirm, yet again, his heroic status.

The film itself concludes with frontal shots of the three high-ranking INA officers, Nawaz Khan, Pawan Kumar Sahgal, and Gurbaksh Singh Dhillon – a Muslim, a Hindu, and a Sikh respectively – put on public trial by the British, speaking directly to the audience about the remarkable accomplishments of Bose and the remarkable outfit (INA) he put together that came to "within an ace" of freeing India (Som 2004: 167). Held at the Red Fort in Delhi, where Bose had anticipated concluding his victory lap against the British, these trials cast an ironic light on Bose's ambition encapsulated in the slogan "Chalo Dilli" ("On to Delhi") (Kurcina 2010: 825; see also Bose 2011: 5–6). On the other hand, characterizing the British as naive in the triumphalism of their efforts to bring these soldiers to trial in such a public fashion, Som observes that these trials were crucial in bringing "into public view" Bose's remarkable achievements, even as they converted the skeptics in the Indian National Congress leadership about Bose's unparalleled heroism and political savvy. Because, having for strategic reasons decided to mount the legal defense for the INA soldiers, Bhulabhai Desai and Nehru had to delve into "the extensive material," says Som, "which proved the extent of the organizing and planning that had gone into the venture [of Bose's efforts to free India]" (2004: 167). According to Kurcina, "the trial took on an all-India versus Britain atmosphere with its secular composition of defendants – a Hindu, a Muslim and a Sikh – reemphasizing the rumoured non-communal attitude of the INA." Kurcina also points out that the Red Fort where the trials were held "is the seat of the former Mughal emperors, which elicited Romantic ruminations of a pre-*Raj* period in Indian history" (2010: 825). Sumit Sarkar, who has spoken of the "impact on the patriotic imagination of an actual army [like the INA] fighting, however ineffectively, for the country's liberation," notes the "decisive shift" among the British regarding India's independence that followed from the Red Fort trials and the tremendous emotion they generated among the masses (1983: 411, 419). Arguably, then, the words with which the film ends capture some of this sentiment and shift in British attitudes to what was soon to become their former empire: "If Netaji had not lived, it is hard to know when Hind [India] would have become free."

In an interview with me, and recalling the contexts from which his documentaries/biopics of Nehru, Gandhi, and Bose emerged, Benegal spoke at some length about the cross currents of various nationalist influences among which he grew up (February 16, 2011). He compared the debates at his family's dinner table to those taking place among Indian nationalists in the years preceding decolonization. Thus, while most members of his family were broadly aligned with the goals and value system of the Congress Party, one of his brothers was sympathetic to the rightwing RSS and an uncle who had been part of Bose's INA; this led to some contentious arguments about what India would be once the British left. With regard to Bose and Nehru, Benegal evinced a personal connection, even an intimacy, which seems at odds with his films about them, given that they are, in fact, portraits of their public life as part of an Indian national pantheon, which conforms with the official or hegemonic national narrative.[29] I think, however, that they are thus *because* of their (mostly state-sponsored) venues of production, and that Benegal has conceived these films in terms that helped them belong within these venues.

Part III

The nation and its ideologies of development

5 “Making these *cause* films”[1]

Cinematic renditions of the developmental agendas of the (nation-) state

> Stories refer to the more contingent processes of narrative construction.... The concept of stories becomes all the more important when we recognize that development or modernity are incomplete projects whose characteristics are subject to disagreement and whose impacts are unevenly felt.... As a construct they are far more useful to represent the incoherence that lurks at the heart of all development efforts.
>
> Sivaramakrishnan and Agarwal 2003b: 49–50

Benegal’s almost four-decade long filmmaking career is dotted with films that engage many of the developmental agendas placed at the center of his efforts to make India modern by Nehru, Prime Minister of the newly independent India. Focusing, among other things, on such subjects as the development of a milk co-operative (*Manthan* [The Churning]; 1976); land reform (*Aarohan* [The Ascent/Ascending Scale]; 1982); the plight of handloom weavers (*Susman* [The Essence]; 1986); untouchability (*Samar* [The Conflict]; 1999); and women’s control of their reproductive rights (*Hari Bhari* [Fertility]; 2000), these films, while evoking debates related to India’s transition to modernity, by virtue of their subject matter and sponsors[2] and the National Awards they have garnered,[3] are, perhaps justifiably, viewed as statist enterprises, not just ideologically, aligning Benegal with the Nehruvian state’s (and then later, Nehru’s daughter, Indira Gandhi’s) developmental agendas, but identifying him as their active proponent. Indeed, both his detractors and supporters have tended to highlight this dimension of Benegal’s *oeuvre*. Thus, while Benegal’s critics, like Prasad and Rajadhyaksha, criticize his films’ “developmental aesthetic” for conforming to official statist ideologies, his admirers emphasize his films’ engagement with socially transformative agendas that development can and does yield. These judgments themselves emerge from, and participate in, the larger analyses – pro and con – of development, frequently perceived as issuing from, and being an instrument of, the state and implicated in a desire for access to modernity: “Development,” says Moore, “has been a signal index of modernity” (2003: 171).

Coming to prominence at an historical conjuncture that included “the Cold War, decolonization, and modern nation-state building in many third world locations," the idea of development, Sivaramakrishnan and Agarwal note, derives some of its power from claims regarding its "promise to redress the misery that continues to be the home of billions," as too it derives some of its power from being viewed as "a naturalized process and commonsense objective" (2003b: 5, 3, 4). For its radical critics, however, who draw their insights mostly from Foucault and other poststructuralist theorists, development remains problematic, indeed inimical to its avowed agendas of relieving poverty, misery, and exploitation because development discourse has not only "created an object of development (Third World countries and their poor)," but also "imposed a western vision of desirable social change on this object, and created institutions through which this change should be accomplished (international donors and agencies)," that, in turn, contribute to "continuing dependency and exploitation" (Agarwal 1991: 468; Sivaramakrishnan and Agarwal 2003b: 26). When applied to individual third world or developing nations like India, this analytical framework defines development as both complicit "with the power of the national ruling elites and the hegemony of international ruling ideologies" and as implicated in the effort to extend "state capacity and its legitimation, instantiation of asymmetric relations of power, and the undermining of the challenges to the status quo" (Sivaramakrishnan and Agarwal 2003b: 26, 28). Emphasizing the victimization of the presumed beneficiaries and objects of development, radical critics of development also emphasize the "tremendous homogeneity" of its operations (Sivaramakrishnan and Agarwal 2003b: 26).

Critics of this radical critique of development, who offer a more modulated, albeit not uncritical, assessment of development, tend to focus on the heterogeneity of its theoretical agendas, practices, and effects. Two such critics, Sivaramakrishnan and Agarwal, note how "Development has always been riven by debate," and against the "lock, stock, and barrel approach" of the radical critics, they invoke those "internalist critiques of development which accept the need for development even as they seek to improve achievements in its name" (2003b: 28; 25–26). Not acceding to an over-determined view of structural constraints endemic to development projects and what Badri Raina describes as the "anti-humanist character of development," with its "denial of a *full* human essence where masses of men and women, instead of being creatively self-fashioning, remain either the inertly suffering objects of a remote hegemonic will or, at best, coerced 'participants' in self-alienating 'nation-building' activity" (1989: 98), they consider, instead, the possibility of empowerment and agency on the part of individuals and collectivities (Sivaramakrishnan and Agarwal 2003b: 47). Above all, they view development and its correlate, modernity, as uneven and "incomplete projects," open to the flux of contestations and contradiction, and thus to change (see epigraph). Adapting Ranajit Guha's terms, one could say these critics view development as a species of hegemony, while the radical critics regard it as an instance of dominance.

In keeping with their investment in a disaggregated, rather than singular or monolithic definition of development theory and practice (and of modernity and the state), Sivaramakrishnan and Agarwal deploy the concept of "regional modernities" to address the need to be alert to "contested histories of development and the shifting links between ideas of development in different locations" (2003b: 24). Analogously, they embrace "stories," as opposed to "discourse," the favored term of the radical critics, as the modality through which to examine development and its purported theories and practices because "stories" allow them to attend to "multiple vocalities, multiple points of production, and the more intimate and unpredictable processes through which development as practice" functions; stories also make it "possible to attend to issues of human agency at many levels – even if some forms of it are thwarted or only partially realized" (2003b: 48; also see epigraph). More significantly, perhaps, they extend the scope of what they see as development, not restricting it only to "iconic expressions such as large dams, super highways, project-based implementation, green revolutions, industrial complexes and planned cities" (2003b: 26).

In her study of Lakshmi Ashram in the Almora District of the Kumaon Division of Uttaranchal State, for example, Klenk (whose essay is included in Sivaramakrishnan and Agarwal's collection) distinguishes between "Nehru's vision of rapid industrialization as the basis of the developmentalist state versus Gandhi's vision of revived village economies as the cornerstone of national development" to demonstrate how in the latter model " 'education' and 'development' have the potential to transform one's life," even though "realizing this potential is always difficult work" (2003: 102, 101). Development, in other words, as Gupta notes, glossing Klenk's essay, is "not just about economics, but about political and social transformation" geared to the "creation of a modern subject" (2003a: 71).

It's instructive that, when speaking of his own practice, Benegal distinguishes didacticism (itself a species of over-determination and restriction of meaning?) from story-telling, aligning his work with the latter: "In my films, I want to tell a story within a specific social milieu," he told me during an interview, while at the same time noting that he is "not a didactic filmmaker," although when "dealing with specific social mores, there is bound to be an element of didacticism – this is discernible in some of the exploitation themes [he has] handled in the past" (March 6, 2006). More to the point, Benegal has consistently cast most of his films about different development projects as "fiction feature[s]" rather than as documentaries, a distinction, addressed in the previous section, that also resonates with some of the attributes Sivaramakrishnan and Agarwal ascribe to "stories": Noting how "it goes against [his] grain to portray people as helpless [victims] because if [he has] any kind of agenda it's to show that people can empower themselves," Benegal speaks about how *Manthan* was scripted:

> It was an original script again, based on research of how the milk co-operatives were developing. It started when I was doing a couple of documentaries about the co-operative movement, particularly milk co-operatives ... I came across many different kinds of incidents and spoke to the man who was behind it all, Dr. Kurien. I told him that if anyone really wants to

> understand this thing it requires a fiction feature rather than a documentary. Documentaries don't have the kind of emotional strength and charge that you need. You have to get to see the motivation of the people themselves and how they work, what their relationships are, what the politics of the village is, what the social characteristics of the village are, what the economic problems are and then how they relate to one another in different ways.
>
> (Interview with van der Heide 2006: 63, 72)

Attending to the motivations of different individuals and relationships along the axes of social, political, and economic circumstances among them inevitably produces differences that disperse and render homogenously conceived agendas heterogeneous, opening up the practices proceeding from such motivations to the uncertainties and multiplicities of interpretation. Benegal's films on development projects facilitate, indeed encourage, such an opening by employing specific strategies of representation that invite the films' audiences to consider multiple, even divergent versions of the same material and/or by making the films self-reflexive. For example, *Manthan* and *Samar* both deploy a documentary-within-a-film or a film-within-a-film structure to dialogically and critically address their analysis of the development projects that are these films' concerns. *Hari Bhari*, on the other hand, uses an ensemble cast and structure to engender more than one position on its thematic concern via the stories of five women from three generations of the same family, each seeking to empower herself in different ways while engaging with the issue of women's reproductive and sexual rights. In its opening, *Aarohan* deploys a form of direct address by Hari Mondal (its protagonist) to draw attention to, and explicitly stage, the "real life" incident that underwrites the film. In each of these films, the statist agendas for development, mediated as they are by the differing investments and modes of representing those who enact them and/or are its recipients, are complicated and opened up for critical examination and analysis.

In what follows, I examine *Manthan* at considerable length because it allows me to explore particularly those strategies of story-telling and visual representation that enable Benegal to present a complicated, nuanced engagement with several interrelated developmental agendas – those designed to address caste discrimination and dalit[4] empowerment, for example – that setting up a milk co-operative was supposed to achieve. I also focus extensively on *Manthan* because it enables me to fulfill the peculiar imperatives of a concluding chapter. Among these is the opportunity to return to subjects with which I began my study. (*Manthan*, after all, is considered part of Benegal's first trilogy, which includes *Ankur* and *Nishant*.) Concomitantly, focusing on *Manthan* allows me to circle back to the critique regarding Benegal's presumably uncritical advocacy of developmental agendas for which *Manthan* has served as the paradigmatic cinematic text.

In this chapter, I also briefly consider two more recent films (*Samar* and *Hari Bhari*) also concerned with developmental issues, that revisit Benegal's prior interests, including those reflected in *Manthan*, and update them. For despite considerable diversity of subject matter and emphases in Benegal's *oeuvre*, there is remarkable continuity and coherence in a career spanning over four decades. A comparative analysis of the subjects of *Manthan* (1976), *Samar* (1999), and *Hari Bhari* (1999–2000), as well as the representational methods through which they are visually articulated, allows me to address both continuities and differences in form and content in Benegal's conceptualization of these subjects over time. For example, *Samar*, like *Manthan*, addresses (albeit more extensively) debilitating discrimination based on caste. The historical moment of its story, however, is different from that of *Manthan*'s: Based on an incident that took place in 1990s, it references a moment when some dalits were able to empower themselves through political representation even as the oppressive aspects of the brutalizing politics of caste persisted. Through the film-within-the-film structure that both use – *Samar* much more comprehensively – Benegal marks both the continuities and differences, in the process historicizing changes and mutations in the politics of caste. For example, development projects since the liberalization of the Indian economy are no longer restricted to state agencies; rather quasi-state, non-state, even para-state organizations and actors also are involved. This is evident in *Samar*, which, unlike *Manthan*, focuses on the making of a film about a "real" incident involving an atrocity against a dalit. *Hari Bhari*, on the other hand, with its virtually exclusive focus on women and their life-worlds allows a return to the many earlier Benegal films in which women's subjectivities are centered and addressed. For, whereas both *Manthan* and *Samar* (and *Aarohan* and *Susman*) focus on male protagonists and stories that put them at the center of the films' concerns, *Hari Bhari* focuses entirely on a set of issues and contexts dealing with reproductive rights that Benegal feels women should have primary, even exclusive, control over, but which they are denied in patriarchal societies: "It should be the right of a woman," he tells Taliculam, "she should have the right to her own body" (1999: n.p.).

Manthan

Made within a couple of years after *Ankur* and a year after *Nishant*, *Manthan* is the third film in what is most often characterized as a trilogy. It deals with efforts to start a dairy co-operative in rural Gujarat, which would challenge the exploitative conditions that have otherwise defined the relationship between milk producers and the intermediaries who buy milk from poor peasant farmers at very low prices and sell it at enormous profit in urban centers; by so doing, these co-operatives seek to wrest economic advantage and self-determination for the poor peasants producing the milk. The film was inspired by the career of Verghese Kurien (credited by Benegal for the story idea behind the film), the mastermind behind the first dairy co-operative established in Anand, the home of Amul dairy, in the Kheda district of Gujarat; this co-operative served as a model for other such co-operatives that were developed subsequently on a national scale under Kurien's stewardship.

With its focus on the rural poor oppressed by feudal political and social arrangements and on an "outsider" who sets the processes of social change in motion, *Manthan* repeats some of the preoccupations of Benegal's first two films. But the two earlier films' centering of female subjectivities and the processes that underwrite their emancipation from the constraints of patriarchy-driven social arrangements appear in significantly attenuated form in *Manthan*. *Manthan* also can be distinguished from the two earlier films by virtue of what Benegal, in an interview with Ryan and Murray at the Melbourne Film Festival, identifies as an activist agenda that can envisage the possibility for the success – if not the actual achievement – of a revolution led by oppressed peasants, even as it takes into account the power relations, both externalized and internalized as a naturalized mentality of domination and subordination, that operate as a significant block to such success (1978:107).

If *Nishant* disappoints Prasad because of its inability or refusal to elaborate the processes through which resistance is organized by peasants or by "a modern political force entering the peasant world and organising them on the basis of a programme of resistance and opposition" (1998a: 207), then *Manthan* should meet with his approval because it seems to conform with the latter imperative. And yet this is not so: *Manthan* earns, instead, Prasad's sharp rebuke because the external agent of change is, according to him, part of "a mobilized state apparatus, which during the Emergency intensified the Congress programme of 'socialist' transformation" (1998a: 209). Thus, Prasad considers the film's "contemporary setting" significant because it locates *Manthan* as an "Emergency film," which, in turn, underwrites his profound suspicion of Benegal's statist politics, evinced particularly in its embrace of the (nation-)state's developmental agendas. Indeed, *Manthan* comes to function as a paradigmatic film in Prasad's evaluation of Benegal's statist credentials that strongly inflects his view of Benegal's early *oeuvre*.

Undoubtedly, the making and release of *Manthan* coincided with the Emergency years. So, too, the making and release of *Manthan* coincided, to some extent, with Operation Flood, the nationwide dairy co-operative program that sought to replicate the first such co-operative set up by Kurien in Anand, which was part of the (nation-)state's developmental agenda during Indira Gandhi's tenure as Prime Minister. Kamath's study of Kurien recovers what is, in effect, a triumphalist narrative about Kurien at an historical moment when "Operation Flood I and II … had become controversial" in order to inform (or remind) people about how "the White Revolution in India got off to a start" – prior to and during the early years of India's independence.[5] Benegal's *Manthan* also is involved in recuperating this earlier moment, albeit shorn of Kamath's triumphalist take on Kurien and the dairy co-operative movement. Additionally, given that the dairy co-operative movement straddles the years from India's independence to the Emergency and beyond, and was, in its earliest manifestation seen as metonymically aligned with nation-building,[6] this recuperation enables Benegal to examine more than the setting up of the milk co-operatives; it enables him to reflect as well on the state of the nation a quarter of a century after independence.

Manthan thus needs to be understood as belonging to two related historical moments: While emerging from the research Benegal did on "how co-operatives were developing" for documentaries that had Operation Flood as its subject, Benegal *returns* to it, as it were, in *Manthan*, and grafts on to this subject, in its later historical moment, the story of these co-operatives' inception in Gujarat in the early years of India's independence. Thus while the Emergency years are significant to the film's making and release, so is its recovery of this earlier moment rooted in the early years of India's independence.

I have argued that one of the salient ways to access Benegal's take on the period of crisis following Nehru's death in 1964 and culminating in the Emergency (1975–1976) – some of which period covers the years during which his first three films were made – is to attend to his recuperation of the possibilities articulated at the time of India's independence as part of the nation-building process.[7] Benegal's recuperation of this earlier historical moment, I suggest, constitutes the lens through which he critically evaluates the period of crisis and the present in which his early films were made. But this does not mean that the earlier moment is evoked and recycled uncritically. Looking back on the heady promise of the first several years of nation-building from the vantage point of a quarter of a century later, Benegal's films bear witness to the possibilities of social justice yet to be fulfilled and ideological structures and mental dispositions still to be transformed. In this regard, one could say the contemporaneity of *Manthan* provides Benegal with an occasion to probe the unfinished business of nation-building, to reflect on what went wrong or remains unaddressed and why. In terms of method, therefore, if the early years of independence provide the lens through which the present of his first few films is to be evaluated, then the reverse is also the case, animating a critique that includes both the politics of the past and the present in its ambit.

For this double-barreled, mutually informing critique of the past and the present, Benegal's choice of form is significant. A fictional rendition of the starting of a dairy co-operative enables him to probe, as he remarks, the motivations – thus, possibly, the agency and psychological make-up – of the various players and relationships among them: Manohar Rao, a veterinary doctor and his cohorts, Deshmukh and Chandravarkar, sent by the Dairy Board to set up the milk co-operative, the local villagers with whom they must interact, including the *sarpanch* (village headman), and the landlord, Mishra, to whom the dalit milk producers, Bindu and Bhola, among others, are forced to sell their milk.

In conjunction with locating the emotional force of the fictional form in its ability to provide psychological density and depth and, therefore, in terms of Benegal's deployment of a realist aesthetic, and the addition of realism to its narrative, the form also enables *Manthan* to interrogate the triumphalist narrative about building the milk co-operatives that inform Kurien's and other official accounts of their successes. These are subsequently reproduced in Benegal's documentary, *The Unquiet Revolution*, but not in *Manthan*. Indeed, *Manthan* self-reflexively thematizes its choice of a fiction feature format within the film itself to make this point. In an early scene, the audience watching the film views villagers within the film watching an informational documentary – Benegal's *The Unquiet Revolution* about Operation Flood (Interview with van der Heide 2006: 76). As part of the effort (by the Dairy Board's team) to persuade the villagers to form a milk co-operative, this documentary is ostensibly being used to present the practical benefits of co-operatives (access to artificial insemination programs that make cattle more productive, the availability of routine veterinary care, and a healthy diet for the cattle and so on) and, perhaps more importantly, their moral benefits, including, not least, the removal of caste- and class-based discrimination. The documentary more or less recycles Kurien's own inevitably self-interested presentation of the successes of the dairy co-operatives he oversaw, emphasizing the transcendence of all forms of caste-and class-based discrimination within them and their establishment of a now empowered and self-determining, formerly impoverished and abject, milk farmer (see Kurien 1984 and 2007). *Manthan*, on the other hand (within which the documentary appears) by showing the ongoing, debilitating presence of caste- and class-based discrimination and the power-laden feudal relationships that keep the poor peasant farmers in their place, complicates, even contradicts, the picture Kurien and, to an extent, Benegal's documentary presents, revealing instead how difficult it is to transform age-old relationships and social arrangements, not least because people who have power seldom give it up easily or willingly. For example, despite Rao and his team's insistence that the co-operative will not discriminate on the basis of caste or class, in one scene where dalit and non-dalit farmers line up in the same queue to sell their milk to what is a fledgling co-operative structure being managed by Rao and his team, the *sarpanch* (headman) orders the farmers to break up into separate queues based on their caste identifications. Only Bhola and Bindu display any hostility to the *sarpanch's* orders, and even they have to finally obey him. (That oppression based on caste continues to haunt Indian society is the basis also for *Samar*, a film based on an actual incident that took place in 1990 – close to fifteen years after *Manthan* was made.)

In this regard the film anticipates some of the criticisms directed against the Anand co-operative particularly in the wake of the controversy surrounding Operation Flood I and II regarding, as George notes, "claims that Anand co-operatives topple caste barriers" (1987: 1659). Analyzing the shortcomings of the "Anand movement," Dogra questions, among other things, whether "the social benefits of the white revolution have filtered down to the small [milk] producers" the co-operative movement was, arguably, designed to benefit, given how effectively "the richer farmers" with many more heads of cattle had "cornered" these benefits (1981: 8). In his account of a visit to Kheda district in the early 1980s, Dogra notes as well the "shock" he felt witnessing, in "villages which have been acclaimed all over the world for their dairy co-operatives and for the spread of benefit to the weaker sections of society," dalit milk producers "living in awe and terror of the [wealthier and higher caste Patels]" who, in order to keep their power intact attack the dalits and, in an uncanny reminder of a scene from *Manthan*, "burn" their huts down "forc[ing]" entire "families ... to flee from their homes" (1981: 16). For Vaidyanathan, "in the scene of the burning of the Harijan huts" *Manthan* "has crossed the Rubicon and the true political cinema of tomorrow seems a distinct possibility" (1996: 85). The burning of Harijan huts becomes an iconic image of the oppression of dalits and the brutality of the landlords and caste Hindus; it is repeated in *Samar* in the film-within-the- film.

Initially, *Manthan's* more skeptical rendition of the milk co-operative movement is not immediately apparent. Instead, its opening scenes, showing the arrival of Dr. Manohar Rao (the leader of the team sent by the Dairy Board to start a milk co-operative in rural Gujarat) establish Rao's idealism and depict the village to which he has come as a virtually utopian space where, as the lyrics of the song playing in the background aver, "milk flows" and where the traveler from afar is invited to enter into "an ideal sense of life" (van der Heide 2006: 75).[8] Rao's idealism is established implicitly at first via his humane response to the malnourished horse pulling the *tonga* on which he is supposed to travel to his residence: Rao opts to walk. Simultaneously, Rao's idealism is presented as a marker of his difference from the villagers when Mahapatra, who has come to receive Rao, is shown as having no compunction whatsoever about boarding the *tonga*, and pokes fun at Rao's compassionate gesture: "Are you feeling sorry for the horse too?" he asks the owner of the *tonga*.

Rao's idealism also is made explicit via claims made on its behalf by Mishra, whose dairy procures all the milk in the village at throwaway prices. Initially, Mishra decries this idealism as "sheer nonsense," and then (hypocritically?) asserts its value through the slogan "this country desperately needs people with idealism." In his conversation with Mahapatra, he and Mahapatra link Rao's idealism with youth and inexperience and "foreign degrees," and oppose it to "experience" that both lay claim to, particularly as it relates to extensive, intimate or insider knowledge of the village and its denizens: "You must be an idealist," Mishra tells Rao sometime later when he rescues him from angry villagers and then adds: "for thirty years, these farmers have been my clients. I know everything about them. You will leave within six months. Apart from destroying my business, you will destroy the village." Since the film shows how much Mishra stands to lose from the setting up of the milk co-operative, it also interrogates his negative characterization of idealism. Concomitantly, the film seems to suggest that idealism's obverse, which Mishra and Mahapatra characterize as experience, is more a form of ideological containment designed to protect the status quo. Inwardness with, and intimate knowledge of, the village and its people that the two of them claim is constitutive of their experience, far from authorizing their view of the village, operates as a handicap, blocking change from taking place by keeping established, coercive power relationships intact. (The radical critique of development, conversely, considers the ongoing maintenance of the status quo a feature of development itself.) For Benegal, Rao (and his idealism) operates as a "catalyst": When queried if change can only result from the exertion of an external force, Benegal demurs, "Not necessarily," and then adds, "For anything to change within the community requires an infusion of a new idea. Otherwise everything remains static. So it always requires some kind of an intervention" (Interview with van der Heide 2006: 75). The film, of course, goes on to complicate the audience's understanding of Rao's idealism, as, too, it complicates Mishra's and Mahapatra's initial take on experience as a function of knowledge internal to the community.

It is interesting that in a film that Prasad aligns with the calibration of the (nation-)state's developmental agenda during the Emergency, so many of the state's pedagogical imperatives, relayed often as slogans, are articulated within contexts that render the pedagogical drive itself problematic, if not altogether coercive. Thus, Mishra, urging Rao to "leave the milk producers alone," asks him to focus instead on "teaching [the villagers, whom he characterizes as 'children'] cleanliness, healthy habits, and family planning." (Family planning was a central ideological plank of the Emergency years and came thereafter to be indelibly associated with it, especially for its critics. Tarlo, for example, points out that, "most post-Emergency writers identify the fear and fury over sterilization as being the primary cause of resistance to the Emergency" (2003: 37). *Manthan*'s primary female subject is also critical of family planning: When Bindu first encounters Rao, who has stopped by her hut to collect a sample of her buffalo's milk to check its fat content, she acerbically remarks, "The have-less-children people came and went. What do you want?") Rao correctly recognizes Mishra's advice as a form of distraction and ideological containment and tells him so. On the one hand, the film's recognition of Mishra's advice – which downgrades and dismisses the (nation-)state's development efforts – as a form of ideological containment implicitly identifies both Rao, and the state's agendas he is linked to, as opposing forces that can transform the power relationships within the village (of which Mishra is a beneficiary and the poor milk producers victims). On the other hand, Mishra's infantilization of the villagers as children who need "teaching" spills over into, and infects, the pedagogical enterprise of the state and Rao and his team as well. For "teaching" is what they set out to do as they show informational documentaries and hold meetings organized around a question-answer format where it is the villagers who pose the questions and Rao and his team who provide the answers, proceeding as if they are the bearers of knowledge and expertise and the former are the recipients of these. Ironically, this characterization can also be extended to encompass a counter- or anti-statist project that calls for, as Prasad does, "a modern political force entering the peasant world and organising them on the basis of a programme of resistance and opposition," in as much as the force entering the political world of the peasants to organize them determines the direction of the "programme of resistance and opposition" that the peasants then learn to follow.

Arguably, projects of social reform and/or more substantive or radical transformations that locate the agent of change in an external, presumably better educated or informed source often run the risk of reproducing the dynamic described above. Cognizant perhaps of this risk, Benegal's *Ankur* and *Nishant*, my analysis has suggested, are both interested in change that is self-directed in terms of an individual and internally driven in terms of a given community of people.

Likewise, in *Manthan*, while the putative agents of change, Dr. Rao and his team, are external to the village, sent by the Dairy Board to start a co-operative, the success of the venture rests finally with Bhola, Moti, and their cohorts – all dalit milk producers – assuming the charge of building and nurturing it. In this regard, it is instructive that Benegal uses the word "catalyst" to characterize Rao's role – he initiates change, but is not there to shepherd it through its many stages, having been recalled by the Dairy Board to the city at the instigation of Mishra and the *sarpanch*. It is also instructive that an event, not a sustained ideological interpellation, incites the villagers to join the co-operative: Dr. Rao, a veterinarian by training, is called upon, and breaches his professional boundaries, to treat a very sick child, which he does successfully; the child's grateful parents become the first to join the co-operative and are soon followed by others whom they bring along.

At first, the dalit milk producers are not convinced that a co-operative is in their (self-) interests. Representing one of what S. Chakravarty calls the "three nodal points" of resistance to the co-operative (1993: 259), the dalits' hostility to Rao and his teammates, unlike Mishra's and the *sarpanch*'s, springs not from power, but from powerlessness. During the information sessions, whereas Rao and his teammates insist that the "co-operative belongs to all of you," and repeat their lesson about self-determination and agency based on a disavowal of dependency, the dalits return again and again to their need for economic assistance: "who will give us loans?" they ask, even though this is the method through which Mishra retains his power, while binding the dalits to an ongoing life of poverty and dependence. Although a far cry from the abject peasants of *Nishant* or *Ankur* by virtue of the vocal manner in which they ask questions and articulate their views, the dalits in *Manthan* are nonetheless unable to see a way out of their severely constrained life circumstances.

Bhola articulates the more powerful reason for the dalits' hostility to Rao and his team, and, by implication, to participating in the effort to set up the milk co-operative. This reason has to do with what Bhola views as an insurmountable distance between the life-worlds and circumstances of the dalits and those of Rao and his team members. Thus, when Rao (whose idealism views the successful setting up of the milk co-operative as function of, indeed, as necessarily flowing from, the participation of the most economically and socially deprived section of the village population) asks Bhola why he is resistant to joining a co-operative which will "better the lives of [his] people," Bhola responds passionately and at length: "What do you know about our lives?... We are the lowest of low. Who cares for us? Our forefathers were your slaves. They cringed before you, you spat on them and got free work out of them." Bhola's response evokes a long history of discrimination, along the axes especially of caste, its resilience a function of its entrenched nature, which casts doubt on the ability of any well-meaning idealist like Rao to dislodge. Like *Ankur* and *Nishant* before it, *Manthan* seems intent on showing why change is slow in coming, and thus why those desiring transformation must commit themselves to the challenges that accrue to a long-range effort.

In some significant ways Bhola is right. One team member, Chadravarkar, seems poised to repeat the unedifying narrative of Bhola's father with the latter's sister. (Bhola's extreme dislike, bordering on an obsession, of city folk, Bindu tells Rao, stems from his own family history. His father, a building contractor from the city – in his brief tenure in the village where a road was being built – seduced Bhola's mother and then abandoned her when it was time for him to return home, despite promising to marry her.) Deshmukh, the other member of the team, is a gradualist, whose conservative cast of mind often makes him uncomfortable with Rao's more activist and interventionist approach. He urges Rao not to treat the severely sick child, reminding him that he is a vet, not a children's doctor; he is also deeply troubled by Rao's vociferous advocacy of the dalit community, having implicitly aligned himself with the more powerful members of the village society like the *sarpanch* whose participation he secures in the co-operative; and he is responsible for Bhola landing up in jail, which puts him at odds – practically and ideologically – with the dalits.

Rao, on the other hand, is distinguished not only from Mishra and Mahapatra, but also from his team members by virtue, primarily, of an idealism whose full force is directed in support of those disadvantaged and oppressed by conditions – structures and ideologies – not of their own making. Thus, for Rao, the success of the co-operative depends crucially on his and his team's success in drawing the dalits into participation. (Rao is visibly excited, for instance, when Bhola finally turns up at his doorstep to complain about the *sarpanch* – he will run the co-operative as if he owns it, Bhola remarks – implying thereby the possibility of his joining the co-operative.) In conversations with Deshmukh and his own wife, Rao expresses his unhappiness with "how things are going. Only the well-to-do have joined. But I want the dalits to join." When Deshmukh accuses him of "ma[king] the dalits the main issue, and not the co-operative" and of favoring the interests of one group, the dalits, over the those of another, the non-dalits, Rao invokes a rationale familiar to advocates of social justice movements that seek to level the playing field for the disadvantaged and/or dispossessed segments of the population: the dalits need more help, Rao implies, because non-dalits have money and power that the dalits don't.

There is, concomitantly, a not-so-admirable dimension to Rao's idealism: his self-righteous belief in the correctness and moral superiority of his views, which makes him impatient with those who hold views different from his. Thus, in response to Rao's insistent argument on behalf of dalit participation in the co-operative to the exclusion, even, of the non-dalit segments in the village ("The co-operative is for the poor and most of the dalits are poor"), Deshmukh rightly challenges him: "If you have already decided, why are you asking me?" Analogously, when confronted by his wife's classist dismissal of his support of the dalits, Rao's self-righteousness expresses itself via a condescending dismissal of her views: Instead of engaging her in conversation, he simply throws up his hands, "I told you, you would not understand." Her complaints about her isolation – "Who else am I able to talk with in this desert?" – are met by his stringent refusal to take her seriously – "you don't understand my responsibilities."

Rao's condescending attitude towards his wife, evident in the way he treats her as a child needing his protection and care, is also a product of his gendered view of the world, which is made particularly apparent during his first encounter with Bindu.[9] When collecting samples to check the fat content in the milk of the cows or buffalos belonging to the farmers, Rao asks Bindu's son repeatedly for his father, and Bindu for her husband, presumably to seek *his* permission to take a sample. When Bindu sharply retorts, "The father is right here" (alluding to herself), Rao proceeds to ignore this statement and takes a sample as soon as she turns her back on him even though she has refused him *her* permission.

This first encounter between Rao and Bindu establishes Bindu as one of the most compelling and sympathetic characters in *Manthan*, even though she is not the central focus of the film's narrative. This encounter also marks the beginnings of a sub-plot delineating the mutual attraction of Bindu and Rao for one another, designed to illuminate, among other things, Rao's repressions versus her openness and willingness to acknowledge her attraction to Rao. The resulting contrast renders her the more courageous, because more forthright, person.[10] (Bindu's forthrightness is made visually explicit: Even when she is an observer, she looks directly at Rao; Rao, on the other hand, unless he is engaged in a direct conversation with her – and sometimes not even then – tends to shy away, looking elsewhere.) For, although Rao constantly seeks Bindu's help to negotiate village politics and, more importantly, to draw Bhola into the co-operative, he sidesteps any attempts at a more personal and individualized relationship with her that can be pursued without necessarily jeopardizing his professional and marital status. Possibly there is a caste- and class-dimension to his resolute distancing of himself from Bindu, but what the film makes clear is that he neither understands nor appreciates her for who she is. For example, when her husband, a drunkard and a wastrel, poisons her buffalo, whose milk is Bindu's only source of income, Rao offers her money, even though he had earlier decried the idea of giving dalits money or loans as it made them dependent. Offering Bindu money for her loss, then, can be seen not only as an instance of a double standard, but also as a sign of Rao's condescension: It's alright, his gesture seems to imply, for a woman to be dependent. Bindu is justifiably livid and remarks on his absolute ignorance about her as she refuses his offer.

In their interview with Benegal, Ryan and Murray locate the connection between Rao's political and social lives in "a degree of repression, reflecting his inability to become involved with either the woman or the [village]." Benegal concurs with them, and then goes on to specify, first, a possible source for the contradiction and then the contradiction itself that runs through Rao's idealism: "One must realize that … [Rao] is an urban, western-educated Indian. He wants to become involved and function as a catalyst for change but cannot overcome his patronizing attitude." To this evaluation of Rao, he adds:

> As one of the straight and true people, he has to live up to the image of being straight and true, not merely to himself, but to people working with him. This is why he holds back. More importantly, however, this [willed]

> aloofness is a mask which prevents him from breaking through to the people.
>
> (1978: 106)

Significantly, in his interview with van der Heide, Benegal also locates Rao, and by implication his idealism, in a particular historical moment: "He's of the generation that came to adulthood soon after independence and who believed that this country needed to change" (2006: 76).

I have suggested earlier that Benegal chooses a fiction feature over a documentary format because the former enables him to give psychological complexity to the events of his narrative and, more importantly, to the characters and the interrelationships among and between them and the events they set in motion or participate in. This, in turn, enables him to produce characters like Rao, rendered admirable through their idealism, but constrained or limited as well by their "desires and fallibilities," including in the case of Rao, as Benegal notes, an "unhappy marriage – he neglects his wife; he feels she doesn't understand him. All sorts of complexities enter into the picture" (Interview with van der Heide 2006: 75). Insofar as complexities and contradictions make him (appear) real, they are a constitutive part of the film's realist aesthetic. But realism also carries another – different – valence, functioning as a counterpoint to idealism. In this regard, one could say that the failures or limitations of Rao are those of a reality that inevitably constrains idealism. I think, however, that Benegal is also making a more specific critique: Rao's idealism, he seems to suggest in his comments above, functions as an alibi for not interacting more substantially, more personally with the dalits, whose dispossession and disadvantage he claims to feel so keenly. To the extent that Benegal situates Rao and his idealism quite precisely as coterminous with that of the westernized national elite during the early years of India's independence, his critique of Rao provides one explanation for why the promises made at independence did not quite materialize.

Just as Rao, as an outsider to the village and as a middle-class, modern subject, exists in a continuum that includes Surya from *Ankur* and the school teacher from *Nishant*, so too the dalit milk farmers in *Manthan* exist in a continuum with the oppressed peasants of *Ankur* and *Nishant* except they are not abject or completely overwhelmed by their powerlessness as the latter are. In fact, among them, Bindu and Bhola are particularly articulate and fiery from the start, with Bhola, in his absolute defiance, analogous to the figure of the homeless drunk in *Nishant*, whose interpellation by any of the hegemonic structures within the village is minimal, if not altogether absent. But, as in *Ankur* and *Nishant*, the dalits in *Manthan* participate in their own subjection, preferring to work with the devil they know, Mishra, rather than engaging in a new set of relationships that participating in the co-operatives represents, but which may carry some risks. What is different from the two earlier films is that they finally do take the risk – not when they start selling their milk to a hastily cobbled together group managed by Rao and his team but, rather, when they decide to participate in the elections for the chairman of the co-operative. Bhola, by nominating Moti, crucially initiates what becomes a contest that has dalit self-empowerment and political self-representation as its *raison d'être*: "all dalits," declares Bhola, "will vote for their man," to which the *sarpanch*'s sidekick responds "If this happens, then the rest will vote for the *sarpanch*." Rao tries to mediate by reiterating that the co-operative "has no caste or creed," and by appealing for unity among the quarreling factions. Rao's vision of an amicably run co-operative that will, overnight, disregard age-old divisions that flow from virulent forms of social discrimination, however, seems to ignore altogether the lesson implicit in his own sustained advocacy of the dalits on the grounds of their profound and long term dispossession. The problem of caste, says Benegal, "will not be sorted out easily" and "it cannot be wished away or changed by legislation." It "will only change by confrontation between castes, by people fighting for their rights and demanding the privileges they have never had before" (Ryan and Murray 1978: 107).

The consequences of the confrontation, however, are ambiguous in *Manthan*. Moti wins the election, which means that the dalits win; but it also means that the *sarpanch*, who loses, pulls out of the co-operative altogether and realigns himself with vested interests, like Mishra, while plotting to take his revenge on Rao. (He succeeds to the extent that he is instrumental in Rao's recall to the city.) Meanwhile, dalit empowerment is not something the vested interests can countenance. Nor do they: The dalits' huts are set on fire so that they lose their homes and worldly goods; Mishra steps in, renewing his "charity" – providing loans, clothes, and household goods – through which he reels them back under his sphere of influence. The only hold out is Bhola, who balks because he wants to "create something new" out of the fragile opportunity the co-operative has made possible. The film ends with, on the one hand, many of the dalit farmers selling their milk to Mishra again and, on the other, Bhola reminding Moti that he is the chairman of the co-operative society; while Moti wonders if they will be able to run the society without Rao and his team, a small group of dalits brings milk to them. The politics of despair, then, vies with the politics of hope, with the lesson to be learned residing somewhere in the tension between opposing positions that both acknowledges the sheer resilience of the power of the status quo and the resistance of the small group led by Bhola, whose leadership, as a member of the dalit community, is organic insofar as it is produced from within, rather than imposed from without.

Samar

While acknowledging that *Samar*, and his earlier film, *Aarohan*, were commissioned by the Ministry of Social Welfare and the West Bengal government respectively, Benegal implicitly claims his own autonomy with respect to the choice of subjects – the problem of untouchability and land reform, – even though these subjects also have been central to the developmental agendas of the (nation-)state from its inception.[11] Thus, for each film, he insists that it "deals with a subject that is very important to [*him*]" or that *he* "was very keen to make a film [about]" each subject and so went looking for a story through which he could address them (van der Heide 2006: 161, 114). In the case of *Samar*, the focus of this section, he finds one in a case study of a real incident that happened in 1991, which he renders as a film-within-a-film – a representational strategy he "enjoyed" deploying "because it allows many more points of view than if you were just to tell a story" presumably from a single point of view.

The bare bones of this real life incident revolve around an atrocity committed in 1991 by the *thakur* (chief) of a village in Madhya Pradesh against a dalit, when the latter dared to enter a temple. (Dalits who were forbidden, by virtue of their caste belonging, to enter a temple, were granted the constitutional right to do so in independent India; such constitutional rights, however, are most often observed in the breach.) The *thakur* punished the dalit by urinating on his head. Seven years after it happened, Benegal visited the village to meet the people who were part of this incident. "The idea was," Benegal tells van der Heide, "to look at the situation ... seven years later and also fifty years later" – that is, from when India became independent and granted dalits constitutional rights, including those of temple-entry – to see how much (or how little) things had changed (2006: 162). Wanting to explore various dimensions of this change or lack thereof, Benegal settled on a film-within-a-film structure, putting his actors in close proximity to the actual people whose roles they were being called upon to play: "You see the actor and you see the actual person. Now this led to many things", says Benegal to van der Heide,

> One was that the urban actor was himself an Untouchable, but he's lived in urban India and had never experienced this. So there is his perception as against the perception of the Untouchable living in the village, their attitude to each other and to the village, and the village's attitude to this group of people who had come a long way to make the film. It becomes clear that the urban middleclass attitude towards these atrocities is completely different from the attitude of the people in the village.
>
> (2006: 162)

Insofar as this film-within-a-film structure fuels the film's critical energy, enabling a complicated and nuanced exploration of a significant, persisting social problem, it is the means by which, I will argue, Benegal enacts his autonomy from a statist developmental approach to the problem. Also at the core of the film's critical energy is the "real" Nathu, the dalit protagonist of *Samar* as Benegal conceives of him; this, in large part, could be seen as a product of the changed circumstances of dalits; but is, perhaps more significantly, a product of this "real" Nathu's refusal to accept a subordination he is no longer required to accept, but which is nonetheless a persistent social fact. This "real" Nathu acts as a foil to the Nathu envisaged by the film-within-the-film, whose director is clearly a liberal in his views and heir to a liberal's contradictions when it comes to social difference and subordination because of this difference. (In an early scene he tells the actor playing Nathu not to cringe – "Don't make your body posture too servile" – only to follow it up with – "you are a dalit, you should know.") The actor, Kishore, who plays Nathu in the film-within-the-film, is himself a dalit, who bristles constantly at the slightest suggestion of discrimination against him. In this regard, his dalit identity operates as a persistent wound, a fact that *Samar* is both sympathetic to and critical of, its criticism emerging immanently from the presence of the more robust resistance of the "real" Nathu, who feels no hesitation about expressing his views and constantly advises the director, who constantly ignores him, about everything that the film gets wrong. As *Samar* moves seamlessly between the film proper and the film-within-the-film, these different figurations of dalit identity emerge in all their heterogeneity and complexity – debated by dalits who are themselves made up of contradictions. (Kishore, for instance, both holds on to his dalit identity as a site of oppression and victimage and wants to escape it through appeals to a more general humanity – his humanity despite his dalit identity.)

Through the film-within-the-film structure, Benegal also enacts one of the bases of a "realist" practice. All the central actors in the film-within-the-film spend time with the "real" people, whose roles they are performing, to get under the skin, as it were, of their characters and to come across as authentic. This, furthermore, serves the purpose of putting them in close contact with their rural counterparts, so that the film also becomes an exploration of the differences that accrue from the urban-rural divide, with Kishore's dalit identity being complicated by his urban identifications. At the same time, however, middle-class or caste Hindu prejudice against dalits is shared across the urban-rural divide. Hence Murali, who plays the role of the *thakur*, goes to meet the *thakur*'s son (the *thakur* having passed away) to portray the *thakur* authentically. As it turns out, he does not need much help to be authentic, since both the son and Murali share a virulent prejudice against dalits, based not least on their sense of entitlement as caste Hindus and resentment, therefore, of any form of dalit assertion. So things have changed, but not necessarily for the better.

On the other hand, comparing Nathu with Bhola in *Manthan* allows viewers to see more than glimmerings of a change: They are both unaccommodating in their resistance, but Bhola is always angry and prickly, whereas Nathu is resilient and displays considerable equanimity and humor – a mark of self-confidence that Bhola lacks – when he challenges the director about his mistakes and for misrepresenting his story. Again this simply might be an individual attribute, but we cannot entirely write off the impact of his historical moment on him. Change also is registered through the young actress, Uma, who plays the role of Nathu's wife, Dulari; she seems more open to the imperatives of a changing relationship with a somewhat more empowered dalit identity, and as Kishore's friend, she is both sensitive to his sense of slight, but also willing to challenge his sensitivity by alluding to things that have changed.

Nevertheless, the prejudice against dalits runs deep, turning up in unexpected quarters and articulated by people who should know better. Kishore believes, rightly, that Murali uses his role as the *thakur* to assault him in his role as Nathu more aggressively than he needs to. This leads Kishore to refuse to play the "punishment" scene, which would involve Murali as the *thakur* urinating on his head, until Murali apologizes to him for his prior roughness. Kishore also refuses the "punishment" because it calls upon him as a dalit to perform his abjection and helplessness. To resolve the impasse, the director asks the writer to research other forms of "punishment" that may be more acceptable to Kishore. Unable to find a reasonable substitute, the writer reveals his latent prejudice when he says that, "Kishore's dalit identity is standing in their way."

As in *Manthan*, the developmental lesson to be learned is presented in the film-within-the-film, thereby subjecting it to mediation, even interrogation. The film proper contains only one didactic interlude, towards the end, when a dalit police officer who has invited the director and some cast members of the film to his house for dinner delivers a mini lecture to his son that concludes with: "What you make of yourself is what counts." The film's "lesson," on the other hand, links genuine social transformation to changing the mindset of people, and this is something the film, temporally situated twenty-five years from when Benegal addressed the problem of untouchability in *Manthan* (and *Ankur* and *Nishant*), suggests is a long-term enterprise. Benegal presents this as a statist conclusion as well when, in response to van der Heide's query – "What did the Ministry of Welfare want to convey about this issue?" – Benegal says:

> They wanted to highlight the fact that there's a long way to go. For these things to disappear, certain mindsets have to change. Mindsets usually change only when there is so much pressure that they can't resist the pressure.... In this case the mindset will only change slowly, because things that have gone on for over three or four thousand years are not going to end in fifty years.
>
> (2006: 163)

From Benegal's comments above and from his comments about constitutional legislation pertaining to discrimination against dalits, it is clear that he greatly admires this legislation, even though his films show again and again, if not the failure of this legislation, then its inability to prevent the brutalities through which such discrimination is enacted. It is in the effort to record – through specific cinematic strategies and stories – the divergent interests and investments that impinge on and affect the actual impact and realization (or not) of this legislation that films like *Samar* (and *Manthan*) make apparent the unevenness and complexities of development.

Hari Bhari

Drawing upon a series of case histories produced by a non-governmental organization, the Population Council, Benegal's usual script writer Shama Zaidi, in collaboration with Priya Chandrashekhar, cobbled together intersecting stories about five women from three generations of an extended Muslim family that Benegal made into *Hari Bhari*. This film, Benegal notes in his interview with

Taliculam, is "about women's rights generally. But more particularly it is an exploration into the concept of women's reproductive rights" (1999: n.p.). It is what the film is about *generally*, rather than what it is about *particularly*, that comes across with greater affective force and resonates with the viewer. This is primarily because, like the other two films I have examined in this chapter, Benegal, eschewing didacticism, lets the imperatives of story-telling inform the shape of his film. Story-telling also helps him "find a new way of looking" – shorn of "propaganda" and a familiarity that elicits indifference – at a subject (women's reproduction rights) "on which many films have been made" (Karnad 2002: n.p.); as he tells Karnad in an interview:

> There's a lot of propaganda, government documentaries and so on, and everyone's blasé about these things. You have to break through this attitude. Because they are real problems continuing to plague us. You cannot just shut your mind to them. So how do you deal with them if you have to go back to them again?... They become challenges; but I like these challenges, because they allow you to explore the medium of film itself in the process.
>
> (2002: n.p.)

Arguably, story-telling also becomes a way of negotiating the pedagogical imperatives of his sponsor, the Ministry of Health, and complicating these via a method designed to render them more complex.[12] To this end, *Hari Bhari* uses an ensemble structure and cast of characters. These conceptualize each of the five women's relationships to issues of reproduction and female (but also male) sexuality as a product of her "environment and also the compulsions within the environment including the weight of [her] background" (Benegal to van der Heide 2006: 164). In so doing, *Hari Bhari* also ends up addressing such subjects as: "ingrained traditional values about sexuality and choice"; internalized versions of patriarchy, which make women into "enforcers of tradition" (van der Heide 2006: 165); anxieties about masculinity, and so on. Pursuing "the compulsions within [each woman's] environment" and the "weight of [her] background," thus makes *Hari Bhari* also, even primarily, a film about female empowerment – the forces, external or internal, that support or impede it – which has been at the center of Benegal films from the outset. In its deployment of an ensemble structure peopled, for the most part, by female characters, *Hari Bhari* most resembles *Mandi*, but in tone and in the disposition of the predicaments that each of the female characters encounters, it is more like his other women-centered films – *Ankur*, *Bhumika*, and *Sardari Begum*, for example. Its focus on women not only sidelines the male characters, but also allows it to show female empowerment as mostly a consequence of female agency. This aspect of the film is further highlighted by the cast of powerful female actresses Benegal has brought together to play the roles of Ghazala (Shabana Azmi), her mother, Hasina (Surekha Sikri), her daughter Salma (Rajeswari Sachdev), and her two sisters-in-law Najma (Alka Trivedi) and Afsana (Nandita Das), all of whom have performed strong female characters – frequently in Benegal's own films.

At the center of the five intersecting women's stories is Ghazala's, which is about an abusive husband who constantly throws her out of the marital home ostensibly because she is unable to give him a male child. When, at the urging of her female doctor, she raises the possibility that he, not she, may be responsible, she triggers a virulently misogynistic response from him, underwritten by anxieties about his "manhood." Her mother, Hasina, who has internalized patriarchal dictates, tries to convince Ghazala to return to her husband, arguing that she must have done something wrong and that it is the wife's duty to look after and not argue with "her man." This despite the fact that Hasina has not been a beneficiary of the ideology she lives by: As a young woman, she was obliged to give up her beloved to marry her much older brother-in-law when her sister died in childbirth. This strand of Hasina's story seems poised on the brink of repetition across generations when her granddaughter, and Ghazala's daughter, Salma, is being readied by her abusive father for marriage with an older man; Hasina, of course, seems more than willing to let this happen. Salma, who has had the opportunity to pursue an education, strongly opposes the fate being prepared for her and runs away from her father's home to her grandmother's. Ghazala's two sisters-in-law represent opposing positions: The older one, after losing a girl child and being thoroughly overworked and malnourished, decides to have an operation to prevent further childbearing, whereas the younger one, a fanatically religious person, considers it a sin to intervene in the (reproductive) role women have been assigned. Each of these stories undoubtedly revolves around "women's reproductive rights," but contextualized through a whole range of particular circumstances and "compulsions," they extend the scope of what it means for these women to empower themselves in very constrained economic, social, and cultural circumstances.

The developmental state and its functionaries operate with a light touch and their roles are primarily geared to providing information that women like Ghazala or her sister-in-law, Najma, don't have access to (see note 12): Ghazala's female doctor raises the possibility that her husband may be the one responsible for her inability to produce a male child; the health worker, who visits Najma after she delivers a girl child (who dies within days of being born) advises her to take care of her health and, because having children so soon after each other has weakened her, to consider the possibility of preventing further pregnancies. In such scenes, when issues involving family planning are invoked, particularly those involving state agents as *Hari Bhari* does, it is hard to ignore the ghost of the Emergency years (1975–1977). But, as noted in my analysis of *Manthan* earlier, Benegal registers his dissent against forcible sterilization both implicitly (via Bindu's sarcastic remark in *Manthan* about people advocating against more children) and explicitly: He concurs with van der Heide's remark about the apparent "aggression" that Ghazala's family directs against the health worker as a response to "the way Mrs. Gandhi and her son dealt with birth control" by describing the sterilization campaign undertaken by the state functionaries during the Emergency as "an absolutely traumatic experience for people," which "recalled Stalin's collectivization plan" (2006: 169).

At the same time, however, Najma does take the health worker's advice and with the help of Ghazala takes action to prevent further pregnancies. Her action, however, is framed by the larger discourse of women's control over their reproductive and sexual rights. In this respect, one could say, adapting Berry's account of development efforts directed at Changar women (Berry 2003: 179),[13] that the development efforts revolving around family planning have objective effects (insofar as they provide Najma with the opportunity to take care of herself) but also subjective ones – empowering her to assert her own autonomy in relationship to her husband (Ghazla's brother) and his family, with whom she lives in an extended family set up. Najma's action, furthermore, exists in dialogue with the beliefs of Ghazala's other sister-in-law who considers preventing pregnancies a sin. And, insofar as her husband both recognizes her need and right to look after her own interests, Najma, in eliciting his support for her action, may well have effected substantive change regarding women's roles and autonomy than is first evident in Ghazala's family.

Benegal's remark to van der Heide that *Hari Bhari*, like *Manthan*[14] "did very well in the market place and it's often shown at conferences. Non-government organizations use it in poorer neighbourhoods in different parts of India" (2006: 164), much like his comment about the continuity of purpose between statist (The Ministry of Welfare's) views and *Samar* regarding what people need to know about the situation of the dalits, asks us to consider not just his films' conformity with statist developmental agendas, but also, perhaps, how these agendas are themselves driven by multiple (or at least more than one) imperatives that are addressed to differing needs and elicit different effects, apart from being riven by contradictions and inconsistencies themselves. In this regard, we arguably can begin to think of the relationship of Benegal's films to developmental agendas in more complicated ways than has been done thus far. For if Benegal's films are indeed of a piece with ideologies of development, they also sometimes have a vexed, conflicted relationship with them. All three Benegal films analyzed in this chapter are, after all, about empowerment – self-empowerment most especially – of individuals and groups. Insofar as they are also about individuals and groups unable to, sometimes even incapable of, empowering themselves, they examine at length the substantive barriers to these individuals and groups' empowerment. These barriers seem coterminous with those identified in critiques of development too: discrimination along the axes of caste, class, and gender; the refusal of power (and the powerful) to yield its many self-defined and self-interested entitlements; the collateral internalization by the powerless of the logic by which power remains powerful, such that they become and remain "inertly suffering objects" of power.

Notes

Preface

1 Although he is routinely invoked in all histories and/or accounts of New Indian Cinema, assessments of Benegal's films, and of his talent as a filmmaker, are restricted to reviews of his many films; a handful of critical/analytical essays, on individual films, mostly confined to his earlier creations, *Ankur, Nishant, Bhumika, Junoon* and chapters (or parts of chapters) of books – also mostly confined to his early films. Only two book-length studies – Datta's *Shyam Benegal* and a collection of interviews with Benegal conducted by William van der Heide, *Bollywood Babylon*, are devoted entirely to Benegal and his films. Van der Heide's interviews, while an important resource for information about the films regarding, not least, Benegal's aesthetic/technical choices, are, by definition almost, not geared to offering the substantive critical analysis that Benegal's *oeuvre* deserves. Analogously, Datta's book (which is primarily an introduction to Benegal and his films) while referencing some of the films' significant contexts (as examples of parallel cinema, their invocation of and relationship to cultural, political and historical aspects of the nation; their deployment of a realist aesthetic), nevertheless offers more exposition than analysis, invested, as it seems to be, in coverage of a fairly extensive range of material rather than sustained argument and critical-theoretical analysis.

Introduction

1 Analogously, in the first issue of *South Asian Cinema*, Joshi finds *Ankur* a "breakthrough" film:

> It defied all the ground rules of popular Hindi cinema. Without a star cast, without a song, and without melodrama, it surged and pulled capacity crowds ... It was happening for the first time in Indian cinema that a filmmaker without any frills was succeeding because of the sheer strength and relevance of his themes.
>
> (2001: 21)

2 Theorists of national (and of the national in) cinema tend to distinguish between nation and state (as Prasad and Rajadhyaksha do in their critiques of Benegal's statism). Thus, Rosen notes:

> Nations are cultural discursive fields. They are imaginary, ideal collective unities that, especially since the nineteenth century era of nationalism, aspire to define the state. The state is an institutional site constructed as an overt repository and manager of legitimated power. Nation is on the side of culture, ideological formations, civil society; state is on the side of political institutions, repressive apparatuses, political society.
>
> (2004: 266)

However, as Rosen himself recognizes, such a demarcation of the two – rendering the one ideological, the other simply coercive – while useful as a heuristic, elides what is in fact a symbiotic, mutually sustaining relationship. In the case of India, for instance, Khilnani argues for the indispensability at the time of India's independence of the state in realizing "Nehru's idea of Indianness" – i.e., national identity and identifications (1999: 167).

3 In a recent essay, Vasudevan views popular Hindi cinema as representing an alternative understanding of secularism (a central ideological plank in official Indian nationalism's self-definition) as "a space beyond bounded [caste- or religion-determined] identity" compared to that privileged by the Indian (nation-)state. In so doing, he suggests, popular Hindi cinema operates as a powerful competitor to the state's representations of secularism. The state's anxiety about the power of popular cinema, which enjoys a "mass constituency," is an anxiety rooted precisely in its popularity (2007: 239, 242). Nor is this anxiety misplaced. For, speaking more generally of "the enormous power of visual images to transform and mobilise self and community," Ramaswamy, following Foucault, notes that "the power to see and the power to make visible is the power to control"; in this regard, the "visual," of which cinema is a particularly powerful instance, "is constitutive of the social realities in which we live and not merely illustrative or reflective of them" (2002: viii).

4 Echoing leading Subaltern Studies scholar Partha Chatterjee's deployment of this Gramscian phrase/concept to characterize the inaugural years of independence associated fundamentally with Nehru in Indian politics, Prasad's deployment of it also resonates with a whole range of positions pertaining, and for the most part antagonistic, to the role of the state, which is seen as a site of repression and coercion, and domestication of any radical impulses. I should note that Prasad uses this phrase/concept to characterize the way in which histories of New Cinema privilege Benegal's films as pioneering efforts of this cinema. Nevertheless, his use of the phrase/concept is aligned with his interest not so much in contesting these histories as in exploring what he considers to be the statism that renders Benegal's films central to New Cinema.

5 Zaidi, who speaks to the "cross-currents of various [nationalist] influences" among which Benegal grew up, describes as decisive an event at the Youth Festivals (to which Benegal led the Osmania University contingent three times) where "Nehru gave a speech on the subliminal influence mass media could exert" (1980: 51, 53). Das Gupta asserts this connection more explicitly when he notes: "If Ray reflected the Tagorean enlightenment, Benegal is undoubtedly the chronicler of Nehruvian India. He shares its 'socialistic' bias and its foundations in secularism, pluralism, democracy, equality of opportunity, human rights, women's rights and their concomitants" (2003–2004:10–11). In his interviews with me (March 16, 2006) and with van der Heide (2006: 23–37), Benegal represented his family as a microcosm of the nation at the time of its independence, with its members investing in and articulating the diverse political positions and affiliations, which were part of debates about what India should be at that time.

6 Khilnani locates the:

> historical success of Nehru's rule in its establishment of the state at the core of India's society. The state was enlarged, its ambitions inflated, and it was transformed from a distant alien object into one that aspired to infiltrate the everyday lives of Indians, proclaiming itself responsible for everything they could desire: jobs, ration cards, educational places, security, cultural recognition.
>
> (1999: 43)

Kapur documents a similar drive on the part of the state with respect to its cultural policy that "favoured a centralized and integrationist functioning" – a claim she supports in a note that points out how the National Museum of Modern Art from its inception:

> functioned under the Ministry of Education (Department of Culture). The Lalit Kala Akademy, one of the three akademies dealing with different arts, was set up in 1954 by a parliamentary committee resolution initiated by Nehru and Maulana Azad, the then Education Minister.
>
> (Kapur 2002)

Among other such initiatives Kapur identifies the FFC, the Film and Television Institute of India, and the National School of Drama. In an earlier version of this piece, she concludes her note: "In India, as in other post-colonial countries … artists have taken this institutional support for granted, nurtured as they have been through the anti-imperialist struggle on the idea of a benign state" (2000: 202; and 228: note 4; 1992: 45, note 5).

7 Addressing the "inherently contradictory and uneven functioning of the postcolonial democratic [Indian] state in response to the social and political consideration of gender," for example, Sunder Rajan remarks on how the state has responded "sometimes inadvertently, sometimes as a result of pressures from outside (including those from women's groups), and sometimes with deliberate, benign or progressive intent … setting aside its own (putatively patriarchal) interests" (2003: ix).

8 Marked by crises within (and of) the (nation-)state, this period witnessed a war with Pakistan in 1965, severe droughts in 1972 and 1973, and a world energy crisis in 1973; all of these caused great economic hardship, which was one of the causes of peasant and working class protests. This period also oversaw a split within a faction-ridden Congress, the ruling party that had, since India's independence, ostensibly governed through consensus. And it oversaw a "cataclysmic split" within the Communist Party of India and the concomitant rise of the Naxalite movement led by a breakaway faction of the party – the Communist Party (Marxist-Leninist). Active in Bengal, Andhra Pradesh, Kerala, and Tamil Nadu, this movement seriously undermined the legitimacy of the (nation-)state by "concentrat[ing] increasingly on creating extra-parliamentary peasant organizations" (Rajadhyaksha 1996: 684), and helping to articulate "the genuine grievances of tribals, low castes and Muslims" (Masselos 2005: 247). The Emergency – a twenty-two month period during which Indira Gandhi's government assumed enormous powers, suspending people's civil liberties, repressing dissent, muzzling the press and other media through severe censorship – accelerated the erosion of the legitimacy of the state. The state remained central, but its character was significantly transformed, not least through the "increased concentration of power within the interiors of a few bungalows and offices in New Delhi" (Khilnani 1999: 46). Benegal's first four feature films – *Ankur* (1973); *Nishant* (Night's End; 1975); *Manthan* (The Churning; 1976); and *Bhumika* (The Role; 1976) – and several documentaries, including *The Quiet Revolution* on milk co-operatives, were all made within a couple of years prior to and during the Emergency years, 1975–1977.

9 Significantly, Benegal is still recuperating these inaugural years: His most recent project is a ten-hour mini-series on the Indian Constitution to be made for the Rajya Sabha channel, although it will be shown on Doordarshan as well. "Revisiting the time from a little before independence," Benegal described this project as one about "how the Constitution came to be, how it strove to enable us to become a nation, seamless despite our diversity"; he also noted that the project is in response to the Constitution's continuing relevance, but also is one that defined "Nehru and the founding fathers' vision of what India was to be, and should be." "The longest, continuous effort at writing a constitution (1946–1949)," Benegal added, "its definition of the idea of India hits one between the eyes" (Interview with me, July 31, 2012). In her own recuperation of the Nehruvian years "when the new nation was attempting to define its being," Uberoi interrogates the dismissal of the "ideals" they embodied "as pious self-delusion" to argue, instead, for "a considered, more sympathetic revisiting" (2002: 198).

10 Interestingly, Meheli Sen's analysis of Benegal's 2008 film *Welcome to Sajjanpur*, while focusing on a different historical conjuncture – of globalization – that constitutes the context of this film, nevertheless views it as Benegal's reflection on the "failure of the Nehruvian project": "At the very beginning of the film," she says, "the postcolonial developmental imperative is unambiguously cast as an incomplete process – a template for social and economic reform that remains profoundly unfinished." Noting, however, that "*Sajjanpur* is simultaneously a critique of modernity and the developmental imperative as well as a celebration of subjectivities that are nurtured within the developmental mode, however compromised," Sen goes on to add that "in tandem with Benegal's other films, the democratic state – however compromised – cannot be abandoned, nor its outreach curtailed" (2011: 13, 16, 18).

11 In counterpoint, Rajagopal marks his own distance from "recent revisionist literature" that "has rejected the idea that the Emergency was exceptional, stressing instead its continuities with the rest of post-independence history," describing the Emergency, instead, as a "watershed in post-independence history." He notes a variety of shifts in the functioning of the state that took place in its aftermath, including not least "an overt reliance on consent over coercion." Furthermore, "the Nehruvian focus on economy as a crucial arena of nation-building, involving labour as the key modality of citizenship" gave way to "culture and community" as "categories that gained in political salience." The Emergency rendered "violence" as both "necessary and productive" – enacted normatively, that is, to yield a nation "as it ought to be." It gave birth to "a form of power" no longer "located in the developmental state … but appearing in civil society and expressed in cultural and political terms but enacting a state-like authority." But Rajagopal's assessment of the break between the pre- and post-Emergency functioning of the state is nuanced, recognizing continuities between the two as well when noting an intensification of the claims made on behalf of the developmental state: "The state's mission of managing economic growth and providing social welfare," he says, "was never conveyed in so public and insistent fashion before, nor were those who crossed prosecuted with greater zeal." He also observes that "the Nehruvian developmental state" for a variety of reasons internal to its functioning was ill-equipped to deal with "vociferous internal dissent and challenges to its legitimacy" and lacked "the mechanisms of assuring political control reliably representing popular consent"; thus, "the Emergency itself may be said to have brought to a crisis the era of the developmental state," revealing "the limits of the state's capacity to govern without actively and continuously seeking and winning popular consent" (2011: 1003, 1013, 1047, 1016, 1004).

12 A caveat is in order here: Insofar as New Cinema, never very robust to begin with, ceased to exist in the late 1980s, and insofar as Benegal has not only survived its demise and continued to make films, his current films have outgrown the label under which they are often placed, and of which he is considered an exemplar. Arguably, Benegal's films always transcended the institutional format of New Cinema given that his first fourteen feature films were privately funded. Nevertheless, certain features indelibly associated with New Cinema define most of the Benegal films discussed in this study, so an account of it seems pertinent, even necessary.

13 Histories of New Cinema, while remarking on Ray's signal import, also mention filmmakers K. A. Abbas, Bimal Roy, the early Raj Kapoor, and Guru Dutt as important precursors. Their films are lauded for their "realism" and strong social and reformist orientation, which are then viewed as continuous with their preoccupation with the nation during an "era of idealism, self-examination, of hope" (Vasudev 1986: 6; see also R. Raina 1981: 8; Masud 1981: 12; Prasad 1998a: 160; and Rajadhyaksha 1996: 681).

14 The anti-statism of Rajadhyaksha and Prasad is part of a historical conjuncture whose most powerful examples include the work of the Subaltern Studies collective, which started appearing in the late 1970s. (Dube notes that Ranajit Guha, a founding member

of this collective, "identifies this period of state repression [the Emergency] as crucial in the formation of the political consciousness of the Subaltern Studies Collective" [2005: 222–223, note 18]. Similar arguments have also been made with respect to the impact of the Naxalite movement on the members of the Subalterns Studies Collective.) Drawing on the Gramscian category of the subaltern, and also, quite extensively, on poststructuralist theories – especially of the Foucaultian and deconstructionist variety – and on the critical re-evaluation of colonialism and nationalism that became prominent in the late 1960s, the Subaltern Studies collective located the motors of social, political, and cultural transformation in a radical openness to (and representation of) subaltern consciousness. An anonymous, unmarked and ignored, if not altogether repressed figure in official nationalism's self-definition and preferred narratives, the subaltern, it was argued, would help reveal what Uberoi characterizes as the Subalternists' understanding of "the invasionary and coercive powers of the modern state" (1996b: x). Following from this understanding, official or hegemonic nationalism, with the state as its instrument, was submitted to rigorous interrogation in the work of this collective, not least for being a product of a Western (i.e., colonial) modernity.

15 Analogously, Aseema Sinha insists that, "the institutional structure of the Indian state was *porous*, generating opportunities and incentives for different kinds of actors . . . to try to change the output of government policy in their favour" (2011: 51; original emphasis).

16 I am drawing upon Raymond Williams's definition of hegemony, which is itself indebted to Gramsci:

> the idea of hegemony, in its wide sense, is then especially important in societies in which electoral politics and public opinion are significant factors, and in which social practice is seen to depend on the consent to certain dominant ideas which in fact express the needs of a dominant class.
>
> (Williams 1983)

Differentiating it from ideology, Williams notes that hegemony "depends for its hold not only on its expression of the interests of the ruling class but also on its acceptance as 'normal reality' or 'commonsense' by those in practice subordinated to it" (1983: 145). Hegemony, in other words requires persuasion, which entailed, in the case of the Indian state under Nehru, what Khilnani characterizes as "practical adjustments in the face of political contingencies" (Khilnani 1999: 30). "The settled coherence of the Nehru era," says Khilnani, "is in fact a retrospective mirage" (ibid. 30).

17 While, for the most part, realism was (and is) the means through which Indian, but also other nationalisms authorize themselves, their ability to do so in an almost clandestine fashion makes them virtually homologous with each other with respect to their interests and formal procedures. For both nationalism and realism aspire to the condition of being self-evident, to the status of objective fact, which both accomplish through their presumed transparency or by effacing the work (including emotional and other kinds of identification they seek to engender with respect to their portrayal of characters, society or a given nation) that goes into their re-presentations. "This typically realist [and nationalist?] ruse: the apparent absence of structure, or structural devices" (Kapur 1992: 26), I would argue, is the necessary ground for an apprehension of their plausibility or naturalness and, thus, of their authority.

18 In her reading of Gillo Pontecorvo's *Battle of Algiers*, Khanna argues for the necessity of a realism/realist aesthetic to Pontecorvo for representing "the struggle of the Algerian people for their liberty" to a hostile audience. To that end, Pontecorvo, says Khanna, "had to believe and make credible the events he portrayed . . . have faith in the power of realism and of *cinema vérite*" (1998: 17). Her argument, however, also demonstrates how intractable "women's presence" is to this realism, "causing a stylistic shift that questions the value of documentary style": "woman, in the film, demonstrates

the impossibility of reflection being faithful" (1998: 19). See also Stam and Phelps for a complex – con and pro – argument about the importance of realism/realist aesthetic for representing the colonized and oppressed subjects by and on behalf of or against them.

19 Curiously, Prasad finds that this aspect of classical realism is not true of the spectatorial position crafted by the developmental realism of Benegal's films; he argues, instead that, as Vasudevan puts it in his review of Prasad's work, developmental realism "exercises" a "vertical control," which positions the spectator in "an external transcendent stance toward the world of the narrative." Thus, "the middle-class spectator is analyzed as an ideological project," bound to the interests of "the nation-state" and not to the particularities of the film narrative's logic (Vasudevan 2001: 120).

20 Referencing Shabana Azmi's "mock serious" remark ("When will you stop making these *cause* films and just make a movie?"), Benegal says:

> Making a film to promote any cause is no recipe for box office success. Yet, somewhere along the way I developed a firm belief that cinema does have a normative role to play in society. It often serves as a platform to initiate, exchange, and extend public debate beyond its signified role as entertainment.... Films, by their very nature, intended or not, reinforce collective prejudices and have the persuasive power to demonize or ridicule individuals or sections of the community, usually constituting the minorities. A film is largely successful on account of its ability to articulate the wish-fulfilling dreams and the aspirational ideals of significant sections of the population. Because of this power, the normative role cannot be overlooked. This is as good a reason as I can offer for my choice of film subjects over the years.
>
> (2002: 189–190)

1 "The places occupied by women": gender, subalternity, and the (nation-)state in *Ankur* and *Nishant*

1 Prasad distinguishes between "audience" and "spectator" to define the former as "an empirical category, referring to actual individuals who frequent the cinema" whereas the latter "is a theoretical concept that stands for the viewing position arising from the text's strategy of representation" (Prasad 1998a: 161). Prasad's definition of the latter draws on French film theory of the 1970s and 1980s (embraced as well by the British journal *Screen*), which itself drew on a combination of Althusserian (neo-)Marxist theory, semiotics, and psychoanalysis, to focus on the determining ideological impact of the "cinematic apparatus." Averring that dominant ideology is " 'built into' " the "cinematic apparatus" (Wees 1982: 50) – which includes both "cinematic 'hardware' " or "the equipment and operations necessary to the (re)production of films" and "*dispositif*" or "the combined physiological, psychological, perceptual, and social mechanisms that provide a means of articulation between spectator and film" (Bryukhovetska n.p.; Wees 1982: 50) – this theory posits that the "cinematic apparatus" interpellates the spectator, constructing her and rendering her an "effect" of the film text (on "cinematic apparatus," see also, Rosen 1977: 273–287 and 1986: 281–285; Rajadhyaksha 2009: 8–9, 11–12). Film scholars, who argue for an altogether more complex interplay of different elements and identifications that render the experience of viewing a film uncertain and variable, as C. Williams suggests, have contested accounts that view the spectator simply as an effect of the "cinematic apparatus" (1994: 279; see also Mayne 2002; Kuhn 2002; Turner 2002b; and Vasudevan 2000b: 25–26).

2 In accounts foregrounding the "cinematic apparatus" as the primary determinant of spectator positioning, "realism" is assigned a very specific meaning and is viewed as "an effect of dominant narrative conventions" that "place[s] a spectator in an ideologically conservative relation to the narrative. Realism, then, means an unproblematic

acceptance of the status quo that is inscribed into the formal structure" (Turner 2002b: 3).

3 Cross's essay, "Shyam Benegal's *Ankur* and the Nehruvian Woman," published a couple of years after I wrote this chapter, argues, in a far more programmatic way than I do, that "it is this initial promise, yet subsequent failure of the 'Nehruvian project' that forms the ideological background to *Ankur*." Addressing substantially different theoretical frameworks and methodological issues from those I do, Cross also considers *Ankur* "the drama of [Lakshmi's] self-empowerment in the face of feudal oppression" (2010: 89).

4 Speaking of the "tremendous effect" that the Telangana movement had on him, Benegal (in his interview with Anand) recalls in particular Ramanand Tirth who "came from an Arya Samaj background. And started a very powerful anti-Nizam movement." "On the other hand," he adds, "there were the communists. In my own family, my eldest brother" who "had been sent off to Calcutta when he was very young … came under the influence of the communists … and used to send many books and journals." In the same interview, he recalls knowing people in college who were jailed because of their participation in the Telangana movement and released "under the general amnesty given by the Nehru government" (2002: 27, 29).

5 In keeping with his negative assessment of Benegal, based on what he views as Benegal's complicity with statist agendas, Rajadhyaksha, dismissing out of hand the fact that Benegal came from the region where the Telangana People's Struggle was waged, also sees Benegal's choice of this region and of the struggle as a context for *Ankur* and *Nishant* as part of "an astonishingly unproblematic turn of a supposedly radical new cinema to Telangana, in order to produce an authoritative symbol of 'Indian feudalism' and to deliver that up to an authoritarian Indian state to use as it may see fit" (2009: 357–359).

6 Those familiar with the (often tendentious but also illuminating) debate surrounding Mulvey's influential "gaze is male" formulation in "Visual Pleasure and Narrative Cinema" will see some of this debate's imprint on my own remarks, albeit modified and appropriated (even, perhaps domesticated) to speak to my understanding of how Benegal's work "places" women (see second epigraph). With respect to Mulvey's essay, Bergstrom and Doane rightly note that it constitutes "an inaugural moment – the condition of possibility – of an extended theorization of the female spectator" (1989: 7), which is ironic given that the female spectator is defined via her "monumental absence" (Rich 1994: 35), an absence that contributors to the debate either seek to redress or confirm, taking issue with (or extending) Mulvey's analysis and assumptions (see, in particular, Bergstrom and Doane 1989; Doane 1982; Rich 1994; de Lauretis 1994; Gledhill 1988; Johnston 2000; Kaplan 2000; Waldman 1988; and Williams, L. 2000; in the context of Indian visual culture, including popular Hindi cinema, see Uberoi 2006: 13–16). Gaines takes issue with feminist theory that focused exclusively on the "cinematic apparatus" on grounds of its "banishment of sociological reference points and historical detail from criticism" (1989: 60). Most of these essays engage the question of "the female spectator" or of the "spectator as female" (de Lauretis 1994: 148), subscribing to, complicating, or contesting Mulvey's embrace of this spectator as an effect of the "cinematic apparatus." I am not interested in analyzing the role of the female spectator per se in Benegal, but rather in what happens to the viewer's understanding of Benegal's film when s/he "foreground[s]" or centers the female protagonist and/as subject.

7 Benegal's deployment of realist details and effects also incorporates something else that is of a somewhat different order, but which is tied to the project of nation building as well. While discussing the "realist *mise-en-scène* and narrative strategies" of "commercial" vs. "emergent art cinema," Vasudevan speaks of the attempt by "art cinema discourse" to "figure, programmatically … a spectator better suited to the perceived goals of an independent and socially dynamic India, but also of a realist

disposition and, more fundamentally, of a reality orientation" (1997: 153). Benegal's realist aesthetic, I think, is directed towards (if it does not altogether assume) such a spectator position.

8 In speaking of "the cinematic imaginings of a new society in the 1950s," Vasudevan's analysis focuses on the "uprootment" of characters "from their familial and social moorings" as the means through which identities could be both "complicate[d] ... and reformulate[d] ... in a socially and geographically extended imagining of nationhood" (1994: 93). The historical moment of *Ankur's* diegesis is virtually the same as the one Vasudevan's essay addresses, and the processes he tracks are, I think, comparable to those Benegal's film suggests in terms of his male protagonist. However, the spectator's simultaneous awareness of the real time of the film's making and viewing (i.e., the mid 1970s) provides an ironic, critical gloss underscoring the failure or postponement, as it were, of this pedagogical project through the continuing need to re-invoke it two and a half decades after formal independence.

9 Surya's boorishness towards his father's mistress and their son in the opening scene of the narrative proper retrospectively acquires morally and socially reprehensible overtones, whereas earlier in the viewing process, it can be seen as a species of adolescent misbehavior.

10 I am drawing here on Smith's tripartite breakdown of the "notion of identification" into "recognition, alignment, and allegiance" that together constitute for him "the structure of sympathy." "*Recognition*," he says, "describes the spectator's construction of character" and "requires the referential notion of the mimetic hypothesis";

> *alignment* describes the process by which spectators are placed in relation to characters in terms of access to their actions, and to what they know and feel ... for the way in which narratives may feed story information to the reader through the "lens" of a particular character.
>
> (Smith 1995)

"*[a]llegiance* pertains to the moral evaluation of characters by the spectators. Here we come closest to what is meant by 'identification'" (ibid: 73; 82–84). Murray's definition of *"allegiance"* is analogous to Vasduevan's understanding of identification constituting a position (or positions) the spectator "incorporates into [her/his] subjectivity." Through this incorporation, Vasudevan, quoting from La Planche and Pontalis, notes that:

> the subject assimilates an aspect, property or an attribute of the other and is transformed, wholly or partially, after the model the other provides. It is by means of a series of identifications that the personality is constituted and specified.
>
> (1996: 89)

11 Rajagopal considers the National Emergency of 1975–1977 crucial to "the formation of the new middle class in India," that, in its earlier, pre-Emergency "phase" was a product of, and "under the hegemony of the [Nehruvian] state," which "focus[ed] on economy as the crucial area of nation-building," its "developmental distinctions premised on an authoritarian relationship between state and the people." The post-Emergency "new middle class," on the other hand, was a product of a shift away from the Nehruvian state to one in which "categories of culture and community, and related forms of social distinction," acquired significance and, in a period marked by economic liberalization, this class "increasingly defines itself through cultural and consumerist forms of identity, and is less identified with the state" (2011: 1011, 1003). Rajagopal also notes that "Middle class in this [latter] instance was only partially a descriptive term. In addition it was a proxy for state strategy, and a heuristic to indicate its changing relationship with civil society" (2011: 1010). Benegal's first three films, we may recall, were made in the years leading up to or during the Emergency, while thematically referencing the immediate aftermath of India's independence;

arguably, then, they could be evoking both phases of the Indian middle class that Rajagopal examines.

12 As a way of accounting for a specific narrative device (which he labels "Fragment B" [fB]) that he says appears in many 1990s Hindi and Tamil films, Prasad points out how these films often segment the film's narrative into three sections comprised of two main sections he labels A and B, with a fragment of the B section excerpted to appear at the beginning of the film, which seems to anticipate the action of the B section, while haunting the film's main body as well (1998a: 222–223). Rajadhyaksha draws attention to this feature of Prasad's argument in order to show how fB's deployment, which constitutes an "interruptive" presence, also constitutes a "spectator-[cinematic] apparatus link": What fB and phenomena like it "attempt to establish to the spectator, in their existence beneath the narrative," he says, "is an explanation of the properties his/her gaze will possess in *this* particular assemblage of apparatus" (2009: 283–287). Arguably, the narrative fragment involving Lakshmi's prayer for a child, *before* the main action of the film begins, performs a role analogous to the one played by fB, in which case what Rajadhyaksha has to say about Prasad's understanding of its function, I suggest, applies to *Ankur* as well, revealing, to my mind, the possibility of more than one spectatorial position even in Prasad's terms if he were to view fB as a phenomenon not restricted to 1990s Indian cinema; the spectator position offered by fB, furthermore, does not quite cohere, as I will demonstrate, with the state's.

13 With regard to Lakshmi as the instrument of social transformation, I think that even though Benegal views the "seedling" of the title to refer to the small boy who throws the stone at the landlord's house (in his interview with Wahed Khan, for example, Benegal explicitly refers to "the small boy throwing the stone at the landlord's house [as] the seedling of the rebellion of the oppressed [against] the exploiters" [1988: 9]), the title could more appropriately be seen as referring to Lakshmi. In fact, my analysis makes a case for Lakshmi as the more appropriate instigator of such a rebellion thereby implying a disjuncture – and a productive contradiction that is also potentially gendered – between what Benegal claims about his film and what his film ends up representing.

14 When discussing different "modes of staging and narrating story events" in cinema, Vasudevan identifies the tableau as a form of representation that while "presum[ing] an underlying narrative structure," conveys the meanings this structure privileges emotionally and ideologically by rendering still or static, and enclosing as if within a frame (like " 'an illustrative painting' ") an event/scene and the participants and interactions between them that constitute it. A "visual summary" (to borrow Peter Brooks's phrase that Vasudevan quotes) of this narrative structure, "the tableau," says Vasudevan, "represents a moment caught between past and future" (2000c: 105–106).

15 At the conference organized by the Postcolonial Study Group at New York University on "Postcolonial Studies and the Hit of the Real" in March 2008, where I presented an early version of this argument, a participant in a session on Indian cinema suggested that the desire for a child was itself subversive during the Emergency years when the state was coercing lower-class and rural populations to restrict the number of children they had through enforced family planning.

16 In another tableau – also a didactic intrusion – Benegal orients the spectator to his ideological agenda by foregrounding, once again, a form of women's agency, this time, however, by mining Indian tradition. In this tableau, a man, gambling with Surya and a couple of other men on Diwali night, stakes his wife after losing all his money; not fully conscious of the implications of his action because intoxicated, he nevertheless views his right to stake his wife as self-evident by virtue of his (hyper)masculinity ("*main mard ki aulad hoon*" [literally, "I am the offspring of a man," but colloquially "I am a man's man"] he repeats several times). When the man who had won the bet turns up the following morning to claim his prize, he

is promptly disabused by the wife who questions, "who is he [the husband, that is] to stake me?" A virtual replay of an episode from *The Mahabharat* in which the oldest Pandava brother, Yudhishtar, bets on and loses Draupadi, who is the joint wife of the five Pandava brothers, the question above is a variation on the question posed by Draupadi to the messenger who comes to claim her: "Did Yudhishtar have a right to stake her if he had already become a slave?" Sunder Rajan points out how Alf Hiltebeitel "regards it as a *feminist* question since it challenges men to consider … their lordship over and 'ownership' of women in contexts of patriarchy." With regard to this question, Sunder Rajan also invokes the interpretation of philosopher B.K. Matilal, who characterizes it as the "sole and 'unique' unanswered dilemma in the epic" and proceeds to note that "'If Draupadi's questions were properly answered, it would have required a 'paradigm shift' in India's social thought'" (2000c: 337).

17 At the time the film was released, Lakshmi's liaison with Surya was, in fact, viewed as a transgression against social norms, especially middle class norms. Reviews often commented that they saw the film's assault on middle class morality as a sign of its subversion of the status quo (Dogra 1978: 15). Rumor has it that Benegal had wanted to cast Waheeda Rehman, a well-known actress highly regarded for her talent, as Lakshmi. She turned down the role, however, because she was concerned about the social respectability of playing a character involved in an extra-marital liaison. In his interview with van der Heide, Benegal comments on the liaison in the following way: agreeing with van der Heide that the film does not see it in "moralistic terms," he notes that it is nevertheless "seen in moral terms that she too has a right as a human being. She [Lakshmi] has the right to a full life" (2006: 61; see also 58).

18 This scene raises some very interesting questions regarding "female spectatorship" by placing Lakshmi at a window from which she looks (much as a movie spectator would at a screen) at the scene of the dead runaway wife being carried to her cremation (see Williams, C. 2000: 46).

19 In this scene, after a long night of drinking, and while Surya lies passed out, Lakshmi tucks him in and stands by the bed looking at him. As she moves around, she displays a kind of confidence that suggests the ease with which she has come to inhabit what thus far has been Surya's space.

20 In his review of *Ankur*, Pym notes:

> When Lakshmi passionately denounces Surya's cruelty and so breaks the accepted rules of deference and submission in another hierarchical country community, one is left … with the implication that nothing will ever be the same for these people, that for the first time they are faced with the possibility of positive change.
>
> (1976: 47)

21 After reading my analysis of *Ankur*, Rashmi Sawhney, who teaches film studies at Dublin Institute of Technology, suggested that the "moment of rupture" *Ankur* offers is "encapsulated within Lakshmi's [unborn] child," whose birth by virtue of "ly[ing] outside the film's text" signals potentiality. Wondering whether this child would be a girl or a boy, Rashmi added that this would "make such a difference in the Indian context." In the same spirit she interrogated Benegal's choice of a boy for throwing the stone at the *zamindar's* house: "Would it have been too radical for a girl to throw that defining (defying) stone?" she asked (personal communication, May 9, 2009).

22 Over the past two decades, several richly complex accounts have addressed Gandhi's signal contribution in mobilizing women for, and empowering them through, their participation in the anti-colonial nationalist struggle. Virtually all these accounts attend to his views on sexuality – especially female sexuality – as it pertains to their participation. Many, though not all, regard Gandhi's views as extremely problematic or debilitating for women. Among those who do, see particularly, Gabriel 2004; Katrak 1991; and Patel 1988; for those who are less critical about his views – regard

them positively or seek to balance the negative resonances with the positive ones – see Forbes 1988, Fox 1996, and Kishwar 1985.

23 Prasad makes much of the text that precedes the film proper, identifying the historical moment of the narrative to unfold as "1945" and its location as "in a feudal state." He considers it a "device of distantiation that enables the spectator to gain access to the fascination and power of the spectacle of feudal oppression and rebellion without being reminded of its proximity in time and space" (1998a: 197). Vasudevan makes a related point but with respect to New Cinema in general: even though "atrocities are located with the dominant group and low castes are championed as victims in the politically correct fashion … backward rural society seems to emerge in a discomfiting way as a space inhabited only by the bestial or the submissive" (2000b: 33–34, n. 45). Benegal, however, has noted, on several occasions that "the reference to a feudal state was really imposed by censors" (van der Heide 2006: 68). Vasudev alludes to the many difficulties *Nishant* ran into with the censors (1976: 176–177), as does Benegal in his interview with van der Heide. More to the point, in the contemporaneous (with the film) interview with Narvekar, already alluded to earlier, Benegal insists on the ongoing relevance of a critique of feudalism in as much as its ideological structures continue to affect the place of women especially within even "modern" nuclear family structures (1976: 7, 15).

24 Visweswaran is right, when considering the "gendering of subalternity" to "distinguish between the figure of 'woman' as subaltern and the question of subaltern women." For:

> women become women not only in relation to men, but also in opposition to other women. Thus, the subject position of the middle-class or elite … "woman" must be counterposed to that of subaltern women. The gendered relation with subalternity means that with regard to the nominal male subject of nationalist ideology, the figure of the woman is subaltern; with regard to subaltern women, the recuperated middle-class woman as nationalist subject certainly is not.
>
> (1996: 87)

25 Richman (1992a) edited *Many Rāmāyaṇas: The Diversity of a Narrative Tradition in South Asia*, which provides a rich resource for examining multiple and alternative re-tellings of this epic, each cued to specific historical, political, and social imperatives.

26 The film also juxtaposes scenes that move the narrative along, giving the viewer access to information s/he needs in order to follow the preceding or succeeding story line. Thus, for example, after the priest's discovery of the loss of the temple jewels and of a gold chain lying close to where they were hidden, the camera cuts to the youngest brother Vishwam's wife Rukmini's discovery of the loss of his gold chain, which, then, places him at the scene, and thereby signals that he is a potential perpetrator of the crime. Later we discover that it was his brothers who incited the theft of the jewels to pay off gambling debts.

27 This swerve or re-routing of the narrative emphasis (and interest) of the opening scenes in *Nishant* is analogous to the method Benegal adopts in *Ankur*, where the film's initial focus on Surya is displaced by its focus on Lakshmi's narrative of development; this re-routing, furthermore, carries some of the same freight as in *Ankur*, centering the female protagonist's narrative as the one that is significant.

28 In "The Mutilation of Surpanakha," Erndl accounts for her own fascination with Surpanakha, and her "feeling [of] both sympathy for [Surpanakha's] plight and admiration for her forthrightness and independence," as stemming from her assessment that Surpanakha, like Kaikeyi, "had gotten a raw deal in a world where rules are made by men" (1992: 68). The mutilation of Surpanakha, she says, constitutes not only a crux in the narrative, setting in motion the "chain of events" that starts with Ravana's abduction of Sita, but is also central "from an ethical point of view, for it sheds light

on Rama's character and on attitudes towards female sexuality in Indian culture" about which "the authors and commentators of various *Rāmāyaṇas*" reflect "a deep ambivalence" (1992: 67–68). Richman suggests that Surpanakha, as a woman who roams the forest independent of male protection and who openly expresses her sexual interest in Rama, also functions as the alter ego that haunts those representations of Sita emphasizing her chastity and subservience as constitutive of the ideal of Indian womanhood in the hegemonic version of *Ramayana* (1992b: 10).

29 Hansen notes how Nehru considered Sita and Savitri, construed as exemplars of chastity and subservience, very problematic role models for Indian women:

> In a speech in 1928, he said, "We hear a good deal about Sita and Savitri. They are revered names in India and rightly so, but I have a feeling that these echoes from the past are raised chiefly to hide our present deficiencies and prevent us from attacking the root cause of women's degradation in India today."
>
> (1988: 29)

Arguably, Benegal's recourse to alternative renditions of Sita can be construed as an implicit attempt to address this problem.

30 If the schoolmaster's non-verbal injunction to Sushila to hide herself from the brothers' prurient gaze parallels, as I think it does, the *Lakshmana rekha* – "a magical line [drawn by Lakshmana to] protect Sita" – then the film's refusal to view Sushila's resistance to it as a transgression, as, for instance, it is in the case of Sita, is significant. And this despite the fact that Sushila's abduction, like Sita's, seems to follow from making herself visible to those entities who pose a threat to her safety. A "tremendously popular episode" that is routinely part of annual Ramlila plays, this episode dealing with the *Lakshmana rekha*, U. Chakravarty tells us, was introduced into the *Ramayana* in medieval times by Tulsidas, his many versions of the epic being composed at a time, as he believed, of crisis, when Hindu society's "norms and values were under threat of complete collapse." "In this situation," Chakravarty adds, "Tulsidas was advocating the dictum that if women remained within the bounds set for them they would be safe – if they stepped out nothing would save them" (1983: 73).

31 Pochamma's "realism" is mirrored in the advice the schoolmaster receives from the various agents of state and civil society, whose job it is to see justice done, when he seeks their help to recover his wife from the feudal landlords. As with the priest and the police earlier, despite having alternative bases for their authority, all these agents uncritically accede to the feudal masters' overriding power, viewing challenges against it as a transgression against the status quo whose stability they want to protect.

32 My research assistant, Max Wolcott, reminded me that Sushila seems to respond in interesting ways to the prospect of violence, which she associates with masculinity. For example, in a scene after her chance encounter with her husband, Vishwam, who is slightly drunk and playing with a whip as he sits on the swing outside, comes to her room bearing the whip; Sushila comes to him of her own accord for the first time, almost as if she is doing so in response to the latent violence he exhibits.

33 As if to underscore that the space for the kind of sexual emancipation for women Benegal endorses is not available even now, Benegal (in the interview with S. Chatterjee) ties the difficulties he experienced securing funding to make *Ankur* with the "difficulty" the "mainstream [Indian film] industry" had with a film that "broke Hindi cinema's female stereotype too violently. Here was a married woman who has a strong moral base but sleeps with another man and bears his child." In *Nishant*, he continues, "the woman is attracted to her abductor.… The industry could not have taken kindly to that sort of characterization" (2003–2004: 23–24). It should be noted, however, that the social space not available for such women in contemporary India is not the same as that depicted by the mainstream Hindi film industry, whose conservatism is notorious.

34 With regard to the ongoing presence of feudal structures and mentality, Benegal, in his interview with S. Chatterjee, notes how "India has the longest history of feudalism,"

even "the relationship of the government and the people is feudal to this day." Feudalism persists, he says, because it "ensures stability … allows the caste system to carry on." However, whereas in the interview he refuses to take a position on it – "I am not saying it is good or bad" – his films are unequivocal about the damage and destruction, exploitation, and oppression that accrue from feudal structures, even though he is not unequivocal about the means to bring it to an end (2003–2004: 24–25).

2 "Performing wom[e]n": the "*Nachne-Ganewalis*" of *Bhumika*, *Mandi*, and *Sardari Begum*

1 Analyzing the "courtesan film genre" in Hindi cinema, within which she incorporates both *Bhumika* and *Mandi*, S. Chakravarty notes:

> Because the figure of the courtesan lends itself to a whole range of interpretation, it is richly invested with allegorical possibilities. Skirting the boundaries of the legitimate and illegitimate, an intricate blend of Hindu and Muslim social graces, this ambiguous icon of Indian womanhood and female power-cum-vulnerability serves as an analog of a national palimpsest inscribed with contradictory social meanings.… Her identity, a play upon impersonation, the figure of the prostitute allows the culture to probe some of its own assumptions regarding sexuality, social mores, and human growth.
>
> (Chakravarty 1993)

She adds: "As both threatened and threatening icon of cultural (in)difference, the figure of the courtesan allows us to explore the psychosexual dimension of the Indian national imaginary" (ibid.: 270, 272). On a more general register, and addressing particularly the subaltern urban figure of the prostitute, Mufti suggests we "read" her as a "re-inscription of what, to borrow Sandhya Shetty's words, is a conventional and tenacious 'moment in the Indian nationalist discourse's production of woman: the allegorical figuration of nation as mother.'" The figure of the prostitute is, thus, "an ironic rewriting of this pervasive familial (and atemporal) semiotic of nationalism that makes it available for historical interrogation" (2007: 179).

2 Although this chapter presents courtesans as casualties, particularly, of nationalist efforts at self-definition, British colonialism, as the scholarship invoked in this chapter makes clear, played a prominent (indeed, originary) role in the displacement and denigration of courtesans and courtesan culture. Colonial denigration was thereafter built into the reformist efforts the nationalists undertook in their own attempt to excise performing women from the (narrative of the) nation they sought to construct.

3 For arguments regarding the former, see Sangari and Vaid 1990b; Banerjee 1990; Chatterjee, P. 1993; Singh 2007; for arguments regarding the latter, see Bakhle 2005; Moro 2004; Peterson and Soneji 2008; Subramanian 2008; and Qureshi 2006. The "middle class" is at least as much an allegorical figuration of certain tendencies in these discussions as it is an empirical category of analysis (see Chapter 1, note 11).

4 In her study of the *nautanki* theatre of North India, Hansen cites Armstrong and Tennenhouse's *Ideology of Conduct* to note the constitutive role the middle classes play across different cultures with regard to the:

> creat[ion] and regulat[ion] of the concept of "desirable" women. Noting that the terms of desire change from one age to the next, [Armstrong and Tennenhouse] suggest "that the redefinition of the female was a crucial feature of the hegemony that brought the middle classes into power."
>
> (Hansen 1992)

Moreover, "If 'the struggle to represent ideal female behavior indeed accompanied the struggle of an emergent middle class,'" Hansen adds:

then changes in the representation of women would be expected to accompany more extensive historical changes … The representation of woman as public entertainer and locus of male desire no longer served the interests of the [nationalist] English educated elite, which put in her place the Indian equivalent of the Victorian domestic angel,… the good housewife.

(Ibid.: 255–256)

5 "The term devadasi," Srinivasan notes, "refers to the class of women who through various ceremonies of 'marriage' dedicated themselves to the deities of temples and other ritual objects" (1988: 175). Among the "markers of devadasi identity," Soneji includes "sing[ing] and danc[ing] in public; …ritual duties in temples; …and bless[ing] homes during auspicious occasions" (2000: 31). Although not permitted to marry, a *devadasi* was free to have sex, bear children, "advertis[ing] in a perfectly open and public manner her availability for sexual liaisons with a proper patron and protector"; indeed, it was a "symbol of social prestige and privilege to maintain her" (Srinivasan 1988: 180). Feldman and Gordon include *devadasis* in the category of "courtesans" – described as "highly educated, creative and skilled women – whose "many linguistic and cultural variants" also include "the Indian *tawaif, ganika,… and baiji*" (2006: 5).

6 The exclusion of performing women was also actively sought because "reformers like Mandlik Kabraji," Bakhle notes:

viewed music as an acceptable means by which to bring respectable women out of seclusion and more squarely into battle with the forces that threatened their marriages. Kabraji wanted women to embrace the ideal of companionate marriage, an ideal under threat from the prostitutes and courtesans he perceived as having commandeered the knowledge of music.

(2005: 71)

7 A range of meanings accrued to the term "home" in nationalist ideology (as it confronted and negotiated the contradictions produced by colonialism) where "home" was opposed to "the world," setting in motion a series of related oppositions that came to define what P. Chatterjee calls "the nationalist resolution of the women's question," since all of them were organized around a foundational opposition that situated "women" within the "home" and "men" in the "world:" "inner" vs. "outer"; "spiritual" vs. "material"; "pure[ly] Indian" vs. "contaminated by colonialism" and so on (1990: 237–240). "Extending Chatterjee's argument," Visweswaran avers that "the nationalist resolution of the woman question must be seen not only as a strategy for contesting colonial hegemony, but as a strategy for the containment of women's agency," with this agency located within the home "itself subjected to a kind of silencing"(1996: 86).

8 The film often shows her running away from home: the first time the viewer sees her doing so – driving away in a cab, having just left her husband, mother, and daughter behind, after a scene of domestic violence involving her husband – she has a flashback about running away as a child. (On yet another occasion – also presented in flashback – she runs away after a violent altercation with her mother.) In the argument that precedes this scene – of her driving away in a cab – Keshav points out to their distraught daughter that this is not the first time she has tried to run away and characterizes Usha's various attempts at running away as a species of drama/melodramatic acting.

9 Even though her mother is married, the film suggests that she nevertheless inhabits (as does Usha as her daughter) a non-normative, loosely defined household in as much as her alcoholic husband has moved into his wife's house and does not provide material or other means of support for its running – these being provided by Keshav instead, who is not a relative, and thus not "organically" connected to the household. The film also suggests that Keshav is her mother's lover. On her father's death, Keshav puts

Usha to work, living off her earnings both before and after marrying her, and thereby continuing to violate those attributes that are seen to define a normative home.

10 In her critical history of the classicization of Indian music as a participant in, and contributor to, national self-definition, Bakhle recounts the career of Hirabai Barodekar, some of whose elements resonate with Usha's efforts to transform herself via a change in her class- and caste-belonging: "Hirabai's life," says Bakhle, "can be characterized as a movement from scandal to respectability couched in middle-class terms. Her grandmother Hirabai Govekar, after whom she was named, was a *baiji*. Her mother, Tarabai, had run away with a Muslim musician." "In stark contrast," Hirabai "became the icon of Marathi, married, middle-class women who pursued her career in the music world without compromising hearth and home." But this could be done only by "tak[ing] over and sidelin[ing]" her "parent's histories" (2005: 243). (The beginning of Hirabai's career, three decades into the twentieth century [Bakhle 2005: 216] conforms with that of Hansa Wadkar's.) Interestingly, as Benegal told me, Hirabai Barodekar's younger step-sister, Saraswati Rane, provides the playback voice for Usha's grandmother in *Bhumika* (February 16, 2011). "In [her] Search [for] Begum Akhtar," Qureshi documents an analogous instance, the transformation of a courtesan singer into a national icon by remarking on her transition, first, from courtesan singer to respectable married woman – a transition premised on an absolute absence of "interaction with her maternal family and the milieu they represented," and thereafter by refusing to perform locally in Lucknow where her husband's family was based, "she eliminated any professional contact with musicians" who would have tied her back to her life as a courtesan (2001: 118).

11 To represent Usha's continuing naiveté regarding her relationships with various men, the film explicitly draws attention to Kale's autocratic behavior as he and Usha travel the long driveway to his mansion. Usha has just found out that Kale is already married and asks him why he did not tell her that, and also that he already had a son, earlier. Kale responds brusquely that he felt no need to do so and that Usha is free to return to her prior life in Bombay if these constitute a problem for her. Usha demurs, almost willfully refusing to consider what Kale's deliberate silence (thus far) on the subject of his marriage seems to presage about her future relationship with him.

12 That, despite all that has happened to her and the "lessons" she has learned, middle-class "respectability" continues to exert its pull on Usha is made apparent through Usha's shocked, even despairing, response to her daughter's news about her pregnancy, until, that is, the daughter reassures her that she is now married, and her child will be a product of a legitimate, conjugal relationship.

13 On the other hand, Mazumdar, who is critical of what she takes to be Benegal's emphasis on the "individual," the "personal," and the "private" as an elision of the "array of social categories," particularly "class (and in the context of India caste)" as these impinge upon "a woman's gender identity," feels that:

> in *Bhoomika* ... Benegal had the golden opportunity to critique the gaze of the cinematic apparatus but chose not to. As an actress, Hansa was continuously dancing and acting on the screen for a camera, yet we only see her dancing and acting on screen for the audience, at no point does Benegal present her through the lens. Having confined himself to a rigidly realist framework, Benegal refuses to draw any attention to the construction of Hansa's personality and character by the cinematic apparatus, for fear of breaking the illusion of "reality."
>
> (1991: WS-81; WS-84)

I find Mazumdar's easy conflation of Urvashi with Hansa, disregarding the fact that the film is an adaptation, problematic; I find her similarly careless about visual details in these scenes. For those familiar with Mazumdar's analysis, mine provides a counter argument – a quite different reading of some of the same scenes and their details.

14 To Behroz Gandhi's query about his use of flashbacks that reconstruct "old Indian cinema," Benegal responds:

> it did two things for me. Firstly, of course, it had a certain nostalgic implication in terms of Indian cinema, its development and its various genres.... For the audience, I think it dealt with an aspect of the way the Indian woman has been treated on the Indian screen.
>
> (1979: 32)

15 As if to hammer this point home, the film depicts Usha looking at herself in a mirror as the flashback reprising her performance of these roles begins. On Benegal's reference to Sita and Savitri, see note 29 in Chapter 1.

16 Kidwai's unpublished essay on "the *tawaif* in Urdu/Hindi Cinema" speaks particularly to "the evidence films provide regarding the history of *tawaifs*, once *kothas* and *mehfils* declined as the main performing spaces for these women" (Kidwai n.d.: 1) I thank Kidwai for making this manuscript available to me to consult.

17 Benegal's use of a Kirana *gharana* singer as the singing voice for the grandmother (van der Heide 2006: 90) is significant. For the "classicization" of music to make it an appropriately modern instrument of national culture entailed the bypassing or transformation of *gharana* musicians, who were also, instructively, mostly Muslims (Bakhle 2005: 6–8; Moro 2004: 193; Qureshi 1991: 161–162).

18 The figure of the mother in *Bhumika*, not least because it is mediated through Usha's resentments and hostility, appears unsympathetic. Extending to *Bhumika* Mufti's and Shetty's assessment (see note 1) of the "figure" of the prostitute as a "re-inscription of ... 'nationalist discourse's production of woman: the allegorical figuration of nation as mother,'" we can translate Usha's unsympathetic/critical view of her mother as continuous with a critical view of the nation she (the mother) allegorizes – a not entirely far-fetched analogy given the mother's investment in respectability that is so central to the national self-definition of middle-class ideology. S. Chakravarty, who suggests that Benegal's *Bhumika* and *Mandi* "draw upon and problematize the conventions of the courtesan film," notes that, "those [conventions] that portray her as the sacrificing mother are closest to Bombay film melodrama and the least ambiguous in terms of representational strategies" (1993: 293).

19 In his analysis of the "performative recollections" undertaken by "*devadasi* women in Telugu-speaking South India," for example, Soneji views "acts of memory" – like the ones these flashbacks represent – as effective at the level of individual identity"(even though they may not be "socially effective") because:

> they keep the matrifocal home of these women intact; they ensure that the *devadasis* remember who they are and from where they have come. Such recollections confer positive self-worth and enable the *devadasis* to retain and express some sense of their fractured identities.
>
> (Soneji 2000)

Re-membering, then, constitutes "a process that 'remakes the self,' and reconstructs identity from scattered fragments and remembrances, knowledge, and experience" (2000: 44).

20 Analogously, regarding the marginality of the courtesans within hegemonic social arrangements (and the resistant or dissident positionality that marginality is almost always seen to represent in postcolonial and feminist theories), Gordon and Feldman note that the courtesans':

> is a complex marginality in which their close consort with those at the centers of power allows them to slide in and out of agency, control, and influence.... Dialectically speaking, the rigid hierarchies of class and gender that allow courtesans to flourish make them powerful because they successfully challenge the delineations

> that keep received social structures in place; but those same social structures also deny courtesans full access to privileges guarded at the very highest strata of society. In all these ways, courtesans and their arts are woven into a dynamic of privilege and constraint that forces a rethinking of the gendering of power.
>
> (2006: 6)

21 S. Chakravarty, for instance, notes that:

> the courtesan ... is one of the most enigmatic figures to haunt the margins of Indian cultural consciousness ... at once celebrated and shunned, used and abused, praised and condemned. Socially decentered, she is yet the object of respect and admiration because of her artistic training and musical accomplishments.... A bazaar entertainer, she is paradoxically the repository of a vanished age and lost way of life.
>
> (1993: 269–270)

22 Visually, one of the ways in which the film establishes this range of reference quickly and efficiently is by pairing scenes whose actions mimic each other even though they are located in quite distinct, ostensibly opposing, social spaces. Thus, for example, the film opens with a scene in which Gupta is negotiating with the owner of the land he wants to acquire. The owner begins by asking for 2 lakhs (Rs.200,0000); when Gupta asks why this precise sum rather than any other, the owner confesses that it is the sum he must pay for his daughter's dowry; Gupta balks, so the owner reduces it to Rs.150,000 then Rs.100,000; as Gupta continues to bargain and negotiate the price down, they finally settle for Rs.35,000 plus smaller additional amounts that the landowner tacks on to the by now much reduced amount. A similar encounter and conversation takes place between Rukminibai and Gupta in the *kotha* when Gupta is trying to persuade her to move from the building that houses the brothel, which he now owns, except that Rukminibai negotiates the amount upwards, not down. The back and forth shots of each combatant, with the camera focusing on one and then the other is identical in both scenes as are the verbal equivalent of offer/counter-offer. In each case, Gupta is the winner, even though Rukminibai thinks she has outsmarted him, much as the landowner of the opening scenes thinks he has managed to squeeze Gupta for the extra sums he negotiates.

23 One of the opening scenes establishes the haggling that goes on *inside* the *kotha* when Phoolmani is brought in after having been kidnapped: Nadira, one of the women in the brothel tells Rukminibai to offer a considerably lower sum to the man who has brought her in as Phoolmani is as yet untried ("can she sing?" she asks) and not knowledgeable about the ways of the *kotha*. Later when Phoolmani is found to be deaf-mute, Nadira regrets not having urged an even lower amount.

24 It seems strange to invoke the term performance, in a chapter on performing women, as something marked by insincerity or as a falsehood as seems to be meant in my comments above. (Perhaps the word "theatrical" would be more accurate, although it does not necessarily address the problem.) For the most part, performance has a different resonance in this chapter – primarily identified as it is with the deployment of aesthetically valuable skills and attributes. Although those skills and attributes are not entirely absent in these examples from *Mandi*, what is being highlighted as well is performance as involving a kind of mendacity, especially with respect to Shantidevi, who, incidentally, is not a performing woman.

25 One of the arguments in support of her claim about courtesans is that their art is centuries old and traditional, not new fangled and modern; she advises one of the guests, who has requested something modern, to go to the cinema instead. This conversation invokes terms that were in circulation in the early years of independence with respect to the definition of national art: Perterson and Soneji note that:

> in the new bourgeois formulation, the high art of the nation had to be simultaneously traditional and modern, an ideal that the system, repertoire and practices of

> hereditary and other traditional performers, including Brahmins, simply could not fit. From the reformist/revivalist perspective, the dance and music of hereditary and other traditional communities were secret, idiosyncratic, heterogeneous, unscientific, non-canonical, hybrid, vernacular and non-modern. They were transmitted and performed through oral, caste-based, and practice-centered processes. The new classical arts, on the other hand, would be based on "ancient" yet suitably reformed, modernized textual and theoretical canons and the performers would be modern professionals untainted by caste associations and non-scientific methods.... A major outcome of the re-invention of a classical tradition would be the displacement of the hereditary performers and the dispersal of their communities and knowledge bases.
>
> (Peterson and Soneji 2008: 7; see also, Bakhle 2005: 3–6; Srinivasan, A. 1989: 197–198; Rao, V. 1996: 296–305)

26 Singh mentions colonialist-nationalist initiatives that undermined these women's power base – "the anti-nautch campaign that culminated in 1947 in the outlawing of temple dancing and the prohibition on dedicating women as *devadasis* in south India." "Female performers," she adds, "were stigmatized as 'prostitutes'" (2007: 94; see also Srinivasan 1989; Soneji and Peterson 2008 and Soneji 2000). Along similar lines, Qureshi mentions the "ban on salons [run by courtesans to conduct their business] enforced by police raids"; the abolishing of princely states, which had served as these courtesans' primary patrons; and the ban instituted by "All India Radio, which had consciously taken over musical patronage from the princes," against "all (women) performers 'whose private life is a public scandal'" (2006: 312).

27 Rukminibai is represented as a surrogate mother figure to Zeenat, particularly and, more generally, to the other women of the *kotha* – a representation that raises all sorts of interesting issues about the allegorical figuration of nation as mother, on which see especially Mufti's claim regarding the "figure of prostitute" as "an ironic rewriting of this pervasive familial (and atemporal) semiotic of nationalism" (2007: 179).

28 Oldenberg views the *kotha* as a site where women "unlearn" the ideological lessons of being a "normal" woman: "The problem, according to Rasulan [one of the courtesans Oldenberg interviewed], was to forget the expectations inherent in the meaning of the word *aurat*, or woman, as it obtained in larger society." Oldenberg then goes on to add, that the "self-affirming ethos of the *kotha*" enables a "radically different socialization process and [provides access to] the lifestyle that gives them the liberation they desire, without jerking the reflexive muscle of a repressive system" (1990: 270–271; 277).

29 Zeenat here seems to be "repeating" the actions of Usha in *Bhumika*, and with Smita Patil paying both roles, the similarity seems almost deliberate. For example, just prior to her escape with Sushil, a *fakir* who lives in proximity to the brothel advises her to "fly away," much like he has sought to free Rukminibai's caged bird to urge it to fly away. "Will it [the bird] be able to live outside the cage?" Zeenat asks him, to which the *fakir* replies, "If it stays in the cage, then too it will die. Perhaps in the act of flying it will discover itself." An obviously symbolic moment, the referent for the "caged bird" is clearly Zeenat herself, whose flight the *fakir* seems to be staging as a flight towards self-discovery.

30 On an earlier occasion, when soon after the *kotha*'s relocation Rukminibai had been enjoined by a similarly disembodied voice to pray to Baba Kharak Shah, she was rewarded with the girl-child born to Kamli and the sudden and unexpected rise in the *kotha*'s business fortunes.

31 The ending also puts into perspective Rukminibai's earlier protectiveness towards Phoolmani, especially given that the only figure she is protective of earlier is Zeenat.

32 Khalid Mohamed, a film critic and former editor of the Indian film magazine *Filmfare*, who has often negatively evaluated Benegal's films, wrote a short story about

his aunt that "moved" Benegal and prodded him to make it into a film, *Mammo*; subsequently Mohamed wrote two more, one about a distant aunt and the other about his mother, both of which Benegal also made into films – *Sardari Begum* and *Zubeida* respectively (van der Heide 2006: 172).

33 About *bol banāv thumri*, du Perron notes that it derives from "*bol banānā* (using phrases extracted from the text as vehicle for melodic improvisation). Short phrases are repeated many times, with a view to emphasizing a different shade of emotional meaning with each repetition." In *bandish thumri*, on the other hand, "as the name suggests, compositions tend to be 'bound': there is little space for melodic elaborations, and improvisations are primarily rhythmic, suitable to dance. The texts are usually narrative in nature, providing the framework for the story-telling in dance performance" (2002: 178).

34 In *Sardari Begum*, Iddanbai and Sardari use the *bol banāv* style of singing *thumri*, for the most part, though on at least one occasion, when Sadiq sees her for the first time, Sardari performs in a style akin to that of a *bandish thumri*.

35 Du Perron notes *thumri*'s integral connection with courtesans, the first-person female narrative voice, and the form's "emphasis on emotional expression" as significant reasons for considering it an instance of "female voice," even though she concedes that "the gendering of a genre is likely to reflect social preconceptions and prejudices as to what constitutes masculinity and femininity, incorporating a hierarchical perspective" (2002: 173). For her "the female voice of *thumrī*" is, almost by definition, "not an empowered woman's voice" because it "locates women's expression of feeling in the realm of excitement for men" (2002: 192).

36 Sardari does marry Sadiq for ostensibly conventional reasons, like providing the child she is expecting from Hemraj with a father. At the same time, the film suggests that she marries Sadiq because she finds Hemraj's attempts to control her movements constricting, especially his desire to keep her confined to small-town Agra for his own pleasure, whereas Sadiq promises to take her to Delhi to expose her remarkable talent to a wider, more cosmopolitan audience. Later she has no difficulty separating herself from Sadiq either and when another admirer, Sen, wants to marry her, she explicitly remarks on her inability or refusal to adhere to qualities a typical Indian wife is supposed to embody when she turns down his proposal of marriage ("*Main pativrata nahin ban saktī*" ["I cannot become a devoted/subservient/loyal wife"]).

37 The film establishes their similarity fairly quickly. When Tehzeeb's father visits her to explain why he had never told her about Sardari's connection with their family, Tehzeeb's boss, with whom she is involved in an extra-marital relationship, turns up to confirm an assignment on which Tehzeeb is supposed to accompany him. The father articulates his disapproval of this unconventional relationship in harsh and disparaging terms very similar to those he uses to characterize Sardari's relationship with her patron Hemraj. The brother's disapproval also mimics Sardari's (and his) father's disapproval of Sardari when the father discovers that Sardari has been singing in *mehfils* (intimate salon gatherings).

38 According to her daughter, Sakina, not only does she give up her family to pursue her music, she is not willing to be a mother either. In one scene where the daughter registers her disagreements with Sardari, she explicitly alludes to the latter's refusal to be seen as her mother ("You have never allowed me to call you 'mother,'" she cries out, adding, "because that would have revealed your age.")

39 Gordon and Feldman point out that: "Courtesans in northern India have typically lacked reference to a wider kin and community – a critical and fascinating lack within a society so strongly marked by the caste system" (2006: 11). Their implication is that courtesans therefore build their own community and networks of solidarity or belonging through affiliative links with other members of the *kotha* who come to stand in for their family. One could argue that in her death, Sardari has come to find such a member in her niece, who while being a member of her family and thus representing

an instance of a filiative relationship, actually exemplifies an affiliative relationship in as much as she (the niece) *affiliates* – that is chooses, to link herself with her aunt – thereby establishing as well, and figuratively speaking, a lineage that proceeds along "matrilineal" lines – also a feature of courtesan culture.

40 Much later, in her interview with the *maulvi*, Tehzeeb asks about and finds out that Sardari was in some ways "responsible" for the communal disturbance because she helped arrange a marriage between a Hindu boy and a Muslim girl. The outrage that followed this incident spilled over into the riot. So, yes, the *maulvi* concedes, despite being uninterested in politics, Sardari inadvertently started the riot.

41 Such a strategy, I want to suggest, also enables Benegal to accurately track the dialectic of empowerment and disempowerment that informs women's positions, more generally, and those of the courtesans (and her art), more particularly, in their search for autonomy.

42 This is a reference to Jabbar's efforts to persuade Sardari to send Sakina to a "convent" like the one Tehzeeb is being sent to. Sardari demurs by saying the "madrassa" is quite alright for someone like Sakina; she is, after all, being trained to become a singer like her mother by her mother. Sakina, on the other hand, views Sardari's refusal to educate her in a convent as an effort on her part to repress any critical consciousness Sakina might develop.

43 This view, incidentally, is also articulated by Sardari's teacher, Iddanbai: When Sardari describes Hemraj as a connoisseur of music, Iddanbai disabuses her by noting that he is more a connoisseur of "beautiful women," thereby also implicitly cautioning Sardari about any involvement with him.

44 On this, see note 10, where I invoke both Bakhle on Hirabai Barodekar's and Qureshi on Begum Akhtar's transformation into national icons by virtue of certain exclusions, primarily of discordant, socially unconventional, parts of their early family histories, including not least their parentage. Sen's desire to exclude Sakina, or uncouple Sardari from her smacks of something similar, for without her, it seems, Sardari can be passed off as a respectable woman.

45 Sadiq and Sen's reminiscences are mobilized much like Jabbar's, the *sarangi* player's and Sakina's are – not only to piece together different strands in Sardari's story, but also to present Sardari's narrative from different perspectives, which are inflected by each recollector's own interests. Sadiq (who introduces Sardari to Sen) and Sen remember the same event – in this instance, when Sadiq voluntarily left or was forced to leave Sardari's house and, presumably, their marriage – differently. But since both are interested parties, the viewer, in the absence of a less interested account, has to negotiate the differences in their accounts, rather than simply grant credence to one over the other. Thus, whereas in Sen's reminiscence Sadiq comes through as a thorough cad, in his own (and in Sakina's), this is not quite the case.

3 Fictional engagements with (national) history: *Junoon*, *Mammo*, and *Trikaal*

1 Speaking of the mutually sustaining relationship between history and realism, Rosen finds that "the notoriously realist impulse of Bazin's film theory is itself congruent with a historicizing cast of mind"; "different modes of writing history often imply," he adds, "different ways of conceiving of or understanding history.... However, there is one constant: historiography always purports to be referential. That is, the construction that is history is necessarily to be read against some standard of the real" (Rosen 2004: 6; see also Nowell-Smith 1990: 163–164).

2 In a more general vein, Nowell-Smith invokes Gramsci's remarks:

> the starting point of critical elaboration is the consciousness of what one really is, and is "knowing thyself" as a product of the historical process to date, which has

> deposited in you an infinity of traces, without leaving an inventory. Such an inventory must, therefore, be made at the outset.
>
> (1990: 169)

This is in order to urge a "return to history – of historicity" so as to enable individuals and collective entities to make sense of the "complex and incoherent ways" in which they are "formed by [and acquire] their culture" (ibid.).

3 Whereas India's takeover of Goa from the Portuguese seldom earns more than a few sentences in dominant histories of the nation, the horrendous violence that accompanied the Partition of South Asia (and which underwrote the founding of the new nations of India and Pakistan), as many recent counter-analyses of Partition make clear, has been actively repressed so that the dominant nationalist narratives can celebrate the birth of the two nations and disregard the brutalities through which they were brought into being. And while some elements of nationalist historiography have sought to construct the 1857 uprising as a national revolt, the event itself has, since its inception, been subjected to an extensive range of diverse and contradictory interpretations, including, not least, its colonial construction as a mutiny. Insofar as until 1944, most accounts of this uprising were, says Guttman, "by pro-British historians, with the Indian perspectives actively repressed … 1857 seems to cry out for national revision" (2003: 276). On the other hand, while acknowledging that the 1857 "rebellion had a genuinely popular basis as well as wide reach," Ramachandra Guha, much like Nehru before him, finds that the:

> uprising was underpinned neither by a sense of a common nationality nor by the modern idea of freedom … it would not have created a new Indian nation-state. Rather, it would have led to the restoration of the pre-colonial political order.
>
> (2011: 47–48).

4 "'Eurasian' was the term most commonly used in the nineteenth century to denote mixed race couples," says Paxton, whereas "'Anglo-Indian' … refer[red] to British residents in India or to British-Indian political relations" (1999: 274; note 8); in the twentieth-century, the term "Anglo-Indian" replaced the term "Eurasian"; Benegal uses the term "Anglo-Indian."

5 Regarding the representation of Muslims – the largest minority among other minority communities in India – in popular Hindi cinema, S. Chakravarty observes that:

> The Bombay film has not so much addressed the Hindu-Muslim relationship as sublimated it by displacing it onto the canvas of history … the historical film [focusing, especially, on the Mughal period] has been the privileged site of the elaboration of Muslim sensibility.… Moreover, the nationalist ideology of historical synthesis found an effective though hardly unproblematic milieu in the Mughal period.
>
> (1993:165–166)

Affirming that the historical film in Hindi popular cinema was "one of the key arenas in which cultural difference [was] conceptualized," Vasudevan considerably complicates such a reading when, through his complex analysis of Sohrab Modi's 1939 film *Pukar* (The Call) that "was understood at the time to be a film about amity between Hindu and Muslim communities, and a salient corrective to the emerging sectarian animosity," he demonstrates how, in fact, it "offer[s] a subtle rewriting of Indian history" whereby "the foreign [Mughal] ruler's formal authority is shown to be ultimately contingent on the real hegemonic authority that the Hindu aristocrats and ruling groups exercised over indigenous society" (2011: 145, 149, 146).

6 Both *Junoon* and *Trikaal* reference historical moments when one ruling class is in the process of being replaced by another: 1857, in some respects, marks the beginning of the erosion of Muslim pre-eminence, though as my colleague Michael Fisher

informed me, since the 1700s, while remaining stronger in places like Rampur and Bengal, Muslim power was in a "holding pattern" (interview, August 11, 2011); and *Trikaal* is set in the months before the Indian army takes over.

7 "Speaking as a novelist," in an essay "addressing … the appropriating appetite of the discourse of history," Coetzee resists the "tendency … to subsume the novel under history" to underscore instead the novel as a rival of, not a supplement to, history: "storytelling is another, an other mode of thinking … more venerable than history"; he speaks particularly on behalf of:

> a novel that evolves its own paradigms and myths, in the process (and here is the point at which true rivalry, even enmity, perhaps enters the picture) perhaps going so far as to show up the mythic status of history – in other words demythologizing history.
>
> (1988: 2–4)

8 Bond notes an earlier iteration of the events presented in his story in J.F. Fanthorne's work, *Mariam: A Tale of the Indian Mutiny of 1857* (1896), which he categorizes as "a mixture of fact and fiction," whereas he has "tried to present," he affirms, his central character, Ruth's "own experiences," which "are true and have been confirmed from other sources … in as factual a manner as possible"(1980: 8). These remarks come from his introduction to the expanded version of *A Flight of Pigeons*, published a couple years after *Junoon* was exhibited – which makes one wonder whether *Junoon* was in some way responsible for the reissue (and expansion) of the story. Benegal adapted his film from the story as it first appeared in a literary magazine, *Imprint*.

9 In an essay that considers "the registers of 1857 in Indian cinema," Gooptu looks at "four films of the historical genre … *Jhansi Ki Rani* (1953), *Shatranj Ke Khilari* (1977), *Junoon* (1978), and *Mangal Pandey: The Rising* (2005)" to suggest that of these only two – Ray's *Shatranj* and Benegal's *Junoon* – aspire to and deliver "authenticity in the rendition of history," evinced in the research they undertake and their "naturalistic period reconstruction"; in so doing they depart from "the principal structures of the mainstream historical genre" (2007: 168, 177–178).

10 That Ruth's grandmother is a Muslim from Rampur, and her mother is the offspring of a French father and Muslim mother are suggested as reasons for the presumed ease with which they can move across these different worlds. Bond's account here is of a piece with Fanthorne's: Describing *Mariam* as a "rare [Mutiny] novel" that views the 1857 "rebellion from a perspective … located between the indigenous and Anglo-Indian social worlds," G. Chakravarty makes an identical point about Fanthorne's protagonists and argues that "the novel's learned appendices and glossary and the familiarity with Hindu-Islamic customs and the Hindustani language" proceed from "a different provenance" than that of Mutiny fiction by the English; the novel "recalls [instead] … those serviceable networks of information that the 'intelligencers' of an earlier generation had access to" (2005: 161–162). On Fanthorne's *Mariam*, see also I. Sen, who in being attentive to the ideological work such representations of cross-racial and inter-racial forms of mediation perform, is somewhat more skeptical about the ease with which Mariam and her family could move across racial divides "in the historical real" (2010: 120–121, 123–126).

11 Benegal's characterization of Javed's ambivalence is co-extensive with that of anti- and postcolonial theorists, such as Frantz Fanon and Ashis Nandy, who speak eloquently of a similar ambivalence as constituting the condition of the colonized male (they both focus on male protagonists), which, in significant ways, has contributed to the persistence of a colonial mindset in former colonial formations long after the physical departure of the colonizer. Significantly, in Fanon's *Black Skin White Masks*, as in *Junoon*, (white) women mediate this ambivalent love-hate relationship of the colonized male with the colonizer. That the film supports the necessity for overcoming this ambivalence can be surmised from what Javed's wife represents as a form of

his (Javed's) abjection. Toward the end, when Delhi has been re-taken by the English, Javed repeats his proposal for her daughter's hand to Mariam ("What do the fortunes of war have to do with relationships between human beings?" he asks); Mariam summarily dismisses his reasoning, but his wife articulates the "shame" she feels ("*mujhko sharam aati hain*") at what she (his wife) sees as his self-debasing, abject pleading ("*tumko aise girh girhate dekh*").

12 In Bond's *A Flight of Pigeons*, Ramjimal's wife only once, briefly, articulates her reservations regarding the Labadoors' "enemy" status in what is a fairly extended account of the Labadoors' otherwise easy incorporation in Ramjimal's family ("We soon fell into the habits of Lala's household and it would have been difficult for anyone who had known us before to recognize us as the Labadoors" [1980: 40]). Similarly, except for Javed's wife, most of the women in Javed's household (and from his extended family) welcome the Labadoor women amongst them, delighted by their fluency in Urdu; the Labadoor women also willingly embrace Indian foods, attires, and names. In *Junoon*, on the other hand, Javed has to force them to wear Indian clothes, partly to keep them "hidden," and when Ruth asks Mariam to comment on her Indian attire – "How do I look, Mamma?" – she receives the acerbic response – "Like a nautch girl."

13 About Fanthorne's text, for instance, I. Sen notes:

> In the historical real, the aftermath of course found a yawning racial divide. [His] novel critiques this growing gap in the post-Rebellion phase. It seeks, as mentioned in the text's preface, to promote racial harmony and help the English "recognise the common fraternity of the two races" (p iii). The construction of female friendship in this novel is strategically geared towards this effort.
>
> (Sen 2010: 124–125)

14 "The thematic of 'inter-racial female friendship'" that, according to Sen, "is a feature of some key 'mutiny' texts, seeks to strategically locate the Indian woman within an anti-Rebellion stance." For a variety of reasons, including the "restrictions of caste and *purdah* (seclusion of females)," in reality such friendships were rare if not altogether non-existent. The Rebellion, however, disrupted "normal" life sufficiently that "middle-class English memsahibs, who were until then notoriously cut off from 'native' India … were sometimes ejected from their sequestered lives in 'British' enclaves and forced into the 'native' areas as they fled from their homes." Inter-racial relationships "however transitory, bitter, hostile, sympathetic or a comingling of all these" could follow from this, and contained the possibility of fracturing "imperial identities." Sen goes on to add, however, that "Victorian gender ideologies of 'separate spheres,' constructions of masculinity and femininity, of 'outer world and inner world,' 'manliness' (namely, aggression and combativeness) and 'womanliness' (namely, gentleness, nurturance, pacifism)" underpin these representations of inter-racial female interactions that then code the violence of the "mutiny" as "male" against which interior spaces of the *zenana* (women's quarters) is counterpointed, thereby insidiously rendering the *zenana* and its women as anti-Rebellion (2010: 121–123).

15 Ruth's lack of range and emotional depth may well be a function of the actress who plays her; Nafisa Ali demonstrates a complete lack of acting talent. But if that is the case, it buttresses rather than contradicts the representation the film seems to want to put forward.

16 Daiya's recent "book about the relation between culture and violence in the modern world … [especially] the relation between contemporary ethnic and gendered violence, and the questions about belonging that haunt nations and nationalisms today" finds in the Partition of the subcontinent its most exemplary illustration (2008: 4).

17 *Mammo* is usually considered as part of a trilogy – including *Sardari Begum* and *Zubeida* – that van der Heide labels "the Khalid Mohamed trilogy" and Datta "the

trilogy on Muslim women." By including *Sardari Begum* in my chapter on "'Performing Women'," and *Mammo* in this chapter, I am not only refusing this usual designation, but also suggesting that they are more resonant as examples of the kinds of films that appear under different rubrics (see Chapter 2, note 32).

18 "The figure of the Indian Muslim," says P. Kumar, "has come to be constituted as the 'intimate enemy' or the 'stranger' in our midst, who is not quite a friend or an external enemy." "The 'strangeness' of Muslims," she adds, "is exacerbated by Partition and the creation of Pakistan as a separate nation for the subcontinent's Muslims" (2008: xv–xvi).

19 On the "permits," "visas," "passports" and other documents that govern and monitor the movement of subjects wishing to travel between Pakistan and India and vice versa see Zamindar 2007: 103–106, 161–184, 190–214. *Mammo* references several details pertaining to such documents – Riyaz resentfully accompanies Mammo to the government office where she must register her arrival; later he accompanies her to renew her visa; the expiration of her visa enforces her deportation.

20 P. Kumar, who situates *Mammo* as a "Muslim minoritarian film," that signals "a very important emergent space for new ways of thinking about Hindu-Muslim relations," identifies the position the spectator is called upon to occupy in a somewhat different, albeit related fashion to the one I have identified, but one with which I am in substantial agreement: Drawing on Vasudevan's work, she notes how mainstream Hindi cinema "by means of its visual culture and characteristic narrative forms … invites the spectator to assume a majoritarian Hindu, North Indian, male identity." The "Muslim minoritarian film," on the other hand, "invit[es] the normative spectator of popular Hindi cinema to identify with the figure of the beleaguered Muslim" thereby "enabl[ing] the majoritarian (and male) Hindu self to come as close as possible to imagining the (Muslim) other as self" (2008: 179, 182).

21 By this I don't mean to suggest that there are *un*mediated versions of Partition that better capture its violence and horror; all representations are mediated. But I do wish to distinguish between different kinds of representational strategies available for representing (or not) such violence and locate that as a matter of choice on Benegal's part.

22 Instructively, the story Mammo tells is not something she experienced, but is itself a piece of literature, as P. Kumar points out, "a distilled version of Gulzar's short story, 'Ravi Paar'" (2008: 223).

23 For a discussion that pertains especially to women in general and Mammo's situation in particular, see Zamindar 2008: 209–214 – the section subtitled "Dependent Women, Chivalrous State." See also, the segment on the "Lucknow Sisters" in Menon and Bhasin (1998: 241 ff).

24 Sarkar addresses the pervasive melancholy and sadness that infuses mainstream Indian cinema in the years following Partition, even as this cinema refuses to take on the subject of Partition, deflecting its trauma onto other subjects: "In these pages," says Sarkar, characterizing his project, "I hope to capture the ways in which the trauma of Partition litters an entire cultural landscape with its melancholy insinuations"; "runes," he adds, "intimating the deep wounds of a traumatized social formation otherwise invested in an ideological itinerary of forgetting" (2009: 96, 97).

25 Consider as an example Manto's acutely horrifying, viscerally felt representation of Sakina, in "Khol Do" ("Open It"), who, after being successively raped, responds reflexively to any request to "open" as if it were a demand to "open" her *salwar* (trousers) and herself for further violation. In a different vein, Saint "speculate[s]" whether "the novel form as a mode of testimony" has now "exhaust[ed]" itself – a "tendency paralleling the possible exhaustion of witness accounts and memory based historical accounts in the domain of partition historiography." He then invokes Hasan's comment that "an element of repetition marks recent historical research based on oral accounts that tends to discover more and more atrocities, without really further amplifying the insights of … Butalia, Menon, Bhasin" (Saint 2010: 361, note 6).

26 With respect to other overlaps between *Trikaal* and the two films that constitute what I have characterized as Benegal's "fictional engagements with (national) history," it's important to note that Benegal often places *Trikaal* alongside *Junoon*, characterizing both, in an interview with Dharkar, for example, as efforts that entail:

> placing yourself into a time in our history and getting that history to become tangible; tangible enough to become part of our environment – including all the trivia of history which are important but which we never get to see in history books … aspects of life hardly ever referred to in most histories. And when you flush them out, they become an extended reality for yourself. That's why *Junoon* was so satisfying … and *Trikaal* … it was not just an evoking of a certain period … but finding your bridges into the past from there.
>
> (1986: n.p.)

27 Of course, the cinematic narrative of *Mammo* is also presented as an act of recall on the part of Riyaz. But the film, after establishing itself as a product of Riyaz's memory of Mammo's earlier visit, does not concern itself with the mechanisms of recall itself.

28 This co-temporality of the two moments – signifying the presence of the past in the present – includes (indeed, is based on) the work of imagination (i.e., of construction/invention) involved in the act of recall. Thus, in his response to van der Heide about the apparent co-temporality of these two moments, Benegal says:

> Recently, I've been reading Jorge Amado … who says in one of his novels that there was always literature, even before the ability to write. So that coffin and this chap [Ruiz] meeting, while I wasn't conscious of it at that time, is very similar in terms of imagination. Ruiz [actively?] recovers that memory.
>
> (2006: 129)

29 Even though the narrator of the film is Ruiz, not all the memories from which the film is constructed are Ruiz's, nor is he present on all the occasions when such recall takes place. For example, he is not present at any of the séances Dona Maria organizes. There are pasts recalled, in other words, that belong to others, to which Ruiz has no access. Memory, in this film, therefore, is not an individual or subjective possession, but the possession, rather, of subjects as social beings and bearers of collective "truths" (see epigraph; Radstone and Hodgkin 2006: 10–11).

30 France and Portugal had both established small imperial domains, mainly on the coasts of the Indian subcontinent, before the British commenced their colonial enterprise in India. Decolonization from the British did not change the status of the French and Portuguese territories in India. These territories were of great symbolic importance to the new nation; hence, India sought to change the status quo by asking France and Portugal to give up their claims to them. France proved amenable to this ambition, Portugal resisted. But, with world opinion favoring the end of imperialism in general and Portugal's continuing presence in Africa in particular, and with frustration growing within India regarding the status of Goa, the Indian army moved in December 1961, quickly bringing to an end the Portuguese empire in Goa (see Brown 2003: 210, 296–297; and Akbar 1988: 502–505; on the Portuguese settlement and trade in the Bay of Bengal, see Subrahmanyam 1990).

31 A fourth alternative, which entails the departure of all those from (or close to) the ruling classes for Portugal, is not mentioned, but is selected by several members of the Souza-Soares family.

32 The doctor clearly views this self-indulgence as an attribute of the class to which Francis and the Souza-Soares family belong, since he says virtually the same thing about Ernesto's life, which he characterizes as "a life of luxury and ease," marked by womanizing and sexual profligacy and, thus, many "illegitimate" children.

33 On the two different occasions when the doctor requests Dona Maria for her granddaughter, Anna's hand for his nephew, Ruiz, she graciously, but firmly, turns him

down: "You know," she says to him, "we only marry within our community." "Goa is a very caste-ridden society," Benegal told me, "Dona Maria's family is Brahmin-Christian whereas Ruiz's family is non-Brahmin-Christian" (February 21, 2011).

34 Rane was housed in the basement before he was beheaded and his head handed over to the Portuguese: "My screams," his ghost recalls, "ring through these walls." Later, Dona Maria's nephew, Leon (who is associated with socialism, supports the Indian National Congress Party, and is also involved in trying to throw the Portuguese out from India) will also hide in the basement after escaping from a Portuguese jail in Lisbon.

35 This is especially, in fact almost exclusively, the case with Benegal's representation of the memories and history that deal with Portuguese colonialism. Rane's appearance incites Dona Maria's memory of rebels' heads hung on trees; the film shows these, but the heads look like (and more than likely are) masks, creating a quite surreal (even crudely horrifying) image through which Portuguese brutality is shown. Rebels' heads hanging on trees, however, is a familiar trope, referring to colonial brutality in the writings on 1857.

36 Yet, while remarking on the lack of success of *Trikaal* at the box office, Benegal says to van der Heide: "somebody asked me why I made a foreign film," to which van Der Heide (rightly, to my mind) responds: "The irony is that you were making a film about India and Indian identity" (2006: 131).

4 A pantheon of national heroes: *Nehru, The Making of the Mahatma*, and *Bose: The Forgotten Hero*

1 Scholarship, more self-consciously critical and/or skeptical of mainstream nationalist self-understandings, provides a different gloss on the three national figures' differential investment in being "inclusive" when it came to India's Muslim population: In Gandhi's explicit and Nehru's implicit presumption of India as Hindu, the terms of Muslim versus Hindu belonging within the nation are configured asymmetrically; Bose's position, on the other hand, is distinguished from Gandhi and Nehru's, with the multi-religious and cultural composition of the Indian National Army he recruited as well his views regarding the equal claim of Muslims on a free India being invoked as a mark of his difference.

2 When discussing FDI's "category of 'Biography and Personality Films,'" Roy observes that "like the educational 'Art Films,' … [this category] was developed with a similar pedagogical motive in mind: that of acquainting Indians with their history and heritage," except that these films "attempt to educate Indians about their past through the use of individual, named exemplars. In their decision to immortalize select heroes for the Indian nation," they "replicate the vertical bond of authority and hierarchy between paternal state and its subject nation, and the chosen heroes standing for, and ultimately standing *above*, the nation and its constituent individuals" (2002: 244).

3 I get this term from Custen, whose comments on the implications of what biopics attempt (and achieve) have a bearing on how Nehru, Gandhi, and Bose are represented in the hegemonic national narrative:

> Most viewers … see history through the lens of a film biography.… [T]he biopic played a powerful part in creating and sustaining public history … provid[ing] many viewers with a version of a life they held to be the truth.
>
> What kinds of lives did the biopic construct?… What parts did these great lives on films play in shaping the audience's notion of the self? What kinds of historical narratives … [were] fabricate[d] in the production and distribution of the lives of the famous?
>
> (1992: 2)

4 Ramaswamy points to another exclusion in the "patriotic pictures," which is also an exclusion in dominant constructions of the nationalist pantheon of the "big men": "Most noticeably," she says:

> Muhammad Ali Jinnah (1876–1948), one of the most important leading men of Indian politics from the early years of the twentieth century does not appear in the company of carto-graphed Mother India.... Indeed, other than the anonymous Muslim body represented invariably by the fez-capped head.... Muslim men who generally appear in patriotic pictures in association with Bharat Mata are "loyalists" associated with Gandhi and the Congress.
>
> (2011: 336, note 13)

5 The rationale for including *Bharat*, even though it is strictly speaking not a biopic or biographical narrative of Nehru, so much as it is a portrayal of his ideas, is that the ideas make the man, thus also constituting his biography of the nation he was to lead through its early decades. Ray, whose worldview is often described as Nehruvian, occupies a similar place to Nehru in Benegal's imagination, albeit in relation to filmmaking.

6 The virtual (but not complete) absence of social, familial, or domestic history in the portrayals of Nehru, Gandhi, and Bose in these documentaries/biopics is quite unlike the portrayal of historical events depicted in *Junoon*, *Trikaal*, and *Mammo*, where the public aspects of those events are presented in a dialectical relationship with their private dimensions; this leads me to think that it is his construction of Nehru, Gandhi, and Bose in their aspect primarily as public figures that commits Benegal to a documentary mode that, in turn, cordons off "the warp and weave of a full life." I also find it instructive that the three or even two of the leaders almost never appear together in the individual biopics devoted to them; the contest of (their) ideas (or conformity between these) through which the nation was defined by being presented in the same frame would have gone some way, I believe, to suggesting the limits (alongside the values) of each leader's vision.

7 In a conversation, during his visit to Oberlin College on October 12, 2011, Salman Rushdie, whose *Midnight's Children*, deploys a similar conceit – "handcuff[ing]" the life of Saleem to that of a post-independence India – told me (in response to a question I had raised about the presence of Nehru's biography in his work) that he had been "reading a lot of Nehru at the time [he] wrote *Midnight's Children*."

8 While examining Nehru's *Autobiography*, Holden makes a similar, but also more ambitious claim about Nehru's significance for his generation of leaders: Nehru's "account of a personal past," he says:

> would become a paradigmatic narrative. In its mapping of individual onto national story, Nehru's text became a model for a series of national autobiographies written by leaders of nations emerging from colonialism: Kwame Nkrumah's *Ghana* and Kenneth Kaunda's *Zambia Must be Free*, for example, and later in the century Nelson K. Mandela's *Long Walk to Freedom* and Lee Kwan Yew's retrospective *The Singapore Story*.
>
> (2005: 89)

Gopal finds that "any study of [Nehru] is bound to be more than merely a personal biography of a great man" because of "the decisive role [he] played in the history of twentieth century – as a leader of the Indian people, as a representative of the new mood in Asia, and as a spokesman for the international conscience" (1975: 5).

9 FDI, which many scholars describe as the nationalist incarnation of what was formerly a colonial institution dedicated to propaganda about Britain's war effort, but involved "equally importantly," says Garga, in the effort "to project a modern and progressive India under British rule to audiences abroad, particularly the United States," retained the content and representational practices of its colonial forbear, though directed this time toward postcolonial, Indian nationalist ends. It was:

described as "the official organ of the Government of India for the production and distribution of information films and newsreels, documentaries and other films required … for public information and education and for instructional and cultural purposes (as well as) to focus attention on important aspects of the country's life and assist growth and development of documentary films as a medium of education and communication."

(2007: 130)

10 Of course, documentaries are not the only visual media involved in this task in what Uberoi characterizes as the "foundational [Nehruvian] moment in the visualizing of independent India"; "popular cinema" and "calendar art," for example were also implicated in "the visual rhetoric of nation-building," which focused on "the project of creating 'unity' out of 'diversity' weaving the 'fragments' into a viable nation-state.… Again Nehruvian rhetoric worked to transform a problem of cultural diversity into a 'resource' for the developmental agenda of the new Indian state" (2002: 199).

11 Not only was "the state the biggest patron of short films," but its instrument, FDI, could promise a large captive audience for its documentaries because "until 1996," FDI, via an official fiat, compelled cinema halls to screen its documentaries and newsreels before each feature film. By securing "rural distribution and viewership," furthermore, FDI "could claim an audience strength of 80 million a week" (Roy 2002: 237, see also Waugh 1988: 29).

12 While revisiting *Nehru* in a recent interview, Benegal told me:

> I wanted to do Nehru in his own voice. A MP [member of Parliament] from Rajasthan had taped Nehru – who spoke about his own life – for eighteen to twenty hours. All these tapes were destroyed in the Janata government period.
>
> (Interview, July 30, 2012)

13 In the same interview, Benegal also noted two other facts regarding the tapes of Nehru speaking about his life, which cast an interesting retrospective light on my analysis: In these, Nehru spoke in Hindi; furthermore, *Nehru* was made in both Hindi and English, since it was an Indian and Soviet co-production. The DVDs I purchased from FDI for my use were, however, in Hindi.

14 In "Voice of Documentary," Nichols defines "voice" to mean "something narrower than style: that which conveys to us a sense of the text's social point of view, of how it is speaking to us and how it is organizing the materials it is presenting to us" (1985: 261). If we understand voiceover as part of a whole cluster of elements through which *Nehru* is organized, then it conforms to what I have been suggesting is the traditional take on Nehru and on India that FDI documentaries sponsored.

15 In fact, Garga arrives at precisely this judgment: "In both films one got the feeling that Benegal was in awe of his material. While the first-person approach can make for purity of a kind, it can also place severe limitations on critical analysis and comment" (1988: 30). The beginning of the documentary seems to support Garga's claim regarding Benegal's approach to Nehru, opening as it does with a fulsome comment from Indira Gandhi about her "father" whom she characterizes as the "humanity in the human being," and, because of his "deep" sensitivity, as possessing the "soul of a poet"; "the more he was influenced by western ideas," she avers, "the more Indian he became." Similarly, with respect to his documentary on Ray, Samik Bandhopadhyay reports that "Ray, we have been told, would have liked this film to be more Benegal than Ray, more of an evaluation of or response to his entire corpus" (quoted in Datta 2003: 225).

16 Guttman, for example, notes:

> What makes *The Discovery* exceptional, in terms of nationalist historiography, is its teleology – the end, and essence of India, for Nehru, is multiculturalism … [*The Discovery* is] perhaps one of the earliest works of nationalist history to overtly privilege cultural diversity and tolerance as national values.
>
> (2003: 263)

She also notes that Nehru's focus falls on "*indigenization*," which is more accurately a form of "*Indianization*," "whereby cultural artifacts (such as languages and customs) are incorporated into a pre-existing civilization" (2003: 270). Analogously, Khilnani remarks: "*The Discovery* is correctly read as an expression of the nationalist imagination, but a highly unusual one, capacious, accepting, and with no desire for purification or hardening of boundaries" (1999: 168).

17 Hyslop says the activity associated with *satyagraha*, if not the term itself, originated with Haji Habib: Gandhi's campaign against compulsory registration, he notes, was "initially built through the Hamidia Islamic Society, an organization centered on the mosque led by H.O. Ally and Haji Habib." "This collaboration in fact was central to the evolution of *satyagraha*," he adds, and "it was not Gandhi but Habib who called on the audience [at the first public meeting in 1906] to take a sacred oath to go to jail rather than to accept the oppressive law"; this "provided the germ of [Gandhi's] lifetime political strategy" (2008: 128).

18 Hyslop allows for a more dialectical relationship of Gandhi's "outsiderness" in South Africa than Brown does, assigning both Gandhi and South Africa, and, within South Africa, Johannesburg especially, almost equal significance by arguing their reciprocal impact on each other.

19 "The script," says Benegal to van der Heide:

> took a long time to do and there were lots of fights between Fatima and I. I then got Shama Zaidi involved in the scripting. So there was this three-way scripting process. After Shama had finished her part of the drafts, Fatima did her own draft. Finally I did my final draft of the script.
>
> (2006: 155)

Despite the contention between at least two of the principals involved, they share their dependence on what are in effect canonical resources for representing Gandhi; and despite Benegal's assertion regarding his scripting of the film, the film follows Meer's biography fairly closely. This is very different from Benegal's substantively critical interaction, as I have demonstrated, with Bond's *Flight of the Pigeons* on which his *Junoon* is based. So the question arises: Is it the case that Bond's work, while based on an actual set of events, but because it is presented and consumed as fiction, opens itself up for interpretation, even a contentious, oppositional one, whereas a biopic on the "Father of the Nation," cast primarily in a documentary register, seems to prevent critical engagement with authoritative sources?

20 This turn away from the political and public to the personal and the domestic as a means of producing a more complex account of an iconic subject is not unique in cinematic or other representations of Gandhi. In his "The Necessity of Harilal," for example, Visvanathan examines and references recent films and biographies about Gandhi that exemplify such a "re-engagement with the concept of Gandhi." Analyzing at length Feroz Abbas Khan's 2007 film *Gandhi, My Father*, Visvanathan finds:

> something different about the Gandhi constructed here; he is a weaker man, a bumbler even when it comes to family.... Both as leader and failed father, it is a quieter Gandhi who has still to discover his own truth, and who effectively erases the Gandhi portrayed by Ben Kingsley.
>
> (Visvanathan 2007)

"*Gandhi, My Father*," Visvanathan concludes, "reveals and tackles a different grid of oppositions, where civil society opposes nation and family opposes state. It creates a family portrait on a national canvas, of Gandhi, father of the nation as, simply, a father" (ibid.: 21, 26, 31).

21 Significantly, Benegal was drawn to Bose precisely because, as he told me, "Bose's thinking had derived from people other than the Congress High Command – people like C.K. Das, who was concerned about the alienation of the Muslims and [who] also

mobilized Muslim women to enter the public sphere" (interview February 19, 2011). This aspect of Bose's significance for our understanding of anti-imperial Indian nationalism – recognizing, that is, his difference from Nehru and Gandhi's embrace of a more "constitutionalist" approach toward acquiring freedom from the British, recognizing, furthermore, Bose as "an alternative beacon of hope" (Bose 2011: 12) – is addressed at some length in two recent books by Som (2004) and Bose (2011) respectively.

22 Interestingly, while both Som and Bose merely reference the relationship between Nehru and Bose, they address the relationship between Gandhi and Bose at some length in recognition of what Som describes as "two diametrically opposed positions in the anti-imperialist struggle." "Subhas," she adds:

> was the only leader in the Congress who dared challenge Gandhi's leadership by advocating an alternative programme. The difference between Gandhi and Subhas made them strike different postures and take up contrary positions.... However, in a situation reminiscent of a familial relationship between a stern father and a rebel son, Subhas was to retain an abiding, albeit grudging, admiration for Gandhi's magnetic popular appeal, the strength of his moral convictions, and the ease with which he could identify with the essential soul of India. Gandhi, in turn, admired Subhas's burning patriotism, his irrepressible zeal, and enthusiasm, his reckless courage and defiance of convention.
>
> (2004: 8)

23 Bose was also forcibly suspended and prevented, therefore, from occupying any position of authority in the Indian National Congress, when, within a week of resigning from his Presidency of the Congress, he "proposed the formation of the 'Forward Bloc' within the Congress to serve as a forum for the more radical elements in the party"; for doing so, the "Congress Working Committee charged him with violating party discipline and banned him from holding elective office for three years" (Bose 2011: 166).

24 In contextualizing this slogan ("Chalo Dilli"), Sugata Bose notes how it is "reminiscent of the 1857 rebellion in India, when Indian soldiers had rebelled against the British under the banner of the last Mughal emperor." "On September 26, 1943 a ceremonial parade and prayers were held in Rangoon, at the tomb of the last Mughal emperor, Bahadur Shah Zafar," Bose adds, "to signal the INA's determination to march to the Red Fort of Delhi" (2011: 4). As with Bose's embrace of violence, the violence of the 1857 uprising has been a thorn in the side of hegemonic Indian nationalism.

25 These slogans, as Ramaswamy notes, not only accompanied renditions of Bose in "popular and public art," they helped inscribe his hypervisibility as well when "for a few years in the 1940s Gandhi and Nehru were rivaled in the barefoot cartographic imaginary by the swashbuckling figure of Subhas Chandra Bose" (2011: 203–204).

26 Interestingly, the recourse to the personal and the domestic sphere in *Making*, while also designed to render Gandhi more complex and human, is deployed to expose his flaws – his inflexibility and tyranny as husband and father. In *Bose*, on the other hand, the recourse to the personal and the familial seeks to display his humanity to enjoin viewer identification with him.

27 In my conversation with him regarding *Bose*, Benegal remarked on how "no political leader in this country [India] has been in the heroic mould," suggesting, thereby, that his interest in Bose stems from his being precisely such a hero – "a hero," that is, "in the Romantic sense – fighting against odds, his failures leading him to levels that transcend those failures until the end when the entire country becomes his constituency" (February 19, 2011).

28 Kurcina's analysis of the Indian National Congress's strategic (some might say, cynical) "appropriation of the INA legacy" to counter the "passions of the Muslim

electorate" that had been roused by "the battle cry for Pakistan and a 'vague Islamic millennialism'" (2010: 823), its "apparent acceptance of violent nationalism" as a tool "to galvanize public opinion at a time when the Indian electorate was preparing to go to the polls for the crucial post-war elections to provincial and central legislatures" in 1945–1946 (2010: 819), which was also the historical moment of the trials of INA soldiers who had been charged by the British for participating in Bose's anti-imperial ventures, is, I think, to the point here. In other words, the INA legacy could be "harness[ed]" in the first place was because emotion(alism) and patriotism are so often part of the same package.

29 Speaking about the uncle who had served in Bose's INA, Benegal recalled how he had wanted to make a film on Bose since having met this uncle as a child. Analogously, he talked about the profound impact Nehru's speech about the subliminal influence of cinema had on him (interview, February 16, 2011).

5 "Making these *cause* films": cinematic renditions of the developmental agendas of the (nation-)state

1 This title derives from a "mock serious" query Shabana Azmi posed to Benegal: "When will you stop making these *cause* films and just make a movie?" (quoted in Benegal 2002: 189).

2 Respectively: Gujarat Milk Marketing Federation Ltd., the Government of West Bengal, Association of Co-operatives and Apex Society of Handloom, National Film Development Corporation/Ministry of Welfare, and National Film Development Corporation/Ministry of Health.

3 For example, the National Award for Best Film on Family Welfare for *Hari Bhari*; National Film Award for Best Actor (*Aarohan*); National Awards for Best Feature Film and for Best Screenplay (*Manthan* and *Samar* and Vijay Tendulkar and Ashok Mishra respectively).

4 The self-chosen designation of those variously defined as scheduled castes, untouchables, or, in Gandhi's words, "harijans," dalit means "crushed or broken."

5 For analyses of Operation Flood I and II as very controversial undertakings, see especially, George 1986 and 1987 and Dogra 1981 and 1982. Analogously, while glossing *Manthan*, Rajadhyaksha and Willemen observe:

> Although the film suggests in its opening title "500,000 farmers of Gujarat present..." that it was publicly financed, it was in fact made through the National Dairy Development Board (NDDB), a controversial organization headed by Dr. V. Kurien, who shares a script credit. Established in 1965 to regularize milk co-operatives and to enhance their productivity with new technology, the NDDB was accused of aggravating India's foreign debt and of diverting resources destined to help the rural poor into servicing the urban upper-class market. Made during this controversy to enhance the NDDB's image, *Manthan* tells a version of the organisation's early years when corrupt local politicians, middlemen, and an uneducated community's prejudices had to be overcome to create local co-operatives.
>
> (1999: 428)

6 Nehru, who was a fan (as was Indira Gandhi) of Kurien and the processes he put in place while building the milk co-operative in Anand, noted how, in doing so, the co-operative's members "ha[d] demonstrated what a lot of benefit can be had by working together." "In building this factory as a co-operative enterprise," he added, "you have set an example to our country as to how a good job has to be executed ... [and performed a] good service to the country" (quoted in Kamath 1996: 2). S. Chakravarty considers *Manthan* "literally" an "allegor[y] of nation building ... centrally informed by building and construction motifs and themes, as these are introduced to the Indian village in the name of modernization" (1993: 257). Kamath explicitly identifies the

milk co-operatives that Kurien masterminded as a Nehruvian developmental enterprise: "Amul [the co-operative set up at Anand] was, in a sense, another of Nehru's 'temples of science' that could be trusted to carry the message of modernity to the villages" (1996: 167).

7 Responding to van der Heide's comment about the folk song that is threaded through the entire film evoking an "ideal sense of life" linked with "the Nehru legacy," Benegal concurs and then goes on to describe the poet who wrote the dialogues for the film, Kaifi Azmi, as someone who "belonged to a generation that understood these ideals," implying thereby that this is the reason Azmi was selected. "He is a person," Benegal adds, "whose value system was very close to this [legacy]" (Interview with van der Heide 2006: 74, 77).

8 My use of the word "utopian" is deliberate here, for, in response to van der Heide's comment that the song associates the village with an "ideal sense of life," Benegal clarifies "it is also a *kind of desire for life to be like that*" (2006: 75; emphasis added). Later the song will acquire a quite different resonance by becoming linked with, and functioning as, van der Heide suggests, "Bindu's voice" (2006: 74). (Bindu, a member of the dalit community, desires and is, in turn, desired by Rao, who, however, resists his attraction to her; the song in this respect can be seen as giving voice to her longing and to its lack of fulfillment, underscoring, as it were, the asymmetry of their desires.)

9 Apart from Benegal's interest in revealing the gender bias that inflects the views of most members – idealistic or not – of Indian society, I wonder if, through his portrayal of Rao, Benegal is not in fact taking a position on the following controversy regarding the dairy co-operative movement. Kurien asserted women's participation and leadership in the co-operatives he oversaw: "Milch cattle in India are tended mainly by women. Amul realized this and built in women's empowerment activities as an important component of its dairy development programme" (2007: 51). But Dogra contests these claims, noting instead, "a study made by the Indian council of Social Science Research from the point of view of the impact of this [i.e., Amul] co-operative on women has yielded pessimistic findings." "Although in the past," he adds:

> dairying used to be primarily in the hands of women, now, in the complex structure of decision-making in the co-operative, women have hardly any place. This case study of 481 co-operatives revealed that women constituted only 10% of the members.
>
> (1980: 15)

10 Although Rao's repression of his attraction to Bindu is shown to be problematic, it cannot be dismissed out of hand as unjustified either: When compared to Chandravarkar's lack of compunction with respect to pursuing an affair with a young woman from the village, Rao's repression can, in part, be seen as a principled act, complicating even further his portrayal within the film.

11 Consider the seamless shift from individual preference to a collective national agenda in the following comment:

> *Samar* deals with a subject that is very important to *me* – the situation regarding untouchability in India today. It's been over fifty years since *we* passed affirmative action legislation to bring this whole community of people ... into the mainstream ... so *we* passed some quite revolutionary legislation in the early years of India's independence.
>
> (Benegal to van der Heide 2006: 161; emphasis added)

12 Representation of state interventions regarding family planning and/or educating women about such matters is kept to a minimum and handled with a light touch in *Hari Bhari*. There is only one scene in which viewers see a health worker visit the household of the extended family at the center of the film and that is soon after one of

the sisters-in-law gives birth; and there is only one other scene involving a visit to a (female) gynaecologist that can be viewed as incorporating a species of "seeing like the state." But that too is brief and subtly handled.

13 Addressing, in particular, subjective efforts of development, Berry notes:

> Changar women, through engagement with programs for their development, are positioned by others and position themselves in relation to their subject position "woman." In doing so, they engage with in new ways of imagining themselves and positioning themselves in relations to others. New desires are created and/or realized, and new actions become possible.
>
> (Berry 2003: 179)

14 *Manthan* has often been put to use in developmental efforts (associated in particular with the setting up of co-operatives) by a whole range of so-called developing and underdeveloped nations – China, Russia, countries in Latin America, and Africa – and by the UNDP (United Nations Development Program) seems to confirm this view of the film (see van der Heide 2006: 73 and Karnad 2002: n.p.).

Bibliography

Agarwal, Arun (1991) "Poststructucturalist Approaches to Development: Some Critical Reflections," *Peace and Change*, 21(4): 464–477.

Agarwal, Bina (ed.) (1989) *Structures of Patriarchy: The State, the Community and the Household*, London; Atlantic Highlands, NJ, USA: Zed Books.

Akbar, M.J. (1988) *Nehru: The Making of India*, London: Viking.

Amin, Shahid (2006) "Of Many Pasts: The 1857 Celebrations Raise Questions Indians Must Confront," *The Telegraph* (India), July 13, available online at: www.telegraphindia.com/1060713/asp/opinion/story_6461478.asp.

Anand, Sukirat (2002) *Gallan Terian … te Kujh Mariyan (And then we talked about…)* New Delhi: Navyug Publishers.

Arnold, David and David Hardiman (eds.) (1994) *Subaltern Studies VIII: Essays in Honor of Ranajit Guha*, Delhi: Oxford University Press.

Bakhle, Janaki (2005) *Two Men and Music: Nationalism in the Making of an Indian Classical Tradition*, New York: Oxford University Press.

Balagopal, K. (1983) "Telangana Movement Revisited," *Economic and Political Weekly*, 18 (18): 709–712.

Banerjee, Sumanta (1990) "Maginalization of Women's Popular Culture in Nineteenth Century Bengal," in Sangari and Vaid (eds.) *Recasting Women*: 127–179.

Banga, Indu (ed.) (1996) *Cultural Re-Orientation in Modern India*, Shimla: Indian Institute of Advanced Study.

Barnouw, Erik and S. Krishnaswamy (1980) *Indian Film*, New York: Oxford University Press.

Baxi, Upendra (1995) "Introduction," in Baxi and Parekh (eds.) *Crisis and Change in Contemporary India*: 8–20.

Baxi, Upendra and Bikhu Parekh (eds.) (1995) *Crisis and Change in Contemporary India*, New Delhi: Sage Publications, in association with The Book Review Literary Trust.

Beattie, Keith (2004) *Documentary Screens: Non-Fiction Film and Television*, New York: Palgrave/Macmillan.

Benegal, Shyam (1973) *Ankur* (The Seedling).

Benegal, Shyam (1975) *Nishant* (Night's End).

Benegal, Shyam (1976) *Manthan* (The Churning).

Benegal, Shyam (1976) *Bhumika* (The Role).

Benegal, Shyam (1978) *Junoon* (Obsession).

Benegal, Shyam (1983) *Mandi* (Marketplace).

Benegal, Shyam (1984) *Nehru*.

Benegal, Shyam (1984) *Satyajit Ray*.

Benegal, Shyam (1985) *Trikaal*, (Past, Present, and Future).

Benegal, Shyam (1988) *Bharat Ek Khoj* (The Discovery of India).

Benegal, Shyam (1994) *Mammo.*

Benegal, Shyam (1996) *Sardari Begum.*

Benegal, Shyam (1996) *The Making of the Mahatma.*

Benegal, Shyam (1999) *Samar* (Conflict).

Benegal, Shyam (2000) *Hari Bhari* (Fertility).

Benegal, Shyam (2005) *Netaji Subhas Chandra Bose.*

Benegal, Shyam (1979) Interview with Behroz Gandhi, *Framework*, 12: 28–30.

Benegal, Shyam (1986) Interview with Sunil John, in Filmotsav 86, *Deccan Chronicle*, January.

Benegal, Shyam (1986) Interview with Anil Dharkar, *Debonair*, February.

Benegal, Shyam (1988) "Secularization Through History: Interview with Shoma Chatterjee," *Cinema-India International*, 5.4: 18–20.

Benegal, Shyam (1988) "Shyam Benegal: Progressive Revolutionary: Interview with A. Wahed Khan," *New Life*, June 3: 9.

Benegal, Shyam (1999) Interview with Sharmila Taliculam, available online at: www.rediff.com/entertai/1999/jul/28shy.htm.

Benegal, Shyam (2002) Interview with Girish Karnad at National Film Theatre, October 18, 2002, available online at: http://bfi-features.blogspot.com/2007/01/shyam-benegal-shyam-benegal-was.html.

Benegal, Shyam (2002) "Making Movies in Mumbai," in Joshi (ed.) *Bollywood: Popular Indian Cinema*, London: Dakini: 170–189.

Benegal, Shyam (2003–2004) "Leaps of Faith: Interview with Saibal Chatterjee," *Cinemaya: The Asian Film Magazine*, nos. 61–62 (Winter–Spring): 20–25.

Benegal, Shyam (2006) *Bollywood Babylon: Interviews with Shyam Benegal*, edited by William van der Heide, Oxford and New York: Berg.

Bergstrom, Janet and Mary Ann Doane (1989) "The Female Spectator: Contexts and Directions," *Camera Obscura*, 20/21: 5–27.

Berry, Kim (2003) "Developing Women: The Traffic in Ideas About Women and their Needs in Kangra, India," in Sivaramakrishnan and Agarwal (eds.) *Regional Modernities: The Cultural Politics of Development in India*: 75–98.

Bhalla, Alok (ed.) (1999) *Stories About the Partition of India*, India: Harper Collins.

Bhalla, Alok and Peter J. Bumke (eds.) (1992) *Images of Rural India in the Twentieth Century*, Delhi: Sterling Publsihers Pvt. Ltd.

Bhatnagar, Rashmi and Rajendar Kaur (eds.) (2011) "Transnational Realisms and Post-realisms in South Asian Literature and Culture," *South Asian Review*, Special Issue, 32: 1.

Bhattacharya, Neeladri (2003) "The Problem," *Rewriting History*, special issue of *Seminar*, 522 (February), avaialble online at: www.india-seminar.com/2003/522/522%20the%20problem.htm.

Binford, Mira Reym (1983) "The New Cinema of India," *Quarterly Review of Film Studies*, 8 (4): 47–61.

Binford, Mira Reym (1987) "The Two Cinemas of India," in Downing (ed.) *Film and Politics in the Third World*: 145–166.

Blunt, Alison (2000) "Embodying War: British Women and Domestic Defilement in the Indian 'Mutiny,' 1857–8," *Journal of Historical Geography*, 26 (3): 403–428.

Bond, Ruskin (1980) *A Flight of Pigeons*, Bombay: IBH Publishing Company.

Bordwell, David and Noël Carroll (eds.) (1996) *Post-Theory: Reconstructing Film Studies*, Madison: University of Wisconsin Press.

Bose, Sugata (2011) *His Majesty's Opponent: Subhas Chandra Bose and India's Struggle Against Empire*, Cambridge, MA: The Belknap Press of Harvard University Press.

Brown, Judith M. (1996a) "The Making of a Critical Outsider," in Brown and Prozesky (eds.) *Gandhi and South Africa*: 21–34.

Brown, Judith M. (1996b) "The Vision of Non-Violence and the Reality," in Brown and Prozesky (eds.) *Gandhi and South Africa*: 111–128.

Brown, Judith M. (2003) *Nehru: A Political Life*, New Haven: Yale University Press.

Brown, Judith M. and Martin Prozesky (eds.) (1996) *Gandhi and South Africa: Principles and Politics*, New York: St. Martin's Press.

Browne, Nick (ed.) (1988) *Refiguring American Film Genres: History and Theory*, Berkeley, Los Angeles, London: University of California Press.

Bruzzi, Stella (2000) *New Documentary: A Critical Introduction*, London and New York: Routledge.

Bryukhovetska, Olga (n.d.) " 'Dispositif' Theory: Returning to the Movie Theater," available online at: www.art-it.asia/u/admin_ed_columns_e/apskOCMPV5ZwoJrGnvxf.

Burnett, Ron (1991) *Explorations in Film Theory: Essays from Ciné Tracts*, Bloomington, IN: Indiana University Press.

Burra, Rani (1985) *Indian Cinema, 1980–1985*, New Delhi: Directorate of Film Festivals.

Butalia, Urvashi (2000) *The Other Side of Silence: Voices from the Partition of India*, Durham: Duke University Press.

Butalia, Urvashi (2002) "Listening for a Change: Narratives of Partition," in S. Settar and Indira Baptista Gupta (eds.) *Pangs of Partition, Vol. II*: 125–143.

Carson, Diane, Linda Dittmar, and Janice Welsch (eds.) (1994) *Multiple Voices in Feminist Film Criticism*, Minneapolis: University of Minnesota Press.

Chabria, Suresh (1992) "Images of Rural India in Post-Independence Cinema," in Bhalla and Bumke (eds.) *Images of Rural India in the Twentieth Century*: 233–238.

Chakrabarty, Dipesh (2007) "Remembering 1857: An Introductory Note," *Economic and Political Weekly*, 42 (19): 1692–1695.

Chakravarty, Gautam (2005) *The Indian Mutiny and the British Imagination*, Cambridge: Cambridge University Press.

Chakravarty, Sumita (1993) *National Identity in Indian Popular Cinema*, Austin, Texas: University of Texas Press.

Chakravarty, Sumita (1999) "Can the Subaltern Weep? Maneuvering as Metaphor in *Rudaali (The Crier)*," in Robin and Jaffe (eds.) *Redirecting the Gaze: Gender, Theory and Cinema in the Third World*: 283–306.

Chakravarty, Uma (1983) "The Development of the Sita Myth: A Case Study of Women in Myth and Literature," *Samya Shakti: A Journal of Women's Studies*, 1 (1): 68–75.

Chanana, Karuna (ed.) (1988) *Socialization, Education and Women: Explorations in Gender Identity*, New Delhi: Orient Longman.

Chatterjee, Partha (1990) "The Nationalist Resolution of the Women's Question," in Sangari and Vaid (eds.) *Recasting Women*: 233–253.

Chatterjee, Partha (1993) *The Nation and its Fragments: Colonial and Postcolonial Histories*, Princeton, NJ: Princeton University Press.

Chatterjee, Partha (ed.) (1998) *The Wages of Freedom: 50 Years of the Indian Nation-State*. New Delhi: Oxford University Press.

Chatterjee, Shoma A (1997) "The Politics of Rape in Indian Cinema," *Deep Focus*, 7 (3/4): 343–350.

Chaudhry, Lubna and Saba Khattak (1994) "Images of White Women and Indian Nationalism: Ambivalent Representations in *Shakespearewallah* and *Junoon*," in Masavisut,

Simson, and Smith (eds.) *Gender and Culture in Literature and Film East and West*: 19–25.

Chopra, Radhika, Caroline Osella, and Filippo Osella (eds.) (2004) *South Asian Masculinities: Contexts for Change, Sites of Continuity*, New Delhi: Kali for Women and Women Unlimited.

Chow, Rey (1995) *Primitive Passions: Visuality, Sexuality, Ethnography, and Contemporary Chinese Cinema*, New York: Columbia University Press.

Coetzee, J.M. (1988) "The Novel Today," *Upstream*, 6 (1): 2–5.

Cook, Pam (2005) *Screening the Past: Memory and Nostalgia in Cinema*, London: Routledge.

Cross, Robert (2010) "Shyam Benegal's *Ankur* and the Nehruvian Woman," *Doshisha Studies in Language and Culture*, 13 (2): 89–115.

Custen, George (1992) *BIO/PICS*: *How Hollywood Constructed Public History*, New Brunswick, NJ: Rutgers University Press.

D'Monte, Darryl (1980) "The Confused Quest for Good Cinema?" *Cinema Vision*, 1 (3): 64–65.

Da Cunha, Uma (ed.) (1981) *Film India: The New Generation 1960–1980*, New Delhi: Directorate of Film Festivals.

Daiya, Kavita (2008) *Violent Belongings: Partition, Gender, and National Culture in Postcolonial India*, Philadelphia: Temple University Press.

Davis, Natalie Zemon (1987) "'Any Resemblance to Persons Living or Dead": Film and the Challenge of Authenticity," *Yale Review*, 76 (4): 457–482.

Das, Veena (1988) "Femininity and the Orientation to the Body," in Chanana (ed.) *Socialization, Education and Women*: 193–207.

Das Gupta, Chidananda (1980) "New Directions in Indian Cinema," *Film Quarterly*, 3 (4): 32–42.

Das Gupta, Chidananda (1983) "The 'New' Cinema: A Wave or a Future?" in Vasudev and Lenglet (eds.) *Indian Cinema Superbazaar*: 39–49.

Das Gupta, Chidananda (2003–2004) "Shyam Benegal: Official Biographies, Personal Cinema," *Cinemaya: The Asian Film Magazine*, 61 (62): 10–19.

Datta, Sangeeta (2003) *Shyam Benegal*, New Delhi: Roli Books.

de Lauretis, Teresa (1994) "Rethinking Women's Cinema: Aesthetics and Film Theory," in Carson, Dittmar, and Welsch (eds.) *Multiple Voices in Feminist Film Criticism*: 140–161.

Deshpande, Anirudh (2009) *Class, Power and Consciousness in Indian Cinema and Television*, Delhi: Primus Books.

Dharkar, Anil (1980) "The FFC Story," *Cinema Vision*, 1 (3): 17–19.

Doane, Mary Ann (1982) "Film and Masquerade: Theorizing the Female Spectator," *Screen*, 23 (3/4): 74–87.

Dogra, Bharat (1978) "The Poor Through Middle-Class Eyes," *Filmfare*, (Bombay) August 16–31: 13–15.

Dogra, Bharat (1981) "The White Revolution: Who Gets the Cream?" *The Economic Scene*, 7: 10–19.

Dogra, Bharat (1982) "Milk Production: Not Such A Flood," *Economic & Political Weekly*, 17 (20): 817.

Downing, D.H. (ed.) (1987) *Film and Politics in the Third World*, New York: Praeger.

Dube, Reena (2005) *Satyajit Ray's The Chess Players and Postcolonial Theory: Culture, Labour and the Value of Alterity*, Houndsmills, Basingstoke: Palgrave MacMillan.

Du Perron, Lalita (2002) "*Thumri*: A Discussion of the Female voice of Hindustani Music," *Modern Asian Studies* 36 (1): 173–193.

Du Perron, Lalita (2007) *Hindi Poetry in a Musical Genre: Thumri Lyrics*, London and New York: Routledge.

Erndl, Kathleen M. (1992) "Mutilation of Surpanakha," in Richman (ed.) *Many Ramayanas*: 67–88.

Fanon, Frantz (1967) *Black Skin, White Masks*, translated by Charles Lam Markmann, New York: Grove Press.

Fanthorne, J.F. (1986) *Mariam: A Story of the Indian Mutiny of 1857*, India: Chadraprabha Press.

Feldman, Martha and Bonnie Gordon (eds.) (2006) *The Courtesan's Arts: Cross Cultural Perspectives*, New York: Oxford University Press.

Ferro, Marc (1988) *Cinema and History*, translated by Naomi Greene, Detroit: Wayne State University Press.

Feuchtwang, Stephen (2000) "Reinscriptions: Commemoration, Restoration and the Interpersonal Transmission of Histories and Memories Under Modern States in Asia and Europe," in Radstone (ed.) *Memory and Methodology*: 59–77.

Forbes, Geraldine (1988) "The Politics of Respectability: Indian Women and the Indian National Congress," in Low, (ed.) *The Indian National Congress*.

Fox, Richard (1996) "Gandhi and Feminized Nationalism in India," in Williams, B. (ed.) *Women Out of Place*: 37–49.

Frankel, Francine R. (2002) "Introduction: Contextual Democracy: Intersection of Society, Culture, and Politics in India," in Frankel, Hasan, Bhargava and Arora (eds.) *Transforming India: Social and Political Dynamics of Democracy*: 1–25.

Frankel, Francine R., Zoya Hasan, Rajeev Bhargava, and Balveer Arora (eds.) (2002) *Transforming India: Social and Political Dynamics of Democracy,* New Delhi: Oxford University Press.

Fuller, C.J. and Veronique Bénéii (eds.) (2000) *The Everyday State and Society in Modern India,* New Delhi: Social Science Press.

Fuller, C.J. and John Harriss (2000) "For an Anthropology of the Modern Indian State," in Fuller and Bénéii (eds.) *The Everyday State and Society*: 1–31.

Gabriel, Karen (2004) "The Importance of Being Gandhi: Gendering and the National Subject in Bombay Cinema," in Chopra, Osella, and Osella (eds.) *South Asian Masculinities*: 264–304.

Gaines, Jane (1989) "White Privilege and looking Relations: Race and Gender in Feminist Film Theory," *Cultural Critique*, 4: 59–79.

Gandhi, Gopalkrishna (2000) "Foreword," in Itzkin, *Gandhi's Johannesburg*: n.p.

Gandhi, M.K. (2004) "In England and South Africa," in Kumar, A. (ed.) *Away: The Indian Writer as an Expatriate*: 87–117.

Gandhi, Rajmohan (2007) "The Gandhi You May Not Know," *India International Center Quarterly*, 34 (2): 1–17.

Garga, B.D. (1988) "The Indian Documentary: Is Anyone Watching?" *Cinema in India*, 3 (2): 26–30.

Garga, B.D. (2007) *From Raj to Swaraj: The Non-Fiction Film in India*, New Delhi: Viking Penguin.

George, Shanti (1986) "Milk & Mud: Review of *Another Revolution Fails: An Investigation into How and Why India's Operation Flood Project, Touted as the World's Largest Dairy Development Programme, Funded by the EEC, Went off the Rails* edited by Claude Alvares; Ajanta Books International, Delhi, 1985," *Economic & Political Weekly*, 21 (8): 337–338.

George, Shanti (1987) "Stemming Operation Flood: Towards an Alternative Dairy Policy for India," *Economic & Political Weekly*, 22 (39): 1654–1663.

Ghosh, Amitav (2002) "The Ghosts of Mrs. Gandhi," in Saint (ed.) *Bruised Memories*: 36–50.

Gledhill, Christine (1987) *Home is Where the Heart is: Studies in Melodrama and the Women's Film*, London: British Film Institute.

Gledhill, Christine (1988) "Pleasurable Negotiations," in Pribram (ed.) *Female Spectators*: 64–89.

Gooptu, Sharmistha and Boria Majumdar (eds.) (2007) *Revisiting 1857: Myth, Memory, History*, New Delhi: Roli Books.

Gooptu, Sharmistha (2007) "Nationalist Spectacle, Authenticity, Historicity: The Registers of 1857 in Indian Cinema," in Gooptu and Majumdar (eds.) *Revisiting 1857*: 166–185.

Gopal, Sarvepalli (1975) *Jawaharlal Nehru: A Biography*, 2 vols, London: Jonathan Cape.

Gordon, Bonnie and Martha Feldman, "Introduction," in Feldman and Gordon (eds.) *The Courtesans Arts*: 3–26.

Grodal, Torben (2002) "The Experience of Realism in Audiovisual Representation," in Jerslev (ed.) *Realism and "Reality" in Film and Media*: 67–91.

Guha, Ramachandra (ed.) (2011) *Makers of Modern India*, Cambridge, MA: The Belknap Press of Harvard University.

Guha, Ranajit (ed.) (1987a) *Subaltern Studies V: Writings on South Asian History and Society*, Delhi: Oxford University Press.

Guha, Ranajit (1987b) "Chandra's Death," in Guha (ed.) *Subaltern Studies V: Writings on South Asian History and Society*: 135–165.

Gupta, Akhil (2003a) "The Transmission of Development: Problems of Scale and Socialization," in Sivaramakrishnan and Agarwal (eds.) *Regional Modernities: The Cultural Politics of Development in India*: 65–74.

Gupta, Akhil and K. Sivaramakrishnan (eds.) (2011) *The State in India after Liberalization*, London & New York: Routledge.

Guttman, Anna (2003) "Compromise and Contradiction in Jawaharlal Nehru's Multicultural Nation-State: Constructing National History in *The Discovery of India*," *Clio*, 32 (3): 263–284.

Habibullah, Shama (1985) "In Their Own Words: *Nehru/Satyajit Ray* (Non-Fiction)," in Burra, (ed.) *Indian Cinema 1980–1985*: 135–138.

Hallam, Julia and Margaret Marshment (2000) *Realism and Popular Cinema*, Manchester and New York: Manchester University Press.

Hansen, Kathryn (1988) "The Virangana in North Indian History, Myth, and Popular Culture," *Economic and Political Weekly*, 23 (18): WS-25-WS-33.

Hansen, Kathryn (1992) *Grounds for Play: The Nautanki Theatre of North India*, Berkeley, Los Angeles, Oxford: California University Press.

Hasan, Mushirul (ed.) (2004) *Nehru's India: Select Speeches*, New Delhi: Oxford University Press.

Hodgkin, Katharine and Susannah Radstone (2006a) *Memory, History, Nation: Contested Pasts*, New Brunswick: Transaction Publishers.

Hodgkin, Katharine and Susannah Radstone (2006b) "Introduction: Contested Pasts," in Hodgkin and Radstone (eds.) *Memory, History, Nation*: 1–21.

Holden, Philip (2005) "Other Modernities: Autobiography and Globalization," *Biography*, 28 (1): 89103.

Hyslop, Jonathan (2008) "Gandhi, Mandela, and the African Modern," in Nuttall and Mbembe (eds.) *Johannesburg*: 119–136.

Itzkin, Eric (2000) *Gandhi's Johannesburg: Birthplace of Satyagraha*, Johannesburg: Witswatersrand University Press, in association with Museum Africa.

Jerslev, Anne (ed.) (2002) *Realism and "Reality" in Film and Media*, Northern Lights: Film and Media Studies Yearbook, 2002, University of Copenhagen: Museum Tusculanum Press.

Johnston, Claire "Women's Cinema as Counter Cinema," in Kaplan (ed.) *Feminism and Film*: 22–33.

Joshi, Lalit Mohan (2001) "*Zubeida*: Shyam Benegal's Second Coming," *South Asian Cinema*, (February): 18–31.

Joshi, Lalit Mohan (ed.) (2002) *Bollywood: Popular Indian Cinema*, London: Dakini.

Kamath, M.V. (1996) *Milkman from Anand: The Story of Verghese Kurien*, 2nd revised edition, Delhi: Konark Publishers Pvt Ltd.

Kannabiran, Vasantha and K. Lalitha (1990) "That Magic Time: Women in the Telangana People's Struggle," in Sangari and Vaid (eds.) *Recasting Women*: 180–203.

Kaplan, E. Ann (ed.) (2000a) *Feminism and Film*, New York: Oxford University Press.

Kaplan, E. Ann (2000b) "Is the Gaze Male?" in Kaplan (ed.) *Feminism and Film*: 119–138.

Kapur, Geeta (1987) "Mythic Material in Indian Cinema," *Journal of Arts and Ideas*, 14–15: 79–108.

Kapur, Geeta (1992) "Cultural Creativity in the First Decade: The Example of Satyajit Ray," *Journal of Arts and Ideas*, 23–24: 17–49.

Kapur, Geeta (2000) *When Was Modernism: Essays on Contemporary Cultural practice in India*, New Delhi: Tulika.

Katrak, Ketu (1991) "Indian Nationalism, Gandhian Satyagraha, and Representations of Female Sexuality," in Parker, Russo, Sommer, and Yaeger (eds.) *Nationalism and Sexualities*: 395–406.

Kaul, Gautam (1999) *Cinema and the Indian Freedom Struggle (Covering the Subcontinent)*, New Delhi: Sterling Publishers Pvt., Ltd.

Kaviraj, Sudipta (2009) "The Post-colonial State: The Special Case of India," *Critical Encounters* (Web Journal), available online at: http://criticalencounters.wordpress.com/2009/01/19.

Kaviraj, Sudipta (2011) "On the Enchantment of the State: Indian Thought on the Role of the State in the Narrative of Modernity," in Gupta and Sivaramakrishnan (eds.) *The State in India*: 31–48.

Khan, Yasmin (2011) "Performing Peace: Gandhi's Assassination as a Critical Moment in the Consolidation of the Nehruvian State," *Modern Asian Studies*, 45 (1): 57–80.

Khanna, Ranjana (1998) "From Third to Fourth Cinema," *Third Text*, 13–32.

Khilnani, Sunil (1999) *The Idea of India*, New York: Farrar Straus, Giroux.

Kidwai, Anis (2004) *In the Shadow of Freedom*, translated by Gillian Wright, New Dehli: Zubaan.

Kidwai, Saleem (2004) "The Singing Ladies Find a Voice," *Seminar* (India), 540: 48–54.

Kidwai, Saleem (n.d.) "The *Tawaif* in Urdu/Hindi Cinema," Unpublished Manuscript.

Kishwar, Madhu (1985) "Gandhi on Women (Parts 1 and 2)," *Economic and Political Weekly*, 20 (40): 1691–1702.

Kishwar, Madhu (1985) "Gandhi on Women (Part 3)" *Economic and Political Weekly* 20 (41): 1753–1758.

Klaver, Claudia (2001) "Domesticity Under Siege: British Women and Imperial Crisis at the Siege of Lucknow, 1857," *Women's Writing*, 8 (1): 21–58.

Klenk, Rebecca (2003a) "'Difficult Work': Becoming Developed," in Sivaramakrishnan and Agarwal (eds.) *Regional Modernities: The Cultural Politics of Development in India*: 99–121.

Krishen, Pradip (1991) "Knocking at the Door of Public Culture: India's Parallel Cinema." *Public Culture* 4.1 (Fall): 25–41.

Kuhn, Annette (2002) "Women's Genres," in Turner (ed.) *The Film Cultures Reader*: 20–27.

Kumar, Amitava (ed.) (2004) *Away: The Indian Writer as an Expatriate*, New York and London: Routledge.

Kumar, Priya (2008) *Limiting Secularism: The Ethics of Co-Existence in Indian Literature and Film*, Minneapolis: University of Minnesota Press.

Kumar, Udaya (2011) "Personal and Public Histories: Nehru and His Vernacular Successors," presentation at a session, "Spectres of Nehru: Perspectives on Culture and Ideology," co-organized by Rajeswari Sunder Rajan and Anuradha Dingwaney Needham, Annual Conference on South Asia, Madison, Wisconsin.

Kurcina, William F. (2010) "Sentiments and Patriotism: The Indian National Army, General Elections and the Congress's Appropriation of the INA Legacy," *Modern Asian Studies*, 44 (4): 817–856.

Kurien, Verghese (2007) "India's Milk Revolution: Investing in Rural Producer Organizations," in Narayan and Glinskaya (eds.) *Ending Poverty in South Asia*: 37–67.

Kurien, Verghese (1984) *Dairy Development Through Co-operatives in India*, Sri Ramchandra Sarvottam Dubhashi Memorial Lectures, Pune: Board of Extra-Mural Studies, University of Pune.

Lakshmi, Aishwarya (2007) "The Mutiny Novel: Creating the Domestic Body of Empire," *Economic & Political Weekly*, 42 (19): 1746–1753.

Landy, Marcia (1996) *Cinematic Uses of the Past*, Minneapolis: University of Minnesota Press.

Landy, Marcia (ed.) (2001a) *The Historical Film: History and Memory in Media*, New Brunswick, NJ: Rutgers University Press.

Landy, Marcia (ed.) (2001b) "Introduction." in Landy (ed.) *The Historical Film*: 1–22.

Low, D.A. (ed.) (1988) *The Indian National Congress: Centenary Highlights*, New Delhi: Oxford University Press.

Lukmani, Yasmin (1997) "Committed Films: A Comparative Study of *Ankur* and *Nishant*," *New Quest*, 1: 41–49.

MacCabe, Colin (1980) "The Classic Realist Text," in Williams, C. (ed.) *Realism and the Cinema: A Reader*: 52–63.

Malcolm, Derek (1988) "National Film Theatre (NFT) Program Notes for Shyam Benegal Retrospective," London, October.

Mankekar, Purnima (1999) *Screening Culture, Viewing Politics: An Ethnography of Television, Womanhood, and Nation in Postcolonial India*, Durham, NC: Duke University Press.

Manuel, Peter (1989) *Thumri in Historical and Stylistic Perspective*, Delhi: Motilal Banarsidass.

Markovits, Claude (2004) *The Ungandhian Gandhi*: *The Life and Afterlife of the Mahatma*, translated from the French by the author, London: Anthem Press.

Masavisut, Nitaya, George Simson, and Larry E. Smith (eds.) (1994) *Gender and Culture in Literature and Film East and West: Issues of Perception and Interpretations: Selected Conference Papers*, Honolulu, HI: College of Language, Linguistics, and Literature, University of Hawaii: East-West Center.

Masselos, Jim (2005) *Indian Nationalism: A History*, 5th revised edition, UK, USA, India: New Dawn Press, Inc.

Masud, Iqbal (1980) "A Fierce Little Bushwar in the Indian Film World," *Cinema Vision*, 1 (3): 83–88.

Masud, Iqbal (1981) "It Was the Time for New Cinema," in Da Cunha (ed.) *Film India: The New Generation 1960–1980*: 11–17.

Mayne, Judith (2002) "Paradoxes of Spectatorship," in Turner (ed.) *The Film Cultures Reader*: 28–45.

Mazumdar, Ranjani (1991) "Dialectic of Public and Private: Representation of Women in *Bhoomika* and *Mirch Masala*," *Economic and Political Weekly*, 26 (43): WS-81-WS-84.

Meer, Fatima (1994) *Apprenticeship of a Mahatma: A Biography of M.K. Gandhi 1869–1914*, 2nd revised edition, published by the Institute for Black Research/Madiba Publishers and the Mahatma Gandhi Institute.

Menon, Ritu and Kamla Bhasin (1998) *Borders and Boundaries: Women in India's Partition*, New Brunswick: Rutgers University Press.

Milne, Tom (1977) "Indian Gambits," *Sight and Sound*, 46 (2): 94–99.

Milne, Tom (1980) "*Junoon* (India 1978)," *Monthly Film Bulletin*, xlvii, (552): 7–8.

Mitra, Royona (2006) "Living a Body Myth, Performing a Body Reality: Reclaiming the Corporeality and Sexuality of the Indian Female Dancer," *Feminist Review*, 84: 67–83.

Mohan, Jag (1969) *Two Decades of Films Division*, New Delhi: Films Division, Ministry of Information and Broadcasting, Govt. of India.

Mohan, Jag (1990) *Documentary Films and National Awakening*, New Delhi: Publications Division, Ministry of Information and Broadcasting, Govt. of India.

Moore, Donald S (2003) "Beyond Blackmail: Multivalent Modernities and the Cultural Politics of Development in India," in Sivaramakrishnan and Agarwal (eds.) *Regional Modernities: The Cultural Politics of Development in India*: 165–214.

Moro, Pamela (2004) "Constructions of Nation and the Classicisation of Music: Comparative Perspectives from Southeast and South Asia," *Journal of Southeast Asian Studies*, 35 (2): 187–211.

Mufti, Aamir (2007) *Enlightenment in the Colony: The Jewish Question and the Crisis of Postcolonial Culture*, Princeton, NJ: Princeton University Press.

Mukherjee, Meenakshi (1996) "Story, History and Her story," in Banga (ed.) *Cultural Re-Orientation in Modern India*: 110–127.

Mulvey, Laura (1975) "Visual Pleasure and Narrative Cinema," *Screen*, 16: 6–18.

Mulvey, Laura (1981) "Afterthoughts on 'Visual Pleasure and Narrative Cinema' Inspired by *Duel in the Sun* (King Vidor, 1946)," *Framework*, 15 (17): 12–15.

Mulvey, Laura (1989) "British Feminist Film Theory's Female Spectators: Presence and Absence," *Camera Obscura*, 7: 68–81.

Murray, S. (ed.) (1997) *Not on any Map: Essays on Postcoloniality and Cultural Nationalism*, Exeter, UK: University of Exeter Press.

Nandy, Ashis (1983) *The Intimate Enemy: Loss and Recovery of Self Under Colonialism*, Delhi: Oxford University Press.

Narayan, Deepa and Glinskaya, Elena (eds.) (2007) *Ending Poverty in South Asia: Ideas That Work*, Washington, DC: World Bank.

Narvekar, Sanjit (1976) "Interview with Shyam Benegal," *Cinema Journal*, March 12: 7, 15.

Needham, Anuradha Dingwaney, and Rajeswari Sunder Rajan (eds.) (2007) *The Crisis of Secularism in India*, Durham and London: Duke University Press and New Delhi: Permanent Black.

Nehru, Jawaharlal (1981) *The Discovery of India*, New Delhi: Oxford University Press.

Nettl, Bruno and Philip V. Bohlman (eds.) (1991) *Comparative Musicology and Anthropology of Music: Essays on History of Musicology*, Chicago: Chicago University Press.

Nichols, Bill (ed.) (1985a) *Movies and Methods: An Anthology, Vol. II*, Berkeley, Los Angeles: University of California Press.

Nichols, Bill (1985b) "The Voice of Documentary," in Nichols (ed.) *Movies and Methods: An Anthology, Vol. II*: 258–73.

Nichols, Bill (1991) *Representing Reality: Issues and Concepts in Documentary Realism*, Bloomington, Indianapolis: Indiana University Press.

Nowell-Smith, Geoffrey (ed.) (1990) "On History and the Cinema," *Screen*, 30 (2): 160–171.

Nowell-Smith, Geoffrey (ed.) (1996) *The Oxford History of World Cinema*, Oxford and New York: Oxford University Press.

Nuttall, Sarah and Achille Mbembe (2008) *Johannesburg: The Elusive Metropolis*, Durham and London: Duke University Press.

Oldenburg, Veena Talwar (1990) "Lifestyle as Resistance: The Case of the Courtesans of Lucknow, India," *Feminist Studies*, 16 (2): 259–287.

Pandey, Gyanendra (1994) "The Prose of Otherness" in Arnold and Hardiman (eds.) *Subaltern Studies VIII: Essays in Honor of Ranajit Guha*: 188–221.

Pandey, Gyanendra (2001) *Remembering Partition: Violence, Nationalism, and History in India*, Cambridge: Cambridge University Press.

Parker, A., M. Russo, D. Sommer, and P. Yaeger (1991) *Nationalism and Sexualities*, London: Routledge: 395–406.

Patel, Sujata (1988) "Construction and Reconstruction of Woman in Gandhi," *Economic and Political Weekly*, 23 (8): 377–387.

Pati, Biswamoy (ed.) (2007a) *The 1857 Rebellion*, Delhi: Oxford University Press, 2007.

Pati, Biswamoy (2007b) "Introduction: The Nature of 1857," in Pati (ed.) *The 1857 Rebellion*: xiii–xliii.

Pati, Biswamoy (ed.) (2010a) *The Great Rebellion of 1857: Exploring Transgressions, Contests, and Diversities*, London and New York: Routledge.

Pati, Biswamoy (2010b) "Introduction: The Great Rebellion of 1857," in Pati (ed.) *The Great Rebellion*: 115.

Pavier, Barry (1974) "The Telangana Armed Struggle," *Economic and Political Weekly*, 9 (32/34): 1413 and 1417–1420.

Paxton, Nancy (1999) *Writing Under the Raj: Gender, Race, and Rape in the British Colonial Imagination 1830–1947*, New Brunswick, NJ: Rutgers University Press.

Peterson, Indira Viswanathan and Davesh Soneji (eds.) (2008) *Performing Pasts: Reinventing the Arts in Modern South India*, New Delhi: Oxford University Press.

Peterson, Indira Viswanathan and Davesh Soneji (2008) "Introduction," in Peterson and Soneji (eds.) *Performing Pasts*: 1–40.

Prakash, Gyan (1990) "Writing Post-Orientalist Histories of the Third World: Perspectives from Indian Historiography," *Comparative Studies in Society and History*, 32 (2): 383–408.

Prasad, Madhava (1998a) *Ideology of the Indian Film: A Historical Reconstruction*, New Delhi: Oxford University Press.

Prasad, Madhava (1998b) "State in/of Cinema," in Chatterjee (ed.) *The Wages of Freedom*: 123–146.

Pribram, E. Deidre (ed.) (1988) *Female Spectators*, London: Verso.

Pym, John (1976) "*Ankur*," *Monthly Film Bulletin*, XLIII (506): 47.

Qureshi, Regula Burckhardt (1991) "Whose Music? Sources and Contexts in Indic Musicology," in Nettl and Bohlman (eds.) *Comparative Musicology and Anthropology of Music*: 152–168.

Qureshi, Regula Burckhardt (2001) "In Search of Begum Akhtar," *The World of Music*, 43 (1): 97–137.

Qureshi, Regula Burckhardt (2006) "Female Agency and Patriarchal Constraints: Situating Courtesans in Twentieth Century India," in Feldman and Gordon (eds.) *The Courtesan's Arts*: 312–331.

Radstone, Susannah (ed.) (2000a) *Memory and Methodology*, Oxford and New York: Berg.

Radstone, Susannah (2000b) "Working with Memory: An Introduction," in Radstone, (ed.) *Memory and Methodology*: 1–22.

Radstone, Susannah and Katharine Hodgkin (eds.) (2006a) *Memory Cultures: Memory, Subjectivity, Recognition*, New Brunswick: Transaction Publishers.

Radstone, Susannah and Katharine Hodgkin (2006b) "Regimes of Memory: An Introduction," in Radstone and Hodgkin (eds.) *Memory Cultures*: 1–22.

Raina, Badri (1989) "The Politics of Development: A Statement and a Case: The Narmada River Project," *Journal of Arts and Ideas*, 17–18: 91–107.

Raina, Raghunath (1981) "Foreword," in Da Cunha (ed.) *Film India: The New Generation 1960–1980*: 1–10.

Rajadhyaksha, Ashish (1996) "India: Filming the Nation," in Nowell-Smith (ed.) *The Oxford History of World Cinema*: 678–690.

Rajadhyaksha, Ashish (2009) *Indian Cinema in the Time of Celluloid: From Bollywood to the Emergency*, Bloomington and Indianapolis: Indiana University Press.

Rajadhyaksha, Ashish and Paul Willemen (1999) *Enclyclopaedia of Indian Cinema*, London: British Film Institute.

Rajagopal, Arvind (1993) "The Rise of National Progamming: The Case of Indian Television," *Media, Culture, Society*, 15: 91–111.

Rajagopal, Arvind (2001) *Politics After Television; Regional Nationalism and the Reshaping of the Indian Public*, Cambridge: Cambridge University Press.

Rajagopal, Arvind (2011) "The Emergency as Pre-history of the Middle Class," *Modern Asian Studies*, 45 (5): 1003–1049.

Ramaswamy, Sumathi (ed.) (2002) *Beyond Appearances? Visual Practices and Ideologies in Modern India*, special issue of *Contributions to Indian Sociology, New Series* 36.1/2 (January–August).

Ramaswamy, Sumathi (2011) *Goddess and the Nation: Mapping Mother India*, Durham, NC: Duke University Press.

Rao, Leela (1989) "Woman in Indian Films – A Paradigm of Continuity and Change," *Media, Culture, and Society*, 11: 443–458.

Rao, Maithili (1998) "A Direction in Search of the Narrative," festival brochure for Shyam Benegal Retrospective, Bombay: Prabhat Chitra Mandal: 9–12.

Rao, Vidya (1990) "*Thumri* as Feminine Voice" *Economic and Political Weekly*, 25: WS-31-WS-39.

Rao, Vidya (1996) "Thumri and Thumri Singers: Changes in Style and Life-Style," in Banga (ed.) *Cultural Re-Orientation in Modern India*: 278–315.

Rao, Velcheru Narayana (1992) "A *Rāmāyaṇa* of their Own: Women's Oral Tradition in Telugu," in Richman (ed.) *Many Ramayanas: The Diversity of a Narrative Tradition in South Asia*: 114–136.

Ray, Satyajit (1976) *Our Films, Their Films*, Delhi and Hyderabad: Orient Longman.

Rich, B. Ruby (1994) "In the Name of Feminist Film Criticism," in Carson, Dittmar, and Welsch (eds.) *Multiple Voices in Feminist Film Criticism*: 27–47.

Richman, Paula (ed.) (1992a) *Many Ramayanas: The Diversity of a Narrative Tradition in South Asia*, Delhi: Oxford University Press.

Richman, Paula (1992b) "Introduction: The Diversity of the Ramayana Tradition," in Richman (ed.) *Many Ramayanas: The Diversity of a Narrative Tradition in South Asia*: 3–21.

Rizvi, Ahmad and Parag Amladi (1980) "Is there a New Cinema Movement," *Cinema Vision*, 1 (3): 4–13.

Robin, Diana and Ira Jaffe (eds.) (1999) *Redirecting the Gaze: Gender, Theory and Cinema in the Third World*, Albany: State of New York Press.

Rosen, Philip (1977) "'Screen' and the Marxist Project in Film Criticism," *Quarterly Review of Film Studies*, 2 (3): 273–287.

Rosen, Philip (ed.) (1986) *Narrative, Apparatus, Ideology: A Film Theory Reader*, New York: Columbia University Press.

Rosen, Philip (2004) *Change Mummified: Cinema, Historicity, Theory*, Minneapolis: University of Minnesota Press.

Rosenstone, Robert A (1988) "History in Images/History in Words: Reflections on the Possibility of Really Putting History onto Film," *American Historical Review*, 93 (5): 1173–1185.

Roy, Srirupa (2002) "Moving Pictures: The Postcolonial State and Visual Representations of India," in Ramaswamy (ed.) *Beyond Appearances?*: 233–263.

Ryan, Tom and Scott Murray (1978) "Indian Cinema: Shyam Benegal," *Cinema Papers*, October/November: 106–107, 163.

Saint, Tarun K. (ed.) (2002) *Bruised Memories: Communal Violence and the Writer*, Calcutta: Seagull.

Saint, Tarun K. (2010) *Witnessing Partition: Memory, History, Fiction*, New Delhi and London: Routledge.

Sangari, Kumkum and Sudesh Vaid (1990a) *Recasting Women: Essays in Colonial History*, New Brunswick, NJ: Rutgers University Press.

Sangari, Kumkum and Sudesh Vaid (1990b) "Recasting Women: An Introduction," in Sangari and Vaid (eds.) *Recasting Women*: 1–26.

Sarkar, Bhaskar (2009) *Mourning the Nation: Indian Cinema in the Wake of Partition*, Durham and London: Duke University Press.

Sarkar, Sumit (1983) *Modern India 1885–1947*, Dehli: MacMillan.

Sen, Geeti (1996) *Image and Imagination: Five Contemporary Artists in India*, Ahmadabad: Mapin Publications Pvt., Ltd. NJ: Grantha Corp.

Sen, Indrani (2010) "Discourses of 'Gendered Loyalty': Indian Women in Nineteenth-Century 'Mutiny' Fiction," in Pati (ed.) *The Great Rebellion of 1857: Exploring Transgressions, Contests, and Diversities*: 111–128.

Sen, Meheli (2011). "Vernacular Modernities and Fitful Globalities in Shyam Benegal's Cinematic Provinces," *many cinemas* 01:*urban/rural*: 8–22, available online at: http://manycinemas.org/available_issues.html.

Settar, S. and Indira Baptista Gupta (eds.) (2002) *Pangs of Partition, Vol. II: The Human Dimension*, New Delhi: Indian Council of Historical Research.

Shanbag, Sunil and Anupam Pruthi (1988) "The Human Face of History: Building for 5000 Years and More," *Cinema in India*, 2 (4): 6–17.

Sharma, Aradhana and Akhil Gupta (eds.) (2006a) *The Anthropology of the State: A Reader*, Malden, MA: Blackwell Publishing.

Sharma, Aradhana and Akhil Gupta (2006b) "Introduction: Rethinking Theories of the State in an Age of Globalization," in Sharma and Gupta (eds.) *The Anthropology of the State*: 1–41.

Sharpe, Jenny (1993) *Allegories of Empire: The Figure of Woman in Colonial Texts*, Minneapolis: University of Minnesota Press.

Siegel, Carol and Ann Kibbey (eds.) (1995) *Forming and Reforming Identity*, New York and London: New York University Press.

Singh, Lata (2007) "Retrieving Voices from the Margins: The Courtesan and the Nation's Narrative," *Indian Journal of Gender Studies*, 14 (1): 93–117.

Sinha, Aseema (2011) "An Institutional Perspective on the Post-Liberalization State in India," In Gupta and Sivaramakrishna (eds.) *The State in India*: 49–68.

Sinha, Mrinalini (1995) "Nationalism and Respectable Sexuality in India," in Siegel and Kibbey (eds.) *Forming and Reforming Identity*: 30–57.

Sivaramakrishnan, K. and Arun Agarwal (eds.) (2003a) *Regional Modernities: The Cultural Politics of Development in India*, New Delhi: Oxford University Press.

Sivaramakrishnan, K. and Arun Agarwal (2003b) "Regional Modernities in Stories and Practices of Development," In Sivaramakrishnan and Agarwal (eds.) *Regional Modernities: The Cultural Politics of Development in India*: 1–62.

Slotkin, Richard (2005) "Fiction for the Purposes of History," *Rethinking History*, 9 (2/3): 147–157.

Smith, Murray (1995) *Engaging Characters: Fiction, Emotion, and the Cinema*, Oxford: Clarendon Press.

Smith, Murray (1996) "Logic and Legacy of Brechtianism," In Bordwell and Carroll (eds.) *Post-Theory: Reconstructing Film Studies*: 130–148.

Som, Reba (2004) *Gandhi, Bose, Nehru and the Making of the Modern Indian Mind*, New Delhi: Penguin/Viking.

Soneji, Davesh (2000) "Living History, Performing Memory: *Devdasi* Women in Telugu-Speaking South India," *Dance Research Journal*, 36 (2): 30–49.

Srinivasan, Amrit (1989) "Reform or Conformity? Temple 'Prostitution' and the Community in the Madras Presidency," In Agarwal (ed.) *Structures of Patriarchy*: 175–198.

Srinivasan, Doris M. (2006) "Royalty's Courtesans and God's Mortal Wives: Keepers of Culture in Pre-colonial India," in Feldman and Gordon (eds.) *The Courtesan's Arts*: 161–181.

Stam, Robert and Louise Phelps (1985) "Colonialism, Racism, and Representation: An Introduction," in Nichols (ed.) *Movies and Methods: An Anthology, Vol.II*: 2–20.

Stoler, Laura A. (2002) *Carnal Knowledge and Imperial Power: Race and the Intimate in Colonial Rule*, Berkeley, Los Angeles, London: California University Press.

Stree Shakti Sanghatana (1989) *We Were Making History: Life Stories of Women in the Telangana People's Struggle*, New York: St. Martin's Press.

Subrahmanayam, Sanjay (1990) *Improvising Empire: Portuguese Trade and Settlement in the Bay of Bengal, 1500–1700*, Delhi: Oxford University Press, 1990.

Subramanian, Lakshmi (2000) "The Master, the Muse, and the Nation: The New Cultural Project and the Reification of Colonial Modernity in India," *South Asia*, XXIII (2): 1–32.

Subramanian, Lakshmi (2008) "Embracing the Canonical: Identity, Tradition, and Modernity in Karnatak Music," in Peterson and Soneji (eds.) *Performing Pasts*: 43–70.

Sunder Rajan, Rajeswari (ed.) (2000a) *Signposts: Gender Issues in Post-Independence India*, New Delhi: Kali for Women.

Sunder Rajan, Rajeswari (2000b) "Introduction," in Sunder Rajan (ed.) *Signposts*: 1–16.

Sunder Rajan, Rajeswari (2000c) "The Story of Draupadi's Disrobing: Meanings for our Times," in Sunder Rajan (ed.) *Signposts:* 332–359.

Sunder Rajan, Rajeswari (2003) *Scandal of the State: Women, Law, and Citizenship in Postcolonial India*, Durham and London: Duke University Press.

Sunderayya, P. (1972) *Telanagana People's Struggle and its Lessons*, Calcutta: The Communist Party of India (Marxist).

Surya, J.S. (1997) "From *Ankur* to *Sardari Begum*: The Evolution of a Filmmaker: An Interview with Shyam Benegal," *Deep Focus: A Film Quarterly* (Bangalore) 7 (2): 52–58.

Swan, Maureen (1985) *Gandhi: The South African Experience*, Johannesburg: Ravan Press.

Tarlo, Emma (n.d.) "Khadi," available online at: www.soas.ac.uk/southasianstudies/keywords/file24807.pdf.

Tarlo, Emma (2003) *Unsettling Memories: Narratives of the Emergency in Delhi*, Berkeley and Los Angeles: University of California Press.

Tejani, Anil (1979) "Behind-the-Screen with Shyam Benegal," *Film World* (April): 27–28.

Thapar, Romila (1989) "The Ramayana Syndrome," *Seminar*, 353 (January): 71–75.

Thomson, Mike (2004) "Hitler's Secret Indian Army," BBC News, September 23, available online at: http://news.bbc.co.uk/2/hi/3684288.stm.

Thorval, Yves (2000) *The Cinemas of India*, New Delhi: MacMillan.

Turner, Graeme (ed.) (2002a) *The Film Cultures Reader*, London and New York: Routledge.

Turner, Graeme (2002b) "Editor's Introduction," in Turner (ed.) *The Film Cultures Reader*: 1–10.

Uberoi, Patricia (ed.) (1996a) *Social Reform, Sexuality and the State*, New Delhi: Sage.

Uberoi, Patricia (1996b) "Introduction: Problematizing Social Reform, Engaging Sexuality, Interrogating the State," in Uberoi (ed.) *Social Reform, Sexuality and The State*: ix–xxvi.

Uberoi, Patricia (2002) " 'Unity in Diversity?' Dilemmas of Nationhood in India Calendar Art," in Ramaswamy (ed.) *Beyond Appearances?*: 191–232.

Uberoi, Patricia (2006) *Freedom and Destiny: Gender, Family and Popular Culture in India*, New Delhi: Oxford University Press.

Vaidyanathan, T.G. (1996) *Hours in the Dark: Essays on Cinema*, Delhi: Oxford University Press.

Valicha, Kishore (1988) "[Benegal's] *Nishant* and the Exorcism of Sita," *New Quest*, 68: 95–99.

Vasudev, Aruna (1978) *Liberty and License in the Indian Cinema*, New Delhi: Vikas Publishing House, Pvt., Ltd.

Vasudev, Aruna (1986) *New Indian Cinema*, Delhi, Bombay, Calcutta, Madras: MacMillan India Ltd.

Vasudev, Aruna and Phillipe Lenglet (eds.) (1983) *Indian Cinema Superbazar*, Ghaziabad U.P. (India): Vikas Publishing House Pvt., Ltd.

Vasudevan, Ravi (1994) "Dislocations: The Cinematic Imagining of a New Society in 1950s India," *Oxford Literary Review*, 16: 93–124 (Special issue on India).

Vasudevan, Ravi (1996) " 'You Cannot Live in Society—and Ignore it," in Uberoi (ed.) *Social Reform, Sexuality and the State*: 83–108.

Vasudevan, Ravi (1997) "Voice, Space, Form: *Roja* (Maniratnam, 1992), Indian Film and National Identity," in Murray (ed.) *Not on any Map:* 153–169.

Vasudevan, Ravi (ed.) (2000a) *Making Meaning in Indian Cinema*, New Delhi: Oxford University Press.

Vasudevan, Ravi (2000b) "Introduction," In Vasudevan (ed.) *Making Meaning in Indian Cinema*: 1–36.

Vasudevan, Ravi (2000c) "Shifting Codes, Dissolving Identities: The Hindi Social Film of the 1950s as Popular Culture," in Vasudevan (ed.) *Making Meaning in Indian Cinema*: 99–121.

Vasudevan, Ravi (2001) "Review of M. Madhava Prasad's *Ideology of the Hindi Film: A Historical Construction*," *Journal of Moving Image*, 1: 117–119.

Vasudevan, Ravi (2007) "Neither State Nor Faith: The Transcendental Significance of the Cinema," in Needham and Sunder Rajan (eds.) *The Crisis of Secularism in India*: 239–263.

Vasudevan, Ravi (2011) *The Melodramatic Public: Film Form and Spectatorship in Indian Cinema*, New York: Palgrave MacMillan.

Visvanathan, Shiv (2007) "The Necessity of Harilal," *India International Centre Quarterly*, 34 (2): 18–32.

Visweswaran, Kamala (1996) "Small Speeches, Subaltern Gender: Nationalist Ideology and its Historiography," in Guha (ed.) *Subaltern Studies V*: 83–125.

Vitali, Valentina and Paul Willemen (eds.) (2006a) *Theorizing National Cinema*, London: British Film Institute.

Vitali, Valentina and Paul Willemen (2006b) "Introduction," in Vitali and Willemen (eds.) *Theorizing National Cinema*: 1–14.

Waldman, Diane (1988) "Film Theory and the Gendered Spectator: The Female or the Feminist Reader?" *Camera Obscura*, 18: 80–94.

Waldman, Diane (1989) "Individual Responses," *Camera Obscura*, 7: 308–313.

Waugh, Tom (1988) "Words of Command: Notes on Cultural and Political Inflections of Direct Cinema in Indian Independent Documentary," *Cineaction*, 23: 28–39.

Wees, William C. (1982) "Review" (of Teresa de Lauretis and Stephen Heath (eds.) *The Cinematic Apparatus*), *Cinema Journal*, 21 (2): 50–54.

Williams, Brackette (ed.) (1996) *Women Out of Place: the Gender of Agency and the Race of Nationality*, New York and London: Routledge.

Williams, Christopher (ed.) (1980) *Realism and the Cinema: A Reader* London and Henley: Routledge, Keegan Paul, in association with the British Film Institute.

Williams, Christopher (1994) "After the Classic, the Classical and Ideology: The Difference of Realism," *Screen*, 35 (3): 275–292.

Williams, Linda (1988) "Melodrama Revised," in Browne (ed.) *Refiguring American Film Genres: History and Theory*: 42–88.

Williams, Linda (2000) " 'Something Else Besides her Mother' " *Stella Dallas* and the Maternal Melodrama" in Kaplan (ed.) *Feminism and Film*: 479–504.

Williams, Raymond (1983) *Keywords: A Vocabulary of Culture and Society*, revised and expanded edition, New York: Oxford University Press.

Williams, Raymond (1991) "Realism, Naturalism and their Alternatives" in Burnett (ed.) *Explorations in Film Theory: Essays from Ciné Tracts*: 121–127.

Zaidi, Shama (1980) "Shyam Benegal," in Da Cunha (ed.) *Film India: The New Generation 1960–1980*: 51–53.

Zaidi, Shama (1980) "After Mahtma What?" *Cinema Vision*, 1 (3): 21–22.

Zamindar, Vazira Fazila Yacoobali (2007) *The Long Partition and the Making of Modern South Asia: Refugees, Boundaries, Histories*, New York: Columbia University Press.

Županov, Ines (2005) *Missionary Tropics: The Catholic Frontier in India (16th-17th Centuries)*, Ann Arbor: University of Michigan Press.

Index